THE
ANTI-SOVIET
SOVIET UNION

ALSO BY VLADIMIR VOINOVICH

The Life and Extraordinary Adventures
of Private Ivan Chonkin

The Ivankiad

In Plain Russian

Pretender to the Throne

THE ANTI-SOVIET SOVIET UNION

Vladimir Voinovich

*Translated from the Russian
by Richard Lourie*

HARCOURT
BRACE
JOVANOVICH,
PUBLISHERS

SAN DIEGO   NEW YORK   LONDON

Library of Congress Cataloging-in-Publication Data

Voĭnovich, Vladimir, 1932–
The anti-Soviet Soviet Union.

Translation of: Antisovetskiĭ Sovetskiĭ Soiuz.
I. Title.
PG3489.4.I53A25   1986   891.74′44   86–327
ISBN 0–15–107840–8

Designed by Michael Farmer
Printed in the United States of America
First edition
A B C D E

Contents

Contents

PART TWO

— SHUT UP AND EAT! —
LITERATURE AND WRITERS
IN THE SOVIET UNION

Contents

A Few Words about Myself

I was born September 26, 1932, in the city of Dushanbe, the capital of Tadzhikistan. My father was a journalist, my mother a teacher of mathematics. My mother is Jewish and my father a Russian of Serbian origin.

A Parisian woman of mixed Russian and Tartar blood was amazed to learn of my roots and asked how I could consider myself a Russian writer. I do not consider myself a Russian writer; I *am* one.

My knowledge of my ancestors on my mother's side breaks off with my grandfather, who was, I think, a miller. On the other hand, I know a great deal about my father's side of the family.

The history begins with a certain Ivan Voin, whose occupation can be guessed by his surname: Voin means soldier in Serbian. There were many military and bellicose people in the family, including some generals and admirals. During the reign of Catherine the Great, one of them, Admiral Marko Ivanovich Voinovich, joined the Russian Navy, beginning his service, as an old encyclopedia notes "in the Archipelago where he distinguished himself for his bravery." He commanded the first Russian battleship, *Catherine's Glory*, in the Black Sea and was the founder and first commander of the Russian Black Sea fleet. The main pier in Sevastopol was named in his honor. Many of his descendants served in the navy as well. That tradition seems to have come to an end after my great-grandfather and his four brothers, all of whom were captains of ships that made long voyages. But our family also included people in the peaceable professions. The works of one of them, Ivo Voinovich, are considered classics of Serbo-Croatian literature; my grandfather's brother, Dragomir Nikolaevich Voinovich, wrote *The History of the Serbian People*, which was well known in prerevolutionary Russia; and my father, Nikolai Pavlovich, translated a considerable portion of the Serbian national epic into Russian (but, unfortunately, published only a small amount of it). I was pleased to learn that Milovan Djilas is also a distant relative of mine; his mother was a Voinovich.

The first part of my life was completely ordinary for a Soviet person of my generation. I had not yet turned four when my father was arrested on an absurd political charge. By Soviet standards he didn't spend all that much time in camps, "just" five years. In May 1941 (a month before the Second World War began), he was not only released but even rehabilitated and offered reinstatement in the Party. To that, my father, who had learned no cunning, replied: "I'll never go back to your Party!"

Aware that his answer could cost him his head, he grabbed me when he came home, and we set off for

Zaporozh'ye (in the Ukraine) where his sister, my aunt Anna Pavlovna, lived with her husband and their two children. My mother stayed on in Tadzhikistan, for she had only a few months to go before graduating from the teachers' institute.

I think that they would have found my father even in the Ukraine, but the war started; he left for the front at once and came home from it disabled.

My own life took the same form as that of millions of others my age. Kindergarten, poems about Lenin, songs about Stalin, first grade, the war, two evacuations, hunger during the war and a half-hungry life after it. My parents were not able to provide me with the basics, and at the age of eleven I began to earn my own way. I worked on a kolkhoz, in construction, in a factory, for the railroad, as an instructor for a village district executive committee, and for a short stint as an editor for radio. I served in the army for four years. I had little schooling, and there were many interruptions, though none in working. But my parents were intelligent people, who were always reading, so I read too. Our principal wealth was our books, a small but select collection.

My father always wrote poetry—prose too later on in life—but since neither the one nor the other met the demands of the time, he succeeded in publishing next to nothing.

My luck was better. While still in the army, I began writing poetry and was published nearly at once. Working with various composers in 1960, I wrote about fifty songs, some of which, without exaggeration, were known to all Soviet people. In that same year, I wrote my first story about village life, "We Live Here," which was published in the first issue of *Novy Mir* (New World) for

1961. On the whole, the story was well received by Soviet critics, and Vladimir Tendryakov, who died recently, greeted my literary debut with an article tellingly titled "A Fresh Voice!" But there were also vigilant critics who at once discerned the budding troublemaker in me. Even back then, in an article called "The Truth of the Age and Sham Objectivity," one of them justly observed that I depicted a down-to-earth, joyless reality and in general adhered to an "alien poetic of depicting life 'as it is.' "

Since I continued attempting to depict "life as it is," trouble was not long in coming. By 1963, one of the chief ideologues of Khrushchev's "thaw," Leonid Ilichev, subjected my story "I Want to Be Honest" to withering criticism, after which the Moscow newspapers (*Izvestiya* [News], *Trud* [Labor], *Stroitelnaya Gazeta* [Construction Newspaper]) published malicious letters which they had fabricated and which were supposedly written by "front-rank workers" and Heroes of Socialist Labor with headlines like "Points of View and Eyesores," "This Is False!," "Writer with a Tar Brush." But the real badgering began in 1968, afer I had signed letters in defense of Yuli Daniel, Andrei Sinyavsky and other writers. This badgering was stepped up when the authorities became acquainted with the opening sections of my novel *The Life and Extraordinary Adventures of Private Ivan Chonkin*. I bore that badgering for five years, hoping to retain my position as an "official" writer, but I came to see that in fact I could retain that title only by renouncing my principal literary plans and my conception of honor and conscience. In 1973, I made a point of sending the first part of *Chonkin* to the West, I signed a collective letter in defense of Alexander Solzhenitsyn, and wrote a satirical letter of my own against the creation of the All-

Union Authors' Rights Agency (VAAP). Subsequently, I wrote a few other such letters, after which, in February 1974, I was expelled from the Writers' Union and for nearly seven years lived under constant KGB pressure, in an atmosphere of incessant threats, blackmail, and provocation.

I continued to write under those circumstances and to make a point of sending to the West my books and satirical letters occasioned by one or another action by Soviet authorities. In January 1980, immediately after Academician Sakharov was deported to Gorky, I wrote a letter to *Izvestiya* in which, parodying the style of those expressing gratitude to the authorities, I spoke my mind as follows: "Allow me via your newspaper to express my profound disgust for all institutions and labor collectives and as well for the individual comrades, including front-rank workers, artists of the words, masters of the stage, heroes of socialist labor, academicians, laureates, and deputies who have already participated or will in the future participate in hounding the best person in our country—Andrei Dmitrievich Sakharov."

Unlike my previous letters, this one did not go unanswered. Approximately one month later, on the day elections to the Russian Supreme Soviet were held, I was visited by a gloomy individual who identified himself as Bogdanov, from the district Party committee.

Standing in the middle of my living room, this Bogdanov said, in the tone of a colonel announcing terms of capitulation to a defeated army: "I have been instructed to inform you that the patience of the Soviet authorities and the people has come to an end."

I thought he was going to execute me on the spot, but that was not the case at all. Unlike other Soviet citizens,

I was presented with a real choice that election day, an either-or. Since the patience of the Soviet authorities and the people had come to an end at the same time mine had, I chose the "or," and less than a year later, on December 21, 1980, I found myself in the West.

Six months after that, I was stripped of my Soviet citizenship by a decree from General Secretary Leonid I. Brezhnev.

The Soviet Context

A BARREL-SHAPED WORLD

One time I spent the summer in a dacha outside Moscow, and apart from doing some writing and making a failed attempt at growing some of the more guileless vegetables, like radishes, I engaged in idle observations of various life forms.

On the grounds of our dacha there was an iron barrel half full of water, long since stagnant, whose level was nearly constant due to the alternation of sunny and rainy days. During the summer some sort of swimming beetles bred in that foul water. They kept darting across the surface and diving deeply for some prey invisible to me. The life of those beetles struck me as extremely mysterious. What did they all live on? How had they or their larvae survived if the barrel had frozen solid in the winter? Still, they had survived, somehow been fruitful and multiplied, living on something or other. But what if those beetles possessed the faculty of thought? What would their idea of the world around them be? Something like this: the world is barrel-shaped and half full of stagnant water. Stagnant is better than fresh (which sometimes falls from above), because it provides an ideal medium for movement, retains heat, and contains an assortment of nutritious elements. The world's frontiers are easily accessible, circular, and created of some hard substance. But beyond the limits of that stable and intelligible world there obviously exist other worlds where things are not so stable, where darkness and light alternate. When it is light out there, something round and hot sails overhead, and when it is dark, shiny, predatory beetles come creeping out. That other world is much worse than this—it must be—because it is from there we get the scorching heat and cold. And sometimes things flash and rumble up there.

Looking at those Diogeneses of nature, all became clear: those beetles are us—Soviet people!

We are born, we live, and we die in a barrel. We do not know what happens outside the limits of the barrel and cannot remember how we ended up in it. No matter how different our backgrounds, after years in that barrel, all come to have a shared view of the world: it is barrel-shaped. Those who live in the barrel have their own conception of good and evil; there are saints among them and villains as well. The most intelligent of them suspect that most likely other worlds exist, that there may be many other such barrels, where life has somehow taken different form. The most freedom-loving ones try to escape; they climb up the barrel's rusty sides, fall back down, then climb up again. The most persistent either lose their lives or make it to the rim. And suddenly a new, never-seen, and many-colored world opens before them—grass, flowers, animals, fish, birds, butterflies, and dragonflies. There is water, solid ground, and air, and each creature moves as best it can in those three elements—some fly, some swim, some crawl. A boundless world. But everyone must obtain his own food and everyone has to take care not to be trampled, bitten, or swallowed. Good God, what's going on here? Quick, back in the barrel!

There are no flowers, no grass, in the barrel, and the food is meager, but life is peaceful. You can cling to one side and have yourself a snooze knowing that no one will attack, no one will peck.

Long live the barrel!

HOW COULD YOU LIVE LIKE THAT?

When landing in the West, I had no intention of stepping forward in the role of propagandist. But wherever I go, people, learning I am Russian, ask me questions. They want to know what the superpower able to destroy the entire world is like. What sort of people live there, and what do they live by? People ask and I answer. But every answer creates another question. It turns out that people in the West find our daily life as mysterious and incomprehensible as the life of beetles in a barrel. And at times I cannot understand that. At times I become irritated. At times I patiently explain that we are also human beings. We are born, we live, we seek happiness, we love, we hate, we rejoice, we suffer, we fall ill, and we die. This general explanation creates no objections, but when it comes down to details, everything becomes cloudy again.

Once, during our stay in the United States, my wife and I decided to visit a woman artist we knew. She lives with her husband, an engineer, and her eleven children on a farm because they can't afford to rent a house or large apartment in the city and they do not wish to live in a small apartment: Americans are spoiled. When I was a young man, I once rented a room in Moscow with a family like hers. The state had lavished a four-room apartment on Kutuzov Prospect on that family of thirteen people. They rented out one of the rooms. "Aren't you all crowded in three rooms?" I asked them. "What do you mean!" said the woman of the house. "Two's a lot for us. Since we left our communal apartment, we're always stuffing ourselves into one room."

But back to Americans. We were off to visit the artist, took a taxi and spoke with the driver about one thing or another along the way. (Taxicab drivers are talkative everywhere.) Hearing our accent, the driver was naturally interested in where we were from. We told him. "Oh, Russia!" he said with respect. "And so how's life over there in Russia?" "What I can tell you?" I told him. "It's worse all the time." "Like here," said the driver. "Life's more expensive every year. Ten years ago this cab cost four thousand and now it costs nine. And I can't even earn three thousand a month." And I said: "Well, that's true, of course. But do you get your meat on ration cards or do you have connections?" He didn't understand my question at first, but when he did, he said that he bought meat and all his other food in the supermarket nearest him. "So then imagine," I said, "that there was no meat, no canned food, no sausage, no frankfurters in your supermarket or the next one or the one in the next city." "Yes," said the driver, "I heard the

Russians have problems with meat. That's no fun, but in the end you can always eat chicken." My wife and I began laughing, to hear the driver sound like Marie Antoinette. The driver became angry with us and said that, unlike Marie Antoinette, he was not cut off from real life; he knew a person could raise as many chickens as he wished. Chicken production was a very simple matter; the chickens hatch from the eggs and grow all by themselves; they just need some feed. I tried to tell him about the Soviet agricultural system, in which nothing is ever so simple, but he didn't want to hear about it. "What are you telling me? What does the system have to do with it? Chicken farms cost next to nothing. You can build as many as you want under any system." And he was so convinced of this that I almost believed it myself.

Well, we arrived and were met by our hostess, who showed us her house. She had had the enormous two-story house rebuilt to her own fanciful specifications, which had resulted in many corners, curves, and passageways. An incredible number of rooms. Each of the eleven children had his own room. She and her husband each had a work space. And there was their bedroom, a living room, and some other sort of room as well, and, counting just bathrooms, there were five, maybe six. The children had all sorts of sports equipment, an Indian playhouse, a pony, and everything else you can think of. There was a swing fastened to the branch of a tall oak tree, and when we had tea on the terrace, the children flew whistling over our heads on that swing.

We sat, drank tea, and talked about life. I prefer that sort of simple conversation to all intellectual discussion. I asked our hosts if life was difficult for them. They said by and large it wasn't easy. A big house, all those children, so much to take care of, and they weren't millionaires, just ordinary people, middle class, as they say in America. Then they began asking us questions, and I gave them a brief account of my life, not in the least intending to astonish them, since my life story is, by Soviet standards, nearly humdrum. I told them of my early life and that, after I became a writer, my subsequent fate took some uncommon turns. I began describing in my books what I had seen in real life, and this brought me trouble. The farther I went, the more trouble there was. Later still, when I began standing up for other people, not with my fists, but on paper, I was no longer published and not allowed to earn a living. Attempts were made to charge me with being a social parasite, my phone service was cut off, I was threatened with death (one time I was slipped poisoned cigarettes), there were staged attacks by hoodlums, my car tires were punctured, and all sorts of other provocations were made (right up to telling my aged parents that I had been killed). All the same, they didn't put me in prison, didn't kill me, but only drove me out of the country, something which some people actively desire. And so the story of my life can be considered a very happy one indeed. The woman of the house did not, however, think it happy.

"How could you live like that? Why didn't you appeal to your government?" she said.

Her elder daughters, college students, began to laugh. They were embarrassed, as children that age often are, by older people's stupidity.

But I didn't laugh. I thought her question reasonable and I explained what sort of government we have and how it responds to that sort of appeal.

"Then you should have taken them to court!"

One daughter began ridiculing her outright.

"All right, I understand. Maybe the courts are the same as the government. But after all, he could have written to the newspapers and appealed to public opinion! Why are you laughing at me? Don't interrupt. I may be old and stupid, and maybe I don't understand a thing. I've never seen governments like that, I haven't read newspapers like that, I didn't know that there were courts like that. But if it's pointless to appeal to them all, in the end you could still go outside and shout: "Hey, everybody, what's going on here?""

We who were raised in the Soviet system sometimes find these remarks by Western people ridiculous; sometimes they irritate us—how can people be so naïve? But I don't see anything to get angry about. Yes, they're naïve. Yes, they can't imagine our life even when they make an honest effort.

But there are also those who do not even try.

THE BEST KEPT SECRET

On one of my first evenings in Germany, I found myself in a conversation that quite quickly turned to the Soviet military threat, to Soviet tanks arriving in Germany in the near future. My new acquaintances seriously discussed what they would do in that situation. One, a horse dealer, said people should flee to Australia today, not wait for the tanks. Another, the owner of a beer brewery, asked me if Russians like beer; he was hoping that the arrival of beer-loving Soviet tankmen might help to expand his business. And, in a way that was beyond me, a young philosopher combined fear of Soviet tanks with the belief that law, social justice, and universal equality reigned in the Soviet Union. He heard my objections with an ironic grin as if he already knew that I would have a prejudiced opinion. He, of course, had read about Soviet camps and Stalin's terror but insisted that it was during the years of Soviet power that Russia had made great strides and become a mighty industrial power whose success in space spoke for itself.

The philosopher further explained to me that the Soviet system had liberated the workers from capitalist exploitation and fear of the future. And I doubted his competence when he told me that in any case Soviet people had never known hunger. I asked him if he had ever heard of the famine in the Ukraine which cost several million people their lives or of the siege of Leningrad. I told him how people died of hunger (I came close myself in Kuibyshev in the winter of forty three and three years later in Zaporozhe). What I said went in one ear and out the other, and he continued to argue. In reply to one point, he said: "Well yes, after all Russia in itself is a small country, no bigger than Bavaria." And in reponse to my stunned look, he explained: "I don't mean the entire Soviet Union, just Russia." I told him that there were different ways of figuring, but Russia itself extended more or less from Smolensk to Vladivostok.

Another time I was asked if Russians understood the languages of other nationalities in the USSR; for example, did I understand Georgian? I was also asked if there were hotels and taxis in Moscow and what Russians needed money for, if there was nothing to buy.

Reading these words, my Russian readers will be quick to nod their heads. People in the West don't know us, they will say. They don't know us and they don't understand us. But I would like to add the following: not only don't they know us, we don't even know ourselves. Among the Russians who emigrated years ago, I have encountered some who are absolutely convinced that only Jews serve in the Politburo, the General Staff, and the KGB. It is impossible to convince them otherwise. I recently attended a lecture by a certain old Russian writer who stated that there was not a single Gypsy left in Russia (they had all been annihilated). And then I have encountered recent emigrés who only heard the name of Sakharov for the first time in the West. In the Soviet Union itself, millions of people know nothing about collectivization, Stalin's purges, or what is happening today.

This ignorance has many causes. Correspondents who have worked in Russia remark that Soviet society is closed to foreigners. The truth is that it is closed not only to foreigners but to Soviet citizens as well. Any information, often the most cursory, is a secret in our country. Certain enterprises are secret, as are entire islands, even cities. Epidemics are secret, as are natural disasters, train wrecks and plane crashes. The true harvest figures are secret and so are most production indices. The number of alcoholics and narcotics addicts is secret. The names of writers exiled from the country is a secret and, of course, their books are too. Even the names of some of the most distinguished figures in the revolution and those of recent Soviet leaders are secret. A curious example: the encyclopedia contains the word "Trotskyism," but not "Trotsky."

From childhood on Soviet people fear foreign spies and their own KGB. They are called on to be vigilant and taught to hold their tongues.

There are also class divisions. In the Soviet Union workers live separately, artists live separately, and so do athletes. The party bureaucrats, diplomats, KGB people, and higher military men are surrounded by fences that will not admit people from other segments of the society. Writers also live apart from everyone else. From time to time "in order to study life" they go off on so-called "creative" assignments, sometimes as individuals but usually in teams, to visit the "front-rank" collective farms or factories where a show is put on for them or, more precisely, they are shown a fictitious side of life—deceived as foreigners are. The overwhelming majority of writers (and there are more than 8,000 in the USSR) have absolutely no knowledge of the life of their own people and those rare few who do know it and who attempt to portray it accurately are persecuted by the authorities, accused of being accomplices of foreign intelligence, and punished.

There are secrets galore in the Soviet Union, but the principal and most carefully guarded state secret is the daily life of Soviet people.

The very idea of a Soviet nation or Soviet people, a term derived from the form of government, has a somewhat unnatural ring to it. It would sound just as unnatural to say "monarchist" or "parliamentary" people or to unite all the common market countries by calling them the "common market" people. All the same, I often use the adjective "Soviet" because I don't know any other term for all the various nationalities inhabiting the USSR. And it's necessary because the general laws, rules of conduct, and conditions of life influencing the entire lives of several generations has already produced traditions and customs common to all, although national differences have not been completely destroyed. In this case

I intend nothing negative in my use of the word "Soviet." Soviet people, like all other people, include many who are intelligent, stupid, gifted, ungifted, noble and ignoble. But try putting a Russian, an American, an Eskimo, and a Thai in the same prison cell, keep them in that cell a sufficient length of time, and you will see that with all their national and personal differences the same bents and habits will arise—they will all write in small letters, will be hostile to bright sunlight, and suffer from claustrophobia. And if their children and grandchildren grow up in that same cell, they will learn from early childhood to deceive their guards, to conceal small objects in the creases of their clothing, hide bread under their pillow. Even when they are released and living freely and well, they may long retain those habits and even pass them on to their descendants.

I avoid using the currently fashionable term *homo sovieticus* because it is inaccurate, unfair. The contemptible creature who possesses a two- or three-fold awareness (he thinks one thing, says another, and does a third) is, of course, to be found in the Soviet Union, but may also be encountered quite often among Western people as well. But more of that later.

Our Daily Bread

Pictures of
Soviet Life

The Soviet Passport

Let's talk about Soviet passports. Consider these lines from a Mayakovsky poem:

From my broad-legged pants I draw
the manifest of my precious cargo.
Read it and envy me,
I am a citizen of the Soviet Union!

Beautifully said, of course. Strong stuff. But the envy part may be overdoing it.

I remember one time when my wife and I were driving through the country in our Zaporozhets. Not one of those little humpbacked models that wits said would run from dogs up a tree like a cat, but a Zaporozhets 968, the more modern design. Naturally, it was better-looking than the old model, but more finicky as well. It would conk out in the most inconvenient of places: at railroad crossings or while passing on narrow roads. All the same, we traveled throughout the Baltic states in it.

We drove back by way of Minsk, where we decided to stop and rest. We tried to get in one of the main hotels, and it was there that Mayakovsky's poem came immediately to mind.

An unseasoned traveler was standing ahead of me in line. He was told: "No rooms. We're expecting guests from West Germany." Having gotten nothing for his pains, he turned to me and said, in a whisper of course: "I was here in Minsk during the war. Back then there was a sign on this same hotel that said, Germans only. And now it turns out that it's Germans only again. So who won the war?"

I, however, was more experienced than he, and I knew that a Soviet passport could do the trick if it contained certain essential supplements, that is, if you inserted the right amount of money in it. You have to know how to gauge the class of the hotel, the season, the personal price of the hotel clerk, and insert an amount that's not too little and not too much. If you put in too much, you'll feel bad, and if you put in too little, the administrator will feel bad, raise hell, and accuse you of bribery. When it comes to money, discretion is advised. In general, it's not everyone who knows how to offer bribes. But if you have a little passport and one that's red in color, it's a different story. Then, it helps to be a hero of the Soviet Union, a deputy to the Supreme Soviet, or a laureate. A passport marked KGB brings a smile as wide as the Cheshire Cat's. Having certification as a journalist also comes in handy—especially from *Krokodil* magazine. Certification from the Writers' Union doesn't mean much, but it does have some effect. Hotel clerks

4

are apprehensive when it comes to people who write.

And so, in Minsk, when my turn came, I pushed my passport through the little window with my writer's certification on top. To avoid any misunderstanding, I said who I was at once: "A writer from Moscow, on special assignment here, accompanied by my wife." This delighted the head clerk and the middle-level one as well. They immediately offered me one of the best rooms and arranged parking for my car. And it was while they were making out the pass for my car that I slipped up. The head clerk asked for my license number and then for the make of the car. And, simple soul that I am, I answered: "A Zaporozhets." The man trembled from the insult that had been inflicted on him, his hand froze, and he was unable to write the word.

Catching my error, my wife rushed up to the window and shouted: "A new Zaporozhets! A new one!"

The hotel clerk could not have cared less whether it was new or old; to him my car was just another sardine can, if somewhat longer. Others may not, but a clerk in a good hotel knows that important people never drive anything less than a Zhiguli.

I learned a lesson from that incident, and afterward, when asked what kind of car I had, I would respond mysteriously: "Foreign." This time, of course, our room had already been assigned to us, and there was no way out for them. The head clerk scowled at me until, in apology for my Zaporozhets, I gave him a package of Hungarian felt-tip pens as a present.

Here another theme comes to mind—the relationship between those in power and makes of cars. Every policeman knows he can always squeeze a ruble out of the driver of a Zaporozhets, even from one who hasn't broken any law. He has to be more polite with the driver of a Zhiguli, and the person behind the wheel of a Volga could well prove important and is better left alone. Chaikas and Zils are to be saluted no matter who's inside. But that's another story in itself; let's get back to passports.

There's an American I know, a professor. Imagine his last name is Rabinovich. This Professor Rabinovich spent a short time in Moscow at the Hotel Rossiya; his friends, also Americans, stayed at the Metropol. Professor Rabinovich decided to go visit them for one reason or another. He presented himself at the Hotel Metropol and proceeded to his friends' room without encountering any obstacles. They sat together for a while, as people do, drinking whiskey or gin, but not chasing them with appetizers the way Russians do, shooting the breeze until it was time for Rabinovich to go. He said good night, left the Hotel Metropol, and turned the corner into Dzerzhinsky Square. There he was grabbed by two hulking guys, who, without a word of warning, twisted his arms behind his back and shoved him into a gray car.

"What's going on?" shouted Rabinovich. "Who are you? What gives you the right . . .?"

"We'll show you that soon enough," said one big guy in a significant tone of voice.

They did not, however, take him to the KGB, but to the police station. They dragged him right in to the chief and reported: "We caught this citizen red-handed, visiting American tourists in the Hotel Metropol."

"Aha," said the chief, fixing his gaze on Rabinovich. "Last name?"

"Rabinovich," said the professor, who was a little shaky from the treatment he'd received.

"Ah, Rabinovich!' said the chief, pleased not that the name was Jewish, but that it was simple. As simple as Ivanov.

"What do you think you're doing, Rabinovich? Who gave you permission? I'll show you, Rabinovich."

And he made a gesture with his hand that came close to Rabinovich's face. Then, overcoming his anger, he said: "Let's see your passport!"

Rabinovich, whose hands were shaking, drew from his pants (they weren't broad-legged) a passport that wasn't red, but blue. And there were none of your usual hammers or farm tools on it, but, instead, a golden bird that looked rather like an eagle.

The chief took the passport in hand, exactly as in Mayakovsky's poem, as if it were a bomb, a hedgehog, a single-edged razor, or a six-foot-long rattlesnake with enough poison to kill twenty men.

"I see. So this means you're Rabinovich," said the chief, beginning to turn the same color blue as the U.S. passport. "Mr. Rabinovich!" he added, with the emphasis on "mister." Then, turning red as a Soviet passport, he said: "I'm very sorry, Mr. Rabinovich. There's been a mistake, Mr. Rabinovich. We thought you were one of *our* Rabinoviches."

His wits about him again, Rabinovich took back his passport.

"I'm not," he said with a sigh of relief. "Thank God, I'm not one of your Rabinoviches. I'm one of theirs."

A Soviet passport, Soviet citizenship . . . How many exalted words have been written about the honor it is to be a citizen of the USSR. It is, of course, a great honor, but anyone who tries to renounce it is in for a rough time. Soviet prisons and camps hold, not only genuine criminals, who, by the way, also have the honor of being Soviet citizens, but prisoners of conscience as well, including those who wished to renounce the honor of citizenship and requested to be deprived of it. That was their crime. A few years ago, a writer I know, Gely Snegirev, sent his passport to Brezhnev, who was then head of state, with a note renouncing his citizenship. For that, Snegirev, who was gravely ill, was arrested, put through hell, and died in a prison hospital.

In the West there are millions of former Soviet citizens who many years ago, either through their own free will or against it, found themselves outside the borders of their native land. I will not go into the subject of why so many people ended up in the West or why so many wanted to return. Many of those who stayed in the West grew old there, they had children and grandchildren, and for a long time now they have been using the passports of the countries in which they live. Some of them have even forgotten their Russian. But the Soviet state still considers them Soviet citizens, despite all their letters, statements, and protests. And why? So that, if given the chance, they can punish them as Soviet citizens with the full severity of Soviet law. And without making any great distinction between those who had at one point actually committed crimes and those who just no longer wished to be citizens of the land of the Soviets.

At the same time, Soviet authorities usually punish people in the arts and literature by depriving them of their citizenship. This punishment has been inflicted on famous people, some world famous—people of whom any country would be proud. The loss of citizenship pains and outrages all those who love their native land and fellow countrymen well.

Sometimes this provides occasion for bitter jokes. One person who was deprived of his citizenship, and was the envy of those who wished to be deprived of theirs, cut the Presidium of the Supreme Soviet's decree on him from the newspaper, framed it, and hung it on his wall. To his visitors he says, "Read this and envy me, I am *not* a citizen of the Soviet Union."

Our Daily Bread

They say you shouldn't eat too much bread or you'll get fat. But they also say you shouldn't consume too much meat either, for the same reason. Take wolves, though; they eat meat, and you don't see many fat wolves. But then, they do their eating in the wild, not scientifically. With us Soviets, however, everything is on a firm scientific footing. As soon as one product or another runs short, up come some doctors who are experts on that very food, and they write long scientific articles proving that it's harmful to eat the food you can't get. It's difficult to disagree with that, of course.

I read an article in a newspaper about an ingenious cook who could make five hundred different dishes from potatoes. That is, if he could get the potatoes. (They used to run out of potatoes even in Moscow from time to time.)

It has to be admitted right away that five hundred different potato dishes is nothing to sneeze at. No matter how I wracked my brains, I couldn't think of more than fifteen. But for a cook who's inventive enough to dream up five hundred, I can suggest dish number five hundred and one.

Our family lived near Kuybyshev for a while during the war. The summer of 1943 wasn't all that bad, but things took a turn for the worse when fall came. Three people in our family worked at a military plant and were given a daily ration of seven hundred grams of bread apiece; my aunt, who worked in an office, got either four or five hundred (I don't remember exactly), and my grandmother and I, as dependents, got two hundred apiece. And none of us were fat either.

We also had a rabbit, which we had acquired to eat later on, but after a week (this always happened with our animals) we grew so used to it, and so fond of it, that killing it simply became out of the question. That, too, kept us from getting fat. Actually, it was the other way around—we were growing thinner from one day to the next more rapidly than on the strictest of modern diets. And our rabbit wasted away along with the rest of us. Later on, when real hunger set in, the rabbit ran away, apparently preferring to die at the hands of a decisive man than to die a slow death with a bunch of starving humanists. To tell the truth, as long as the rabbit was with us, we fed it decently enough, but after he was gone, we exploited his good name for our own purposes. I would go to the mess of the soldiers billeted near us and ask them for some potato peels for "my rabbit." The soldiers were all surprised: How can one rabbit eat so much? They didn't know that the rabbit had six hangers-on. The soldiers probably would have given us potatoes too if we hadn't been too shy to ask; they had so many they didn't even take the trouble to peel them carefully. We fried those potato peels in the form of pancakes, cooking them in something like machine oil. At the time, I found them madly delicious. And so I am able to offer that clever cook a five hundred and first dish, which just might come in handy someday.

But let's get back to bread. From time to time our entire Party press literally overflows with scientific articles, journalistic pieces, columns, poems short and long, and even novels about bread.

Indeed, the very word *bread* says much more to our hearts and minds than the name of any other food. Bread contains everything necessary to sustain life: proteins, carbohydrates, and so forth. A person with bread cannot be said to be going hungry. Even in his prayers, the first thing man asks God for is bread: "Give us this day our daily bread." Nearly all of us who grew up under the Soviet system experienced war and hunger at one time or another, and we grew used to thinking of bread as something almost holy. Despite the meat shortage, no one will blame you for throwing out a chop that's gone bad, but it's a different story with a piece of bread.

How many angry lines in verse and prose have I read about people who have forgotten the war and the siege of Leningrad and have tossed bread down the incinerator! There are more poems written about this than there are actual cases.

If they would only confine themselves to talking about *loaves* of bread. Wrathfully, lyrically, romantically, the press calls on the nation to cherish and use every morsel, every crust, every crumb. If you drop a piece on the floor, first blow on it, spit on it, and then you can eat it. If a piece of bread is too stale to chew, soak it in water and then eat it. And even if it's turned green, you shouldn't forget that the mold contains penicillin.

I once read in a newspaper supplement that serious measures had been adopted in the Zhovtneev district of Kiev. Not only were recipes for dishes made from stale bread posted in the stores (those recipes deserve an epic all to themselves), but also a crumb-collection campaign was organized.

What's going on here, comrades? Of course we have to be thrifty with bread, but surely we don't have to pick up every little piece we happen to step on or every little crumb that falls under the table. What are we, sparrows? Crumb bums? And why do they keep throwing the war and the siege of Leningrad in our faces? The people who were born after the war and especially after the siege are already bald and potbellied.

A day doesn't go by without them showing some village on TV, the workers, with dust-caked faces, driving combines and tractors, fighting the battle of the harvest. I've been living in the West for five years now and I haven't noticed any special battles going on. I've never once seen people driving tractors or combines on television. I don't see any newspapers calling on people to save every crumb—and the stores are stuffed with goods.

So, with all those gigantic efforts, where's our bread?

Well, they say there are still some unenlightened citizens who feed their pigs bread. These pig-keepers are written up in the newspapers and even put in jail every once in a while.

By the way, while we're on the subject of pigs, for about ten years I spent a month in the town of Klintsy, in the Smolensk region. And of course I visited the local food stores. Naturally, there was no meat there regularly.

It was only on holidays that you could buy sausages with a sort of greenish tinge to them. On the other hand, there was an abundance of pigs' feet and pigs' tails. The locals made meat jellies from them.

Well, there were a few grumblers who cursed and said that they were being fed on only pigs' feet and tails. Other, more sensible, people said: "Hmph, so it's not good enough for them," as they brought up the war and the siege yet again. And, without taking one side or the other, I thought to myself: Where do all those pigs' feet and pigs' tails come from? What ever happened to their original source, meaning the pigs themselves? Of course, Klintsy is a small Soviet town. It had, however, a regional committee and a regional executive committee. But could high-level officials, no matter how many of them there were, devour all those pigs, leaving only the tails and feet for the non-high-level local populace? Especially since that's basically an agricultural region, and, no matter what the circumstances, there should be more pigs than there are comrades in the leadership.

And in another city, where there were no pigs' feet or pigs' tails and where bread was a problem, I began to do some thinking. All right, there's no bread—that you can understand; the pigs ate it. But where are the pigs?

It was only later on, in Moscow, that I got an idea. I was on a bus, taking my cat to the veterinarian. I was minding my own business, and the cat wasn't bothering anybody either. All of a sudden an aggressive old woman attacked me savagely. "The reason there's no meat," she said, "is because all sorts of selfish people are keeping cats and dogs." And the other passengers were with her one hundred percent. I was worried that they might lynch my cat. And me with it. To avoid trouble, I got off the bus and, cat in arms, went home, not to the vet's. Then I got into an argument with my wife because the cat hadn't gotten its shot. That was the last straw. In a foul mood, I had a drink of vodka. The vodka was lousy rotgut, made from sawdust. After all, if they won't let you feed bread to pigs, they're not going to waste it to make vodka.

So I had a vodka and then I started looking around for a bite to eat. No bread; the pigs had eaten it all. No pork; the cat had eaten it. I got a pickle. Pigs and cats don't eat pickles. Then the cat started whining around my feet for something to eat. I gave it some milk (good thing the woman from the bus wasn't there). I drank another shot of rotgut, took out a book by a prerevolutionary writer, Vlas Doroshevich, lay down on the couch, and started reading. Doroshevich described a performance by the great tenor Chaliapin in Italy after which the Italian newspapers wrote that it was just as crazy for Russia to export singers to Italy as it was for Russia to import wheat. I thought: Hold on a minute! Had it really seemed like a crazy idea for Russia to import wheat back then? But the truth can be bizarre. After all, Russia, or, more precisely, the Soviet Union, is such an enormous country that it has land that is dried up, swampy, and frozen, and it also has some that's not bad, some that's good, and some that's even excellent. But then there's the climate. That, plus the collective-farm system, spells trouble, of course. That aside, though, the land is bad in some places and entirely decent in others. And even with our climate, enough food—for us, the pigs, and the cats—could be grown there.

Even when bread is in abundance, it has to be respected like all products of human labor. But not to the extent of making special dishes from stale crusts or gathering crumbs from the floor. That, you can give to the pigs. It won't sound so blasphemous if you remember that we'll end up eating those pigs anyway. When we can get hold of one, that is.

For Crying Out Loud!

ON THE DOWNING OF THE KOREAN AIR LINES PLANE

"For crying out loud!" exclaimed the Soviet pilot taking aim at the foreign jetliner. "I'm going; I mean, my RF light is on."

For a long time afterward, United Nations' translators racked their brains over what crying and loudness had to do with anything thirty thousand feet above the ground.

I don't know what RF stands for: reserve fuel or rocket fire. I only know that "for crying out loud" expresses excitement, delight, irritation, anxiety. There are other words for this, which are often used in regular life, but it is strictly forbidden to say them on the air. Even when shooting down a passenger plane, a person should express himself in a cultivated manner.

Despotic regimes always excel in their rejection of crude words and expressions, and unbelievable cruelty is always accompanied by verbal hypocrisy. The Nazis called the annihilation of millions of Jews the "final solution to the Jewish question." In the USSR, mass repression is termed "collectivization" or the "struggle with the opposition" and, afterward, the "mistakes of the cult of personality." Aggression against other countries is given the high-sounding name "fraternal aid."

When three Soviet cosmonauts were killed in 1971, the television newsman did not say: "Dear comrades, there's been a disaster," but, in the invariable exalted tone, reported that the spacecraft's flight had been completed successfully, such and such achievements were made during the flight, the braking motors were switched on, on time, the craft entered the thicker layers of the atmosphere and made a soft landing right on target, and the cosmonauts were found in their places—here the announcer switched from a tone of exalted triumph to one of exalted sorrow and finished his sentence with "showing no signs of life."

The same was true in the case of the Korean airliner. Why not say simply that the plane was shot down? No, the plane went off in the direction of the Sea of Japan. And it was only intense pressure that forced the appearance of a new expression, one concerning measures taken to cut off the flight. The flight was cut off—the plane went off in the direction of the Sea of Japan, and the Sea of Japan was right beneath them. It was there—down—that the plane had gone. One of the world's largest jumbo jets fell end over end like an autumn leaf. The passengers went flying from their chairs, crashing against the ceiling, chair backs, and each other. The heartrending screams of more than two hundred people were not recorded by any ground-control station, but they are not difficult to imagine. Ground control heard only the Soviet pilot's voice. He was worried—for crying out loud!—that he did not have fuel enough to return to base.

At this point I'd like to say a few words in defense of that Soviet pilot. Some say that he could not have made an error, could not have confused a passenger liner with a spy plane, a Boeing 747 with a Boeing 707, especially with the plane's name on its side. The Soviet pilot might have seen pictures of a Boeing 747 and then again he might not have. And pictures are one thing, but real life is something else. And as for the words *Korean Air Lines*, you can write whatever you want on the side of a plane. We Soviets know that all Soviet spy trucks rolling through Europe are marked SOVAIRTRANS.

All Soviet people, and especially military people, are taught to be paranoid about spies; everyone is instilled with the belief that a foreigner is a spy, and everyone is told horror stories about the machinations of foreign intelligence. When I was a soldier, we were told a story (it was even printed in our textbook) about a dog that used to run around in a military airport and later it turned out that one of the dog's eyes had been replaced with a camera. In Poland, we were told that in no case were we to have any contact with the local population—all Polish girls worked for U.S. intelligence. And we also heard a story about an insufficiently vigilant officer who had only helped a Polish woman lift her suitcase onto a train, and the next day the Western newspapers apparently printed a photograph of this with a caption explaining that Soviet troops were sending Poles to Siberia.

Intimidated as they are, Soviet citizens are ready to suspect anyone wearing dark glasses, carrying a camera, or worse, binoculars, of being a spy. In Moscow, my neighbor, a writer who liked to dictate his stories into a tape recorder while taking a walk through the park, was forever being detained on suspicion of making radio contact in some espionage caper.

In the sixties, Soviet papers carried a story about an old man who walked barefoot and in his shorts through the snow in winter to toughen himself up. His plan was to strengthen his health and live a longer life. He did not succeed. One day, barefoot and in his shorts, he somehow got lost in the woods and ended up near a military installation. Catching sight of this odd individual, the sentry immediately thought: For crying out loud, a spy. It is true that at first the sentry tried to detain the old man, and shot him only after he had taken to his heels in panic. The newspapers, which had been so fervent in recommending his way of life, did not report a word about that final walk of his.

By the way, nineteen years ago, I happened to spend some time on Sakhalin Island. Just before my plane arrived, an Il-18 passenger liner had crashed. Needless to say, it had not been reported by the papers. The plane had crashed into a hill, and the bodies of passengers were spread across the hillside. When my friend tried to photograph that hill (not the corpses), some vigilant citizens nearly smashed his camera over his head.

I gave lectures on literature to many army units on Sakhalin, and the major who shot down the Korean Boeing may have been stationed there at the time. One pilot, also a major (though he may now have risen to general), told me that he was with two friends in Moscow near the Central Telegraph Office and they noticed a foreigner—for crying out loud!—taking their picture. They stopped him, grabbed his camera, exposed the film, and took him to a police station.

"Why did you do that?" I asked the major.

"Don't you understand?" he asked.

"No, I don't."

"We were in uniform and he took our picture."

"So what? What could he do with those photographs?"

"You don't understand?"

"No, I don't."

"What if he published them in a newspaper?"

"All right," I said. "Suppose he did. Let's even suppose that foreigners found out that one day three officers were standing near the Central Telegraph Office. What of it?"

"You don't understand?"

I didn't. I still don't. It's impossible to understand without a psychiatrist's assistance. But even though the major could not explain why he had been upset, he stuck to his opinion—if something that cannot be expressed in words can be called an opinion.

Let's imagine a major who takes fright at seeing a foreign tourist with a camera. What can be expected of him if, ordered to fly at night at an altitude of thirty thousand feet, he sees an enormous thing flying by with non-Russian lettering on the side? For crying out loud! How is he to know this is just a passenger plane that has gone off course? He's a military man, and his job is to carry out orders, not discuss them.

Many are to blame for the loss of that plane. And they include the Korean pilot who made a fatal error, the American and Japanese ground-control staff for not picking up a plane straying off course, and that Soviet general who, also the product of paranoia, gave the order to open fire. I would place the Soviet pilot last among the guilty. He was only obeying an order.

Still . . .

In 1945, an American major, Claude Eatherly, who

21

was also carrying out orders, was among those who dropped the atomic bomb on Hiroshima. That bomb was one of the two that decided the outcome of the war. Had it not been for those bombs, Japan might have prolonged its resistance, and the number of casualties would have been even higher. So everything was correct, strategically and mathematically. But what can you do about the fact that thousands of innocent people were killed as a result of the explosion? War is war, and bombs make no distinction between the innocent and the guilty. Of course, justice would have been better served had the bomb blown up only selected Japanese generals.

Eatherly's conscience, however, took no account of logic, strategy, or mathematics. When he realized what had taken place below after the button had been pushed, he went out of his mind.

And what about the Soviet major? Does he suffer pangs of conscience if he happens to learn that the headless corpse of a child was retrieved off the coast of Japan? And the body of a woman? And a corpse without a head, arms, or legs? The hunk of human flesh soaked in sea water?

I imagine that the major is an ordinary, peaceful man when he's on the ground. He reads newspapers, goes to the officers' club with his wife, helps his children with their arithmetic, and takes them out fishing. No criminal he. If he meets a pedestrian who's lost his way at night, he doesn't shoot or stab him.

Nevertheless, I would like to ask him: "Major! Do you really sleep soundly under the sky you defend and never dream of that headless child?"

For crying out loud!

A Few Words on
Sacred Cows

Soviet citizenship, our Motherland's borders—we hold quite a number of similar words and concepts sacred. Let's talk about a few of them. I'm even something of an expert in these matters. One American newspaper dubbed me "the kicker of sacred cows." And to tell the truth, that name did not embarrass me. On the contrary, it gave me pleasure.

In our language (I don't mean Russian, but Soviet officialese), the epithet "sacred" is applied far too often, and sometimes to things that are not in the least holy.

Take our "sacred borders," for example. Those borders are inviolable, not to be crossed from without or within. The incident of the Korean airliner is a perfect case in point—not the first example of its sort, either. Sacred this and sacred that are drummed into our heads so often that we ourselves can't see what nonsense we're talking. I recently read a report in *Nedelya* (The Week) about two skyjackers who had intended to violate our sacred borders. While one sat with a bomb in his lap, the other ordered the pilot of the TU-134 to fly to Sweden. But he landed the plane in Leningrad. The skyjackers were shot on the spot, before they knew what was happening. And what did the passengers have to say after the incident? One of them said (and, I believe he was completely sincere): "I thank the crew who saved our lives." But did they really? The crew had exposed their lives to danger and not out of the slightest concern for their passengers' safety, but solely because if the skyjackers were successful in escaping to the West, the crew would be in serious trouble. For now, I will leave aside the important issue of why people would in general defect to Sweden or anywhere else. Why can't they simply purchase a ticket and fly there without jeopardizing themselves or others? Why can't they cross those sacred borders on foot with an ordinary knapsack on their back? Here, in the West, it's quite easy to walk across sacred borders; all you have to do is show your passport. Once, crossing the border between France and Switzerland during a very important soccer match, I found no one at all at the border station. I even stopped my car and got out to find some uniformed man to check my papers and be assured that I was not crossing that sacred border haphazardly but in the most legal manner. Not finding a soul, I gave up, got back in the car, and drove off. That's how people cross borders in the countries of the West.

Within the Soviet Union, the borders between republics can also be crossed without obstacle. But not always. One time, in my Zhiguli, I attempted to enter the Russian Republic from the Don Province, which is located in the

Ukraine. I was stopped and ordered to open my trunk, which then underwent a thorough examination. And what do you think they were looking for? Not dynamite, not narcotics, not even forbidden literature. They were looking for sausage, which the residents of Rostov were often bringing in from the better-supplied city of Donetsk. But that's not the point here. My point is that the adjective *sacred* should not be applied to every last idea, and, in general, the less the word is used the better.

Various countries have their revered symbols and relics. In England, for example, great reverence is shown to the English monarchs. But sometimes the English speak of such sentiments with a sense of humor. You don't find them asserting that the English monarchy is the most advanced political system in the world. They usually say: "Yes, we're not against the monarchy. We're used to it, it's used to us. It doesn't bother us on the whole."

About fifteen years ago, an English student told me about a Soviet literary scholar, Professor Mashinsky, who had come to Oxford. Speaking before an audience, the professor told the students of the life and work of Soviet writers, of the innumerable rights they enjoy in comparison with their Western colleagues. Soviet literature, he maintained, was not only the greatest but also the freest in the world. The student who told me the story had raised his hand and asked, "If yours is the freest literature, why are Sinyavsky and Daniel in jail?"

The professor smiled condescendingly, as if to say that the student was still young and green, and required enlightening. "The point is," said the professor, "that Sinyavsky and Daniel insulted Lenin in their works. And Lenin's name is *sacred* to us. It's natural for every country to have its sacred symbols and ideas, which must not be insulted. In some countries it's the flag, in others the national seal, and in your country, for example, the Queen must not be insulted."

"You're saying we can't insult the Queen?" asked the student. "I, for one, want to bring that old cow here, put her up against the wall, and shoot her dead on the spot." He paused, then said: "Well, do you see any police? Is anyone dragging me off?"

When telling me the story, the student confided that he did not in the least consider the Queen an old cow. She is a charming woman and he was as fond of her as the next Englishman.

In the Soviet Union too, you can say whatever you want about our leaders. That is, if you can imagine the impossible—that there won't be a single stool pigeon in the audience. But in Stalin's time, to have said to an audience anything resembling what that student said . . . well, the audience itself would have torn the person to pieces without waiting for the comrades from State Security. And for that reason Stalin's name, like Lenin's, became sacred.

Sacred words. Sacred borders, graves, names, ideas, stones, banners.

The very word *sacred*, taken from church use, is exploited as much as possible by the Soviet authorities. They try to find substitutes for religious rites and rituals, to substitute the hammer and sickle for the cross.

After leaving the Wedding Palace, where they take their vows beneath a portrait of Lenin, newlyweds in their wedding dress go to the grave of the Unknown Soldier. What a bizarre mixture of the religious and the atheistic, and what hypocrisy and blasphemy it contains!

Those newlyweds are not paying tribute to the soldier, but to barbarism and military propaganda. In inculcating this new ritual, the authorities are unscrupulously exploiting people's need to preserve the memory of those who were killed and those who have died. Each of us holds dear those we loved and lost in war or in the camps. Each of us has relatives who fell in battle, at Kursk, say, or at the Elbe, or who are buried somewhere along the shores of the Kolyma or the Pechora. If tribute is to be paid, then it should be paid not only to the Unknown Soldier, but also to the Unknown Prisoner as well.

We all hold dear, not only those who fall with a submachine gun or a pickax in hand, but those who simply die from sickness, old age, or accident. Yet it's not a duty to visit their graves on one's wedding day. There's the anniversary of their death for that. Some countries have memorial days; in Russia the custom is to go to the cemetery at Easter. After all, when entering into marriage, people do not swear a military oath; they just intend to live together and have children.

On the whole, we have lost all sense of measure when it comes to elevating things to the rank of sacred. Property, for example. It is a noble thing when one person saves another person's life, risking his own life for the other's. But Soviet propaganda encourages people to risk their lives, make sacrifices, and act heroically to save socialist property. Here, a different adjective is used, but it is employed in an exalted sense and could easily be replaced by the word *sacred*.

All sorts of things have been written about people who have sacrificed themselves to save socialist property, such as farm equipment, foot cloths, reserve supplies of detergents. This inspires yet another sacred ritual. In various Soviet military units, a name is called out at evening roll call, and the soldier on the right flank responds by rote: "Private (or Sergeant) So-and-so was killed while carrying out his battle orders" (or "while saving the flag"). These rituals encourage people to die, not only to save their country, their freedom, or other people, but also for things that, no matter how sentimental we may be about them, are not worth dying for.

Take the flag, for example. Of course, it's a relic, and maybe even a precious one. But when it's a choice between losing the flag and losing a human life, it has to be remembered that a flag, no matter what sort, even one pierced by bullets and surrounded by the glory of battles past, is still just a piece of cloth fastened to a pole. And a life? Surely there can be nothing more sacred.

Without Lenin's Party

If someone had told me, ten or even five years ago, that I would be living in a German village and saying "Guten tag," "Danke schön," and "auf Wiedersehen" to my neighbors, I wouldn't have believed him for anything in the world.

But that's just what's happened. I now live in a village outside Munich called Stockdorf. In German, *stock* means stick and *dorf* means village. In Russian, stick is *palka*, and so we sometimes refer to our village as Palkino. Our friends from Moscow call it Perepalkino, because that sounds like Peredelkino, the writers' dacha settlement outside Moscow.

Naturally, it's mostly Germans who live in Stockdorf. But not entirely. Nastya, a former collective-farm worker from outside Kharkov, lives right across from us. During the war, when she was a young girl, the Germans deported her to work in Germany. She didn't return to the Soviet Union after the war. Life wasn't easy for her here;

even so, she couldn't bring herself to return to her native land—to the collective farm where her back was bent from dawn to dusk, her body swollen from hunger. Her father had been taken away—no one knew why, no one knew where. And had she returned, her own fate would have been uncertain, to say the least. Stalin had no liking for people who had spent time in foreign countries, even if they hadn't done so of their own free will. Stalin disliked all who had seen life in the West and who could make comparisons.

That's why Nastya had been afraid to return home. She stayed on in Germany, married, had a daughter. She became Germanized. She spoke German with her husband, German with her daughter, and with her grandchildren there's no question of speaking anything but German. Then all of a sudden she has Russian neighbors. She can visit them, open her heart, speak her native tongue. The language she had spoken at home was that of the so-called simple people, neither quite Russian nor Ukrainian, but a mixture of the two. Now she threw German into that mixture, especially for postwar words. For *television*, for example, she uses the German word *Fernsehen*. A couple of days ago, she called and said: "Turn on the Fernsehen; they're showing Moscow."

We turned on the television, and there was Moscow. Red Square. The leaders' portraits, GUM. The camera dollied in on GUM.

A line. An enormous line. Around the store. Inside the store. Spreading from department to department. I don't know what was on sale. They might have thrown Yugoslavian boots on the market, or school uniforms. Who knows what? Whatever's on sale, a line always forms, because everybody needs everything. A suffocating crowd, those in back pressing on those in front. Some faces are brimming with the resolution to stick it out and triumph; others have a look of doom about them. They already know that you will stand there all day, elbowed in the ribs, and when you finally get to the counter, you'll hear the saleswoman yell to the cashier: "Stop accepting money for school uniforms! We're all out!" and to the customers: "Citizens, don't waste your time crowding around here!"

But one citizen, still hoping for a miracle, will call to the saleswoman: "What do you mean? I came here specially from Voronezh!"

And she'll be told: "Everybody came specially!"

"But I need only one!"

That's no argument. Everyone needs only one. There are thousands of people needing only one.

It made me sad to see all that. It had been my old life. I had lived forty-eight years in the Soviet Union and had stood in lines that, if set end to end, would reach from Moscow to Vladivostok. I remember the lines for bread, for hot water at railroad stations, for some meaningless document or other in governmental institutions, and the long, long lines in front of the women's rooms during the war. Now, with the increase in prosperity, people stand in line for beer, detergent, gloves, toothpaste, toilet paper, and even Rubik's cubes.

There are various types of lines. In some you have to wait a few minutes; some, overnight; some, for a few days. For years if you are waiting for a car or an apartment.

All the same, I had no idea how awful a line of human beings looked when seen from the outside.

After showing all the lines in all the different departments on all the floors, the camera focused on a fat elderly woman who was an employee of GUM. I didn't catch what her position was—Party organizer or section head—but she was high up politically. She explained to West German viewers that the abundance of goods that they were seeing with their own eyes had been produced by the Soviet people under the leadership of Lenin's Party and with its untiring encouragement.

Watching and listening to her, I lamented. What fools the Soviet people have become! That woman has no idea she's talking nonsense. A Westerner would only ridicule the miserable goods on display at GUM.

There's a joke about an American who walked over to a line and asked what they were waiting for. "Boots on sale!" he was told. He went over, looked at the boots, and said: "They *should* be on sale."

Well, perhaps that old lady at GUM was not allowed to travel, had never been outside the country, and is unable to imagine the difference between her wretched GUM and any simple little store in the West. But surely Felix Kuznetsov, the secretary of the Moscow branch of the Writers' Union, knows the difference. He's allowed to travel, he's been abroad. When he's in the West and has a moment free from the struggle for peace, he's in the stores and gasping at what he sees. So he ought to be ashamed to be caught saying the sort of things the old lady at GUM said. But no. In his article "Don't Be Late" (*Literaturnaya Gazeta*, November 1983), a diatribe against pernicious imperialists, Kuznetsov writes that at a time when the West is gripped by panic and psychosis at the prospect of nuclear holocaust, Westerners who travel to the Soviet Union find surprising (and here I quote) "the calm, collected, businesslike atmosphere in our country." And later on he says: "We are working calmly, solving the problems in the Food Program, and perfecting socialism."

If there's anything foreigners find surprising about the Food Program, it's the very fact it exists—after sixty-seven years of Soviet rule and nearly forty years since the end of the war.

Now that's surprising.

In the West there's no one engaged in solving the problems of a food program, simply because none exists. Here a person just heads for a store and buys what he needs.

I recently heard a story about a very orthodox Soviet citizen, a woman professor of Marxism-Leninism. It was her first trip to the West, to Munich, to be more exact. She went into a store with the Germans who were showing her around. When she saw the shelves full of goods, she immediately thought that the entire display had been especially set up for purposes of provocation. She knew, for she had been taught well, that in the West you have to be on your guard. Seeing twelve varieties of oranges, she remarked: "We have those too." Seeing a dozen types of sausages, she said: "We have those too." Then she walked over to another shelf, one with toilet paper—white, pink, flowered, polka-dotted, checked; regular or two-ply; smooth or textured. "We have those too," she said . . . and fainted. When she came to, she was on a stretcher being loaded into the back of a van. Afraid it was a Black Maria, she asked: "What's this?" "An ambulance." "Ah ha," she said, reassured, "we have them too."

Another person, an elderly man from the Soviet Union, came to visit his daughter, who had married a German.

He too went to a store. The daughter began to brag: "Look, we have everything here."

He looked around and frowned. "Come on," he said, "show me a real store."

"What kind do you think this is?"

"I don't know," he said. "Maybe it's a special store for foreigners. Show me a real store, where regular people go." His daughter tried to convince him that anyone could shop there, regular or not. But the old man wouldn't change his tune: "Can't be. Show me a real one."

And so she began taking him from one store to another. He'd walk around, take a good look, and, not believing his own eyes, demand again to see a real store.

"So what would you call a real store?" asked the daughter, growing exasperated. "A grocery store like the one on Sokol Street?"

"Yes, something like that," he said.

"But we don't have any stores like that! There aren't any crummy stores like that here. Would you like me to show you a general store out in the country?"

"Yes, show me," said her father.

Fine. She put her father in the car and drove about thirty miles out into the country. Again he went into the store. When he came out, he looked around and saw a few one- and two-story houses, all well made, built of stone, with tiled roofs, huge windows, flowers on all the balconies. Not even one tumbled-down shed. "Is this an ordinary German village?" asked the father.

"Yes," said the daughter, "couldn't be more ordinary."

"Come on!" said the father. "Show me a real village!"

I want to be correctly understood here. Personally, I am not moved or tempted by wealth. I'd prefer a modest life in a free society to a rich life in an unfree society.

But, as practice indicates (theory, too), free people produce more and better goods than people who are not free. Even Karl Marx noticed that.

People in the West have achieved a level of economic abundance beyond Soviet people's ability to imagine. Interestingly enough, they have managed that without one drop of encouragement from Lenin's Party.

Soviet Anti-Soviet
Propaganda

ON THE RIGHT ROAD

About fifteen years ago, my wife and I were driving
back to Moscow from the Black Sea and somewhere in
the district of Armavir, I think it was, we came upon a
large road—by Soviet standards, quite a good one—that
ran between Pyatigorsk and Rostov-on-Don. There were
no signs at the point where we entered the road so we
took what seemed to us the right direction. We figured
we'd come to a sign soon enough and, with luck, we'd
keep on going.

The road was almost deserted. It was rare that we saw
a car approach us going in the other direction, and I
don't believe there was anyone on our side except us.
Still, we weren't worried. The main thing was to reach
the nearest sign. One seemed to be up ahead. . . .

It seemed to be a large roadside billboard. When we
drew closer, we saw that it was an enormous portrait of

Lenin, a kindly looking old man with a modest red ribbon on the lapel of his jacket and a cloth cap in his half-bent hand. Vladimir Ilich squinted tenderly, seemingly approving the direction we had chosen. YOU'RE ON THE RIGHT ROAD, COMRADES! was written in large letters under his portrait.

In the case at hand, we could not be satisfied by the leader of the world proletariat's words and would have liked more detailed information. But what could we do? We kept on going. We continued on that deserted road, which had no gas stations, no road signs, not even the usual (and equally meaningless) plywood billboards on which the local kolkhozes report how much milk or how many eggs they plan to give to the state during the current Five-Year Plan. Only those same portraits of Lenin with that same smile and those same words YOU'RE ON THE RIGHT ROAD, COMRADES! kept reappearing with irritating regularity along the roadside.

Having driven something like sixty miles, we finally came across a tractor, whose driver informed us that we were of course on the right road, but traveling in exactly the wrong direction. We turned around and headed back, and those Lenin faces with their assurance about "the right road" kept rising up, approaching us, and vanishing.

Whenever I think about Soviet propaganda, I remember that drive.

PRODUCERS AND CONSUMERS

To compare Soviet propaganda with its American or Western counterpart is difficult, though perhaps not impossible, because Soviet propaganda is a basic product of the Soviet system; its production far exceeds that of agriculture and of light, heavy, and even military industry.

Naturally, it is primarily the propaganda agencies of the Communist Party, the Komsomol, and the Committee for State Security (KGB) that engage in the production of propaganda. These include all newspapers, magazines, television, radio, movies, theaters, the unions of writers, artists, and composers, and even the official church. In addition to the above-mentioned organizations, all factories, kolkhozes, hospitals, construction companies, and military groups, without exception, engage in the manufacture of propaganda. Every director, manager, department head, chairman, and military officer is supposed to see to it that the area under his charge has the requisite number of portraits of Lenin and the current members of the Politburo (if one of them is removed from office, his portrait should disappear immediately and permanently), as well as banners with meaningless captions on the order of "The nation and the Party are one," "Marx's teachings are invincible because they are true," or "The victory of Communism is inevitable." There should also be a wall of newspapers filled with anything at all (just so long as they're there), a board of honor with the portraits of so-called leading workers (in order to be numbered among them you have to be not only a good worker but also an active producer, or, at least, consumer, of propaganda), and posters of every sort with slogans, quotations, figures, and percentages that promise overfulfillment of the production plan. Figures bearing no relationship to reality are hung everywhere. Once, in a dentist's office, I even saw a pledge to be economical with materials.

Every manager of every operation knows that if a check

is run on him, he or those under him might be forgiven for failing to fulfill the plan, for drunkenness, theft, absenteeism, and bribe-taking, but irregularities with portraits, posters, slogans, quotations, and figures will not be forgiven.

And who are the consumers of the propaganda? Every Soviet person, beginning with the nursery or the elementary school, in which the child first becomes a member of the collective. Depending on age, social position, Party membership, and educational level, every person is given propaganda in a form that the authorities deem appropriate for him.

Regardless of what they major in, university students are given classes in Marxism-Leninism and the history of the Communist Party of the Soviet Union, classes that keep changing to suit the changing needs of propaganda. Workers, kolkhozniks, and soldiers are supposed to attend political classes and study groups. Once, they studied the biography of Comrade Stalin, later the "works of Comrade Brezhnev"; now, even Comrade Gorbachev has created a masterpiece worthy of study. These classes are officially voluntary and free of charge, but everybody knows that attending them or avoiding them will have an effect on one's standard of living, and will be taken into account when job transfers, citations, honors, trips to resorts, or imported holiday hens are being given out.

As one boss put it to his subordinates, somewhat ironically: "Work unselfishly and you'll get paid for it."

AN INTERESTING EFFECT OF
SOVIET PROPAGANDA

Long gone now are those happy days for Soviet propaganda when the masses responded to the Party's contradictory appeals, built factories in Siberia with a will, "defended" freedom in Spain, brandished flags and portraits of their leaders enthusiastically at demonstrations, went mad with happiness if they caught even a distant glimpse of Lenin, Trotsky, or Stalin, fastened red ribbons to their shirts, and gave their children revolutionary names like Vladilen (Vladimir Lenin), Melor (Marx, Engels, Lenin, October Revolution), Kim (Communist Youth International), and even Traktorina or Industriya.

In those hallowed days, Soviet youth did not turn up its nose at Soviet symbols. Young people decorated their soccer balls and shirts with pins from MOPR (International Aid Organization for Fighting Revolutionaries) or Voroshilov Marskmen badges, and the girls wore red kerchiefs. I can remember when army caps, Stalin jackets, and even Stalin mustaches were in style.

But those times were long ago and are long forgotten.

Now, people go to demonstrations and wave flags and slogans, but only in exchange for an extra free day, a bit of time off, or a bonus.

Today's fashion has changed too. Now, it is not revolutionary slogans, but names of Western firms and their products that young Soviets, and those not so young, utter with a thrill in their soul. The words *Chesterfield*, *Panasonic*, *Mercedes* speak to their hearts more than *liberty*, *equality*, *fraternity*; foreign clothing is preferred not only for its quality. The price of a pair of jeans rises steeply if the rear pocket bears the name Mustang or Lee and falls steeply if it does not. Shirts and T shirts marked "Coca-Cola" or "I Love New York" are very much in style. Muscovites even report having seen T shirts marked "I'm voting for Reagan." If a person can't get hold of a foreign T shirt or can't afford one, he can buy an imitation (the same words on a T shirt of Soviet manufacture). But just try to sell a T shirt, even one of the highest quality, with Cyrillic letters on it—"I love Moscow" or "Lenin," or, let's suppose, "I'm voting for Gorbachev." Not only will you get no takers, you'll probably be sent for psychiatric evaluation, for such captions would be viewed as dissident mockery.

Soviet people are drawn to anything Western. Any tone-deaf American singer or dull American exhibit will be packed regardless. This, naturally, unsettles Soviet propagandists.

At one time, one of the most orthodox Soviet writers, the hard-line Stalinist Vsevolod Kochetov, wrote an entire novel about the CIA sending an American jazz band to the Soviet Union along with an absolutely outrageous black woman singer who wiggled her big behind onstage (also, of course, on CIA orders) so that the unstable element in Soviet youth would be permeated by that corrupting Western spirit and would stop studying Marxism-Leninism and be diverted from fulfilling tasks essential to the national economy. Kochetov was one hundred percent right. The young people *have* been diverted. Instead of singing "Vast is the country of my birth," they have for some reason taken to the ideologically dangerous and even blasphemous

Rasputin, Rasputin
Greatest Russian love machine . . .

I happened to see a Soviet television program not long ago in London. A doctor of philosophy gave a lecture in which he spoke about the amoral and insidious methods to which the international imperialists were resorting in order to undermine the Soviet people's monolithic unity and to smash the unsmashable Soviet system. During the Revolution, they had attempted to smash Soviet power by means of direct intervention. It didn't work. Then they tried to strangle it by means of economic sanctions of every sort. It didn't work. They hoped to destroy the Soviet people through Hitler's hordes. That didn't work. They tried to shatter us by using so-called dissidents. That didn't work either. Now they are spending millions of dollars to send us jeans and T shirts adorned with bourgeois symbols. And they have sunk so low as to affix their own American flag to the part of the garment that covers the buttocks. Flags on buttocks so incensed the doctor of philosophy that he devoted the greater part of his talk to that particular subject.

By the way, the very people who fight Western "product propaganda" also prove to be the principal suppliers and distributors of such products. Soviet journalists, diplomats, delegates, and Party figures on all levels who are allowed to leave the country, not only prefer foreign clothing to Soviet themselves, not only obtain it for their children and other family members, but they use their exceptional opportunities to buy up enormous quantities of glad rags at a discount abroad and deliver them by rail, sea, or air to the Soviet Union, where they sell them for a high profit on the black market.

But statements such as that professor's always produce contrary reactions. Over the years, Soviet propaganda has completely exhausted its credit among its consumers. The tireless lies and unscrupulousness have produced a stunning effect: Soviet people are deeply interested in whatever it is the propaganda repudiates, and no less deeply disgusted by everything it extols. This applies to all spheres of culture and society. For example, if the Soviet press praises one writer or another, he will, of course, be published, but next to no one will read him. At one point, Mikhail Zoshchenko, Anna Akhmatova, Boris Pasternak, and Alexander Solzhenitsyn became considerably more popular after Soviet propaganda subjected them to withering criticism, whereas Vasily Grossman, entirely deserving of an equal place among them, is little known only because he was smothered quietly without a lot of propaganda hullaballoo.

Every day of the week, Soviet newspapers, radio, and television curse the United States and paint it in the darkest colors—unemployment, racial discrimination, crime, inflation, poverty. As a result of that propaganda, there are many Soviet people who think that America has no serious problems, that there money grows on trees, one lives in luxury, gambling at the casinos, driving a Cadillac, never lifting a finger. For this reason, when they encounter real American life rather than the charmed life they had imagined, some émigrés are disappointed and curse Soviet propaganda for having caused them to lose their bearings. It's like the old joke about one passenger on a train asking another where he's going. "To Zhmerinka." "You trickster!" says the first. "You say you're going to Zhmerinka so I'll think you're going to Zhitomir, even though in fact you *are* going to Zhmerinka!"

SOVIET ANTI-SOVIET PROPAGANDA

Having now lost its own bearings, Soviet Communist propaganda is gradually merging with anti-Communist and anti-Soviet propaganda. For example, anti-Soviet

43

propaganda asserts that since the time of its creation, the Soviet state has been ruled solely by criminals. Soviet propaganda asserts nearly the same thing. Dozens of high state leaders, from Trotsky to Khrushchev, have been declared and are still considered enemies of the people, agents of imperialism and foreign intelligence, or, at best, anti-Party factionalists and voluntarists.

Both anti-Soviet and Soviet propaganda maintain that there is no socialism with a human face, nor can there ever be.

Soviet propaganda is extremely indignant in its rejection of all suggestion by Western futurologists of the possible evolution of the Soviet system, and contends there is no such evolution, nor will there ever be. (That contention is both unscientific and anti-Communist: unscientific because evolution is an objective factor and is always occurring in one country or another, and anti-Communist because what else will produce the final stage of Communism if not evolution?)

Attempts by Western Communists to save the "scientific world view" from utter ruin meet with even greater hostility. The Soviet press sharply attacks anyone undertaking any such attempt, as it attacked Carrilo and Berlinguer. Distributing their speeches to Soviet citizens was punished no less severely than distributing *The Gulag Archipelago*. Even distributing certain articles by Marx, Engels, or Lenin can also result in big trouble. I won't even mention what's in store for anyone distributing the Twentieth Party Congress documents unmasking Stalin. But here's a more telling example: At the beginning of the seventies, in the Urals, a group of workers was arrested, not for distributing leaflets, no, and not CIA forgeries, but for distributing a document that had not been countermanded and that promised that Communism would soon be built. The document was, needless to say, the majestic and grandiose *Program of the Communist Party of the Soviet Union.*

Our Man in Istanbul

A very important part is played in Soviet life by the questionnaire. And its praises truly deserve to be sung. Were I a writer of odes, I would devote one to that singular invention of the bureaucratic mind.

There are various types of questionnaires. Some are a bit easier than others, some a bit more difficult; then there are those that could trip up the devil himself. A questionnaire's complexity increases in direct relation to the importance of the place a person seeks to occupy and for which filling out that questionnaire is part of the process. For example, when I worked as a carpenter, I was presented the simplest of questionnaires upon starting a job. Actually, it was more of a registration card than a questionnaire. I don't remember exactly, but it seems to me it asked only my last name, first name, patronymic, year of birth, profession, and rating. And then they'd hand you an ax and say, "Go to work. The Party trusts you." But the better the place one comrade or another wishes to occupy, the less the Party trusts him, the more questions it asks, and the more suspiciously it views the answers.

I saw my first more complicated questionnaire when I joined the Zaporozhye Flying Club in 1950. I no longer recall how many questions there were—forty, fifty—but some of them made an impression on me and I can still remember them. Despite the fact that I was born in 1932, that is, fifteen years after the Revolution, I had to answer a question asking whether I had served in the White Army, where, when, and with what rank. Also, was I a member of any political party? And, of course, did I have any relatives abroad, and if so, who were they and what did they do? I answered nearly all the questions sincerely and truthfully. No, I did not serve in the White Army, I belonged to no political party, and I had no relatives abroad. I did learn later that my distant relative Milovan Djilas had been a close comrade of Tito, who at this time was invariably referred to as a bloody dog by the Soviet press, but when filling out the questionnaire, I had no idea I had such a relative. Maybe I did lie knowingly once. I answered "No" to the question asking if any of my relatives had ever been on trial, even though I was perfectly aware that my father had spent five years in Stalin's camps. To make a long story short, my answers were found satisfactory by those who read them, and the Motherland entrusted me with a glider that could attain a speed of forty miles per hour.

The small trust shown me then was later to be overturned by a greater distrust. Three years later, I served as an airplane mechanic in Poland. Though it's really neither quite fish nor fowl, Poland is still outside the Soviet Union, and we lived a slightly better life there

47

than on our own territory. We were paid more money, fed better, given butter, which soldiers never lay eyes on in the Soviet Union, and we didn't roll our own cigarettes there, but smoked Belomorkanals.

Then all of a sudden I was called in to the regimental commander and told: "Listen, we found out you're a flier!"

"What do you mean a flier? I used to fly a glider."

"So that means you know how to fly a glider?"

"I don't see the point, but yes, I can fly a glider. You push the handle away from you or toward you, nothing too tricky."

"Well, since you already know how to deal with a glider handle, you'll go back to the Soviet Union and train as a helicopter pilot."

I packed my bag and went back to the Soviet Union. When I arrived in the city of Kinel, in Kuybyshev Province, I saw that about a hundred other aces like myself had been assembled there. Some had been in Poland, some in East Germany, and some in Austria, where we had troops stationed at the time. And it was then that I learned they had no intention of training me to be a helicopter pilot; they simply had wanted me away from the border. It turned out that, not long before, in Germany, an airplane mechanic had flown from the Soviet Zone to the American in a staff biplane.

And so I was done in by a questionnaire in the most unexpected way.

At the end of the fifties, after I was out of the army, I worked as a carpenter in Moscow and wrote poetry that no one would publish. I did not find my job suitable and wanted to be closer to art. One day, walking past the Moscow Art Theater, I noticed a sign saying that stage-set workers were needed. That's the job for me, I decided. I went to personnel, where I was given a friendly reception. They thought me a good find, because stage-set workers were paid little and no one wanted the job. "Well, here's your questionnaire," they said. "Read it carefully, fill it out, and bring it back. They'll run a check on you over the next three weeks or so; then we'll inform you when to come to work." I was surprised. Why such a long questionnaire and why such a long time to check it out? "You should understand," they said, "that our theater is special, that Party and government leaders sometimes attend our performances. Not only that, but we go on tour abroad from time to time."

I took the questionnaire home with me and studied it carefully. It contained innumerable questions concerning not only me and my parents, but my grandparents and my wife's relatives as well, questions I was simply unable to answer. I tossed the questionnaire out, and never did work at that illustrious theater.

I think there is not a single person in the Soviet Union who does not experience some fear when filling out a questionnaire. Everyone is aware of the mysterious eminence who will read the questionnaire, carefully checking it against the attached autobiography, comparing one answer with another, combing for contradictions, and putting a plus or a minus after each answer. Member of the Party—plus; non-Party—minus. Was not on German-occupied territory forty years ago—plus. Relatives abroad—minus. Russian—plus. Jew—minus.

In the brief period of Soviet history when the door to Israel was opened partway, it turned out that being Jewish and having relatives abroad provided an unprecedented opportunity to be delivered forever from those questionnaires and their unpleasant probing. But when applying for a job in the Soviet Union, a Jew always encounters obstacles, sometimes surmountable, sometimes not. The same can be said of Crimean Tartars and ethnic Germans (the latter, however, have or have had a chance to leave the country). Representatives of certain other, smaller, nationalities sometimes have advantages over all the rest, including Russians.

I know of a case in which a physicist applied for a position at a prestigious research institute. As a Jew, the director of the institute was sensitive to the ethnic composition of the staff (meaning he tried to avoid the accusation of hiring too many Jews), and after a chat with his future co-worker in which he determined his professional level and sphere of scientific interests, the director hemmed and hawed, then asked: "And how about everything else?" The physicist seeking the position understood the question at once and was quick to reply: "As for all the rest, everything's in good shape, I'm a Tadzhik."

But despite the fact that all personnel managers do nothing but pore over questionnaires seeking out inconsistencies and flaws in the biographies of employees of one institution or another, the most incredible absurdities do sometimes slip past their watchful eyes. Some mischievous people write utter nonsense, for example, that they served in the White Army with the rank of general. Others write nonsense not because they're mischievous but out of practical considerations. At times this can fuel scandals. Suddenly it will come to light that the director of some institute, a Ph.D. in science, in fact never got past the seventh grade, never wrote a dissertation, and hasn't the foggiest notion about the branch of science he is overseeing.

I was once privy to one of those extraordinary cases. In the mid-sixties, as a board member of the prose section of the Writers' Union, I was invited to a hearing in the case of a writer named Novbari. He had been accused by a woman of plagiarizing her play and publishing it under his own name. During the first stage of the investigation, we looked at Novbari's questionnaire and read his autobiography. And a very colorful biography it was. Born in Iraq, he had been sold into slavery for four years. He escaped from his master and joined the Communist Party of Turkey. In time he became the *rezident* for Soviet intelligence in Istanbul. When the questionnaire and the autobiography were compared, it turned out that he had joined the Communist Party at the age of nine and had become the *rezident* at eleven. And there were all sorts of other fantastic fabrications that did not jibe at all. His actual biography was more modest than the one he had invented. He was not born in Iraq, but in Azerbaijan, and he had never been abroad. It turned out that he had joined the Writers' Union twice, the first time in Tadzhikistan, where he had been expelled for plagiarism and other shady dealings.

It's a curious thing that, before the scandal broke, Novbari's papers, filled with the most absurd concoctions, had roused no suspicion in the so-called creative personnel section of the Writers' Union, where highly qualified KGB people work.

The board meeting at which Novbari's case was examined took place, needless to say, behind closed doors. The defendant, an elderly and melancholy Eastern type, seemed not in the least embarrassed; on the contrary, he assumed a very bellicose attitude. At the very start, he said that the hearing was of no interest to him; he had brought an application with him and requested that he be recommended for a trip to Syria, where he would gather material for his book on the Arab nations' struggle for liberation. He was told: "Hold on. First we have to look into the facts of your biography. Is it possible that you joined the Party at the age of nine?"

To this and the other questions, Novbari replied enigmatically: "Those who need to know, know."

"But you couldn't have been the intelligence *rezident* at the age of eleven!"

"Those who need to know, know."

"So where were you born then, in Baghdad or Baku?"

"Those who need to know, know."

To my surprise, some of the other board members, of whose literary activities I had not the slightest notion, at once displayed an interest in those to whom the defendant kept making vague reference. "Who is it who knows? Give us a name? What department is he in?" And then they began naming names and departments, showing themselves to be well informed about such matters.

Unlike them, Novbari was able to keep military secrets; he did not reveal names and department numbers, he just kept on with his dull incantation: "Those who need to know, know." Not only that, but he continued to insist that he be recommended for a trip to Syria.

That issue was put to a vote and all the board members voted against it, except me. I abstained, for which I almost received a reprimand. Why had I abstained? they wanted to know. I replied that I was prepared to vote for Novbari's expulsion from the Writers' Union for plagiarism and lies, but did not think I had the right either to forbid or to allow him to travel, especially since I did not have the right of travel myself.

The board meeting ended then and there. The secretary of the Moscow branch of the Writers' Union, KGB General Victor Ilin, proceeded to call certain board members, including me, into the next room. (I think he wanted to involve me in more active "public" work.) He said that the next time we should prepare better for exposing Novbari. "He must be surrounded like a wolf!" said Ilin, a rapacious gleam in his eye. Then he shifted his gaze to me, his expression becoming somewhat sour. "And you'll probably stay out of the picture, won't you?"

"I will," I promised confidently, seeing no place for myself in that pack of predators. I kept my promise and therefore know nothing about the further investigation into the former *rezident* in Istanbul. I know only that it all turned out well for Novbari, because he was still listed as a member of the Writers' Union when I left for the West in 1980. And no doubt he is a member to this day, if he's still alive. That is to say, the people to whom Novbari kept referring—the ones who needed to know what was behind the answers on his questionnaire—must, in fact, have known.

A Few Words
on Defectors

People are taking to their heels. And they're running fast—fleet as deer, as a poet once said. That's putting it mildly! A deer, of course, is a fleet animal, but there are limits on its speed. Take the pilot Viktor Belenko (remember him?), who stole a MIG a few years ago and flew off to Japan faster than the speed of sound. That's when the joke about "eMIGrating to Japan" started making the rounds.

Well, there are quite a few jokes about Soviet citizens and their brothers in the socialist countries fleeing to the West. I remember when the Polish passenger liner *Stefan Batory* was sailing around Europe. The passengers were jumping ship in nearly every port, alone or in groups, and to such an extent that the ship was practically deserted. At the time, the Poles quipped that it shouldn't be called the *Stefan Batory*, but the *Flying Dutchman*. And another joke popped up after several ballet dancers de-

fected: "How do you make a string quartet?" "You send
a Soviet orchestra abroad."

Jokes are jokes, but people *are* fleeing the country.
And what people! Artists, conductors, directors, chess
masters, champion athletes, Ph.D.'s in every science there
is, winners of socialist medals, laureates, deputies, diplomats, and, needless to say, employees of the Committee on State Security, the KGB. And there are probably
more of the last than of anybody else. There are so many
running that you could make a track team out of them.
Small fry do it; big shots too. Even the assistant to the
Foreign Minister, Arkady Shevchenko, decided to take
a powder. And people say that not long ago a lieutenant
general in full uniform crossed the Turkish border on
foot. And there was the quite recent case of Oleg Bitov,
a correspondent for *Literaturnaya Gazeta*.

They didn't seem that sort at all! They'd all been checked
out. The local Party organizations had run checks. Their
files had been approved by the district committees. The
Central Committee and the KGB commission on travel
had vigilantly scrutinized all the ins and outs. Everything
was, as they say, tiptop—the right social background, the
right position at work. They were politically disciplined,
morally stable. They fulfilled production quotas, spoke
out at meetings, took part in voluntary Saturday work
projects, didn't cheat on their wives, weren't in trouble
with the law, had no venereal diseases. And they paid
their Party dues on time.

That is to say, people without defect defect.

I had a friend who was a film director. He made doc-
umentaries. One time he was making a film about the
ballet. When he started filming a soloist, he was told:
"Don't film that one; he's no good." The dancer had

once signed a letter that wasn't so good itself. The comrades in charge told the director: "Film this one; he's good. He's a national talent, a national treasure. He can leap higher, attends political-information sessions regularly, takes the lead in social campaigns as a deputy to the City Soviet, *and* he's a candidate for membership in the Party." The director says of course. He's a Soviet man too, politically disciplined and morally stable. He does what they tell him. He cuts the no-good one out of the film and shoots a mile of film of the good one. Pleased with himself, he runs to show the higher-ups his new masterpiece.

They take their seats in the screening room. The lights fade, the music comes up, and then, half-naked, the candidate Party member leaps across the screen as if he were already a full member of the Party. The director steals a glance at the officials, who steal glances back at him, their frowns visible even in the dark.

One of them asks: "Who's this you're showing us?"

"What do you mean? That's . . ." He provides the ballet dancer's name. "An incomparable Soviet artist, a national treasure, a candidate member, *and* a deputy to the City Soviet."

"Are you aware that this deputy only yesterday requested political asylum in the West?"

"That can't be!" says the director. "I can't imagine such a thing!"

"Why not? Do you mean to say you never listen to foreign radio broadcasts?"

"Of course I don't, of course not," says the director. "I don't listen to them and I don't allow my children to listen to that junk either. And as for that dancer, it was you people who told me to film him and not the other one."

That, of course, he said without thinking. He would have been better off accepting the false accusation and admitting that he listened to foreign radio. Instead, he had hinted to higher-ups that they were the ones to blame for the foul-up.

It all ended badly. Secret orders were issued regarding the director. The movie was shelved. The director was barred from working in films and reprimanded for allowing his political vigilance to grow blunt and for parading dubious characters across the screen.

After that, the director became politically undisciplined and much less morally stable. He took to drink, went to seed, grew a beard, and began listening to foreign radio broadcasts. Later on, however, he mended his ways. He stopped drinking, shaved, and sold his radio at a secondhand store. He began attending meetings again, paid his membership dues, and had nothing to do with radios. He watched only hockey and figure skating on television, and when our side won, he would cheer so loudly that even his neighbors could hear.

The higher-ups got the message: he's one of us after all. Of course he made a few missteps, but that happens to the best. They took the ban off him and began throwing him work. Then, having fully regained their trust, the director was emboldened to apply for permission to make a very important film. I don't remember exactly what it was to be called—"In the Footsteps of Lenin"—something like that. As we know, the greater part of those footsteps occurred outside the borders of our country. Because Comrade Lenin at one time had been something of a defector himself. He had hidden from the Tsarist authorities in Zurich and Geneva, Paris and London.

The higher-ups were a little hesitant. They had already allowed one slip. They took a close look at him. He had filled out his forms to a tee, he supported Soviet sport, knew the Secretary of the French Communist Party, and had won the fight with his own moral decline. So they told him not to succumb to provocation over there, to avoid connections with the enemy camp, not to go crazy shopping, and if asked about Sakharov, he was to say: "I don't know him personally, so I can't say anything good about the man." And in regard to Afghanistan: "I still don't know exactly where it is, but I have heard that a limited contingent of ours is providing temporary aid to the peasants in harvesting the cotton and repairing the roads."

OVIR, the visa department, issued him a passport to travel, a limited amount of foreign currency was deposited for him in a bank abroad, and then he purchased a round-trip ticket from Aeroflot.

To this day he is still following in Lenin's footsteps, from Zurich to Geneva, from Paris to London.

When some reliable person defects, of course, new information is immediately forthcoming to prove that he was a So-and-so, in love with dollars, wore jeans, had a weakness for loose women, and even that he was not indifferent to persons of his own sex.

And naturally they attack all the defector's weak points. They force his close relations to weep and wail in newspaper articles. Official government representatives seek out meetings with him and tell him, with a sweet lilt to their voices: "Come home! Your country will forgive everything, and you'll be given more than you had before. If you don't come back, you So-and-so [here they whisper the most forceful expressions], we'll get you all the same, no matter where you are." Then they start reproaching him for every little thing he took from the Party: his education, his upbringing, his dacha and car, access to stores for the privileged. They ask him what was it he lacked.

Perhaps it was freedom he lacked. Not the freedom that is the recognition of necessity. But one which is itself a conscious or unconscious necessity. Maybe he was running away from those special stores for the privileged. Maybe he was ashamed to walk out of secret establishments with a hunk of salami or sturgeon wrapped in gray paper so as not to attract any attention. Maybe he was disgusted by the humiliating procedure of the loyalty check, to which everyone wishing to travel abroad is subjected. Maybe he couldn't twist his tongue into saying he didn't know who Sakharov was or where Afghanistan was located.

Come to think of it, why don't Westerners defect to the Soviet Union if things are so good here? We have no unemployment, apartments are cheap, medical care is absolutely free, and people treat each other like friends, comrades, brothers. But what happens when Angela Davis, Georges Marche, James Aldridge, or some other foreign comrade comes here to the land of their dreams? For one thing, they get a different reception from that given Soviet people when they go abroad. They're driven around in limos, put up in the best hotels, shown only the most beautiful things and places, and fed black caviar on top of red. They hang around for a while and then, feeling at loose ends, go back to where they came from. They don't defect. Even though no one ran checks on them. Even though there are no travel commissions in their countries. Or could that be the very reason? Maybe all those travel commissions are the very reason people flee the Soviet Union. Because even if you only want to visit your grandfather in Los Angeles or your aunt in Amsterdam or just spend a couple of weeks by the Mediterranean, you have to swear an oath that you'll be vigilant, resist everything, and treat smiles from passing women as preplanned provocations.

Since it's inconceivable that the Soviet authorities will ever abolish travel commissions, I'd like to give the Security people who work on them some useful advice: Step up the vigilance. Choose only the cream of the crop—dedicated Communists, active, public-spirited people. Study their forms closely, their personal files, and the reports on them by informers. And once the most dedicated, the worthiest, the best of the best have been winnowed out, do not allow them to go abroad under any conditions. They're just the ones most likely to defect.

My Fellow Russians

I no longer remember in which book I read it, because
I've read it in so many, and it has become something of
a set piece: during the war and especially on foreign soil,
whenever Russian Soviet soldiers met, they'd call out in
delight: "You Russian? Where're you from?" Answers
would come flying from all sides: Voronezh! Tambov!
Ussuriysk! Fellow Russians. And even though they called
each other derisive names like Tambov wolf, Vologda
jailbird, Ryazan potbelly, they were just showing affec-
tion for one another. Potbellies, jailbirds, and wolves
aside, they were countrymen—born in the same country,
speaking the same language, raised on the same songs.

Of course, there's nothing especially Russian about all
that. It's true of all people. If two Americans meet, it's
"Where ya from?" "Oklahoma." "Michigan here!" "Great!"

It's always like that. The farther a person is from his
native land, the happier he is to meet someone from
home. When a German meets a German, or a French-

man meets a Frenchman, they're as happy to see each other as they would be if they were related. The people who live in other countries may be interesting, but for some reason your own's your own. And sometimes a person feels like sharing something that is mutual but select, something others would not understand in the slightest.

Let's suppose two Congolese meet. They immediately have a set of shared associations: the Congo, crocodiles maybe, Patrice Lumumba University in Moscow. These things have some special meaning for them, some secret significance. And what is the significance for us Russians who run into each other abroad, on the street, in a bar, a theater?

It so happens that my first memory of a meeting of that sort is connected with a store in Munich. My wife and I were in a very large one, something on the order of GUM, with this difference: GUM is packed with people and there are no goods to speak of; in our store it's the exact opposite. Anyway, we were pushing our shopping cart down the aisles and discussing the various products aloud in Russian, thinking that we wouldn't be understood. Suddenly, another couple came running over.

"Are you Russian?"

"What else? Of course!"

"Us too! From Moscow!"

"So are we."

"Perfect, someone from home! We live on Dybenko Street. And you?"

"We live on Chernyakhovsky Street."

"Of course, of course. We know where that is, by the Airport Metro station. That's where the writers' building is. So that means you live right next to the writers."

"That's right, we did, but now we've moved."

"You moved? From such a nice neighborhood? What street do you live on now?"

"Now we live on Hans-Karossastrasse."

I could see the wife already tugging at her husband's sleeve and stepping on his foot, but he was a little slow and the meaning did not register at once.

"You say . . . Hans-Karossa . . . So that means—pardon me for asking—that you're émigrés?"

"You've got it! Emigrés. Renegades."

"In that case you'll excuse me."

They dashed away and that was the last we saw of them.

Though this was the first such meeting, it was by no means the last. It's the same every time. If a fellow Russian is abroad for a short while, first he runs up to you like you were his own brother, but when he realizes what's what, he runs away with equal speed. Because Soviet citizens with the right to travel are, as a rule, cautious people. It was their cautious behavior that earned them the trip in the first place. And before leaving on that trip, they've had the fear of provocation drummed into them; they've been instructed not to gape at shop windows and to avoid émigrés like the plague. That's just what they do—not so much out of fear of provocation by émigrés, as fear of the eagle eyes watching them.

Those chance meetings leave me so unsettled that now I do not dash over to speak with my fellow countrymen; on the contrary, I pretend not to understand a word of Russian.

Sometimes it's hard to avoid, however.

Quite recently we decided to go skiing. The weather's

not dependable in Munich. Sometimes it snows and sometimes it doesn't. So we decided to go to Austria. We arrived at the ski resort, which, though it once had been a vacation spot for the rich, was now full of all sorts of people. We skied down small hills, fell, and yelled "Careful!" to one another. All of a sudden a beautiful, dark-eyed girl about ten years old ran over to us. Looking at our daughter, she said: "Are you Russian?"

"We are."

"Where from?"

"Where are *you* from?"

"I'm from Moscow."

And of course we're from Moscow too, and we ask her where she's living now, where she had come to the resort from—Vienna, or Munich like us.

"What do you mean where from? I told you, from Moscow."

She didn't understand me and I didn't understand her. I said: "And how it is you came here?"

"Very simple. Mama's on vacation, Papa's on vacation, and it's school break, so we came to ski for five days."

"You just up and came?"

"That's right. Why not? We just up and came."

She was still young and hadn't yet taken all the elementary political-education courses. She already knew, though, that in the Soviet Union there were two kinds of people—those who could come here and those who could not. But she was not yet aware that not all those who came could go back. She did have some sense of it, however, for doubt and suspicion clouded her eyes and she began gradually sidling away from us.

As I looked at her, I thought, Could her parents be up to any good if they were simply allowed to come here with their daughter for vacation and had no fears on any score?

As any Soviet knows, Soviet children are not only flowers of life, they are useful hostages as well. The well-known writers, actors, artists, and academicians I knew who were able to leave the country at one time or another could be counted on the fingers of one hand. I don't seem to recall that any would have been allowed out with their children.

But that's not counting my former neighbor Ivanko, who at that time was a KGB colonel and who by now most likely has risen to the rank of general. Ivanko can travel. With both his wife and his child. Both on official business and for no reason at all, for pleasure. I don't know his preferences these days, but he used to be fond of spending his leave in Nice. To hike through the area outside Moscow with a knapsack on his back or camp out in Karadag, like other people, was not for him. Having gotten himself a good toehold, risen, and put in his time, he enjoyed a privilege beyond the comprehension of normal Soviet people. He traveled wherever he wished—just like, more or less, we do.

But to go back to that little girl, Varya. She had come there, that little Russian, to vacation in an Austrian resort. No other girl or boy there—German, French, Italian, American—had anything over her. Varya was wearing brightly colored European clothes with labels that children love the world over. For her that was possible. But the children of ordinary parents without the right to travel are dragged into people's militia headquarters for wearing such clothes.

It is those fathers and mothers with the right to travel who have created the conditions that divide us Russians into those who either cannot go abroad or cannot return home. And so, hearing our own language we first run like madmen toward the sound, saying: "Are you Russian?" But then at once we come to our senses and, without waiting for an answer, dash away as fast as our feet will carry us.

A Simple
Woman Worker

Many stories, novels, plays, and film scripts have been written about that unique breed, the Communists. Generations have been raised on their image. Every Soviet person knows that Communists are made of special stuff. They're tough as nails; you can pour molten lead down their throats, carve stars in their backs, burn them in the fireboxes of locomotives, but they don't care. Either they say nothing, or, if really pressed, they sing the "Internationale" or shout out proudly that their cause will be victorious in the end.

Not all readers have yet shown, however, a desire to emulate Pavel Korchagin or Alexander Matrosov. For some reason, certain readers feel more affinity for non-Party types like Natasha Rostov, Pierre Bezukhov, or Prince Mishkin. I personally prefer antiheroes to positive heroes in literature. For example, my favorite character is Gogol's Sobakevich, who said the only good person in town was the prosecuting attorney and, if you looked close enough, you'd see he was a real pig too. When speaking of food, Sobakevich said: "You can sprinkle a frog with sugar but I still won't eat it." I would apply those words to the image of the Communist, which they've been sprinkling with sugar for seventy years now and which still is inedible.

The Communists . . . Judging by Soviet literature, they're staunch, uncompromising champions of the people's good. They are by nature selflessly devoted to the cause, courteous and comradely to women. They're first in work and first in battle. And if it so happens that they have to give their lives for something, then it's like these lines:

> *Very softly said the commissar:*
> *Communists, forward! Communists, forward!*

I don't know about that, of course—I was too young to have been in any of the major battles—but in daily life most of the Communists I've run into bear little resemblance to their counterparts in literature. Either they're dull, slack-jowled bureaucrats who scowl at those beneath them and fawn shamelessly on their superiors, or else they're slinking out of the special stores for the privileged, their briefcases bulging. In general, they are cowed little people who never have anything to say on any subject, great or small. "Come on," they say, "how can I do that? I'll get in trouble. Don't forget I'm a Communist." I'm not even talking about the crooks who build themselves dachas with government money, sell caviar and ikons abroad by the trainload, or throw orgies. It's usually high-ranking Communists who engage in that sort of activity, and I would rather tell about the rank and file.

One time, my wife and I drove to a southern city on the sea. There was a crowd gathered in the town's dusty square. This was what they called there the "housing office." Landlords on one side, "wild men" on the other. Not wild men in animal skins; that's just what we call people who don't have passes for Soviet health resorts and whose passports, with all their hammers and sickles, won't get them through the front door of a hotel. We ended up in that crowd too, and were immediately besieged by profit-mad home and apartment owners. "Need a room? For how long?" We proved unpromising customers, because we had come for only a week, and the landlords preferred people there for the season or at least for a month.

We had been turned down by everyone when one last chance turned up—a sickly old man with a sunken chest and steel teeth. He approached us timidly. "Need a room? For how long? A week? Sorry, can't help you." He walked away.

But the way he walked made me think he was not dead set against us. I went after him. "Why not for a week?"

He nodded, a doomed look in his eyes, and said: "Well, if you like." Then he noticed we had a car and said, "I don't take people with cars."

"Maybe this time you could," I pressed.

He nodded again and said: "Well, if you like."

As time passed, that was what he always did—first he'd refuse, then say: "Well, if you like." We nicknamed him Wellifyoulikov.

We asked him if he lived far away.

He said, no—a mile, a mile and a half. "I'll show you

the way. I'll run up ahead, and you follow in the car."

"Why should you run ahead?" I said. "Get in; we'll give you a lift."

"No, no. I'd feel funny about it."

After I explained that we'd feel even funnier about him running ahead of us, he got in the front seat and sat huddled, as if trying to take up as little room as possible.

Wellifyoulikov turned out to live on the outskirts of town, on a dusty, bumpy street that after a rain would be passable only by tractor. His house, however, was large and well made. A powerfully built woman of around forty, wearing a torn sundress, was standing on the porch. Loudly and with great gusto, she was slapping mosquitoes on her sunburned shoulders and thighs.

"Who's that with you?" she called out, looking first at her husband and then at us, as if we were low-grade goods.

"Summer people, Egorovna, here for a week."

"Summer people?" she repeated. "For a week? What kind of summer people come for a week. That's all there was? Nobody else?"

"That's all, Egorovna," he said in a frightened voice. "Just them."

"All right then," she said and began to regard us with a more kindly eye. "Since you're rich people with a car, I have a room for you for ten rubles."

"A week?" asked my wife.

"No, a day."

"Ten rubles is too high," I said.

"No, it's not," she said, killing a mosquito on her leg.

"And there are mosquitoes here."

"What are you talking about?" she said, slapping her cheek. "These aren't mosquitoes."

"Then what are they?"

"Just plain bugs."

One way or the other we came to terms, and that evening we sat out on the terrace with our hosts, treating them to the wine we had also purchased from them. Wellifyoulikov said very little; his wife, Egorovna, did the talking.

"I work as a brigade leader in the vineyards, Volodya," she said to me. "Oh, it's hard work, it's tough work. Five in the morning till dark. I'm telling you, it's tough. But I love hard work. You feel good about yourself when you do hard work."

Their good-sized house was packed with people on vacation. We rented a private room. There were rows of cots, hostel-style, at two rubles a night, in the other rooms.

We got up late the next morning; the sun was already high. I went out to the washstand in the garden. Way at the back of the garden I noticed a shed. The shed door was open, and inside was Egorovna, lying face down on a folding cot and still wearing that torn and tattered sundress. She hadn't gone to work. Must be sick, I thought.

After breakfast, I went out to the garden again and saw Egorovna coming out of the shed stretching like a weight lifter before the lift.

"You didn't go to work today. Are you sick?" I asked.

"Not at all. We're in session today."

"A village soviet session?" I asked with some surprise.

"No. Town soviet. I'm on the cultural commission."

My wife and I went off to the beach, saw a film, and had dinner in a restaurant. So our hosts were asleep when we returned. The next morning I went out to the garden, and there was Egorovna again, sleeping in the shed.

"Another session today?" I asked.

"No. A Party meeting."

On the next day, she had a conference of front-line workers in industry. And the day after that it was something else. The only person in the house who did any real work was the husband, who was not a member of the Party. In the morning, while she was still asleep, he'd be running after customers on her command and then later on would either do some planing or sawing or work in the garden.

Since we would leave the house before she was up, and return after she was home, we never saw Egorovna in clothes befitting her position. She always had that same sundress on.

She liked to talk and was always saying that she loved hard work, that she had been a truck driver in the Altai during the war and had brought her husband back from there. She had only recently joined the Party.

"Our Party organizer, Ivan Semyonovich, calls me in and says, Egorovna, what's going on, a good worker like you not in the Party; it's not right. And so I got to thinking, if us leading workers don't join the Party, then who will? Especially since the Party leads our country and the Party is wise and peace-loving. Isn't that right?"

I had told her that I was a writer, and she was evidently hoping that if she expressed herself with true Party spirit, I would write something about her. Not that she hadn't been written up already. She'd been in the local paper and in an illustrated Moscow magazine.

Meanwhile, her husband, Wellifyoulikov, who was retired and not a member of the Party, was pained by having a lower standing than his wife and had become something of a domestic dissident. For the longest time, he said nothing, and then he exploded:

"You say their policy's correct? Is that it, correct? No one's saying it isn't, but just tell me why they're arguing with the Chinese? You're a member of the Party and you don't know. Well, I'll tell you why. The Chinese sold us coats at forty rubles apiece, and then they go in our stores and see those same coats going for a hundred and twenty."

"You don't understand anything," she said with a dismissive gesture. Then she turned to me: "Volodya, make a note—he's stupid and backward."

Only gradually did she reveal her secrets to me. On the eve of our departure, we sat out on the terrace drinking wine again.

"It's embarrassing to say, Volodya, but I got awarded a prize."

"Which one?" I asked, not surprised, but thinking it would be one of the smaller ones.

"The order of Lenin. I was received in Krasnodar by Politburo member Comrade Dmitri Polyansky. Very polite; he took my coat. If you had had some other medal before, even the badge of honor, he says to me, we would have given you the order of Lenin long before now."

We had ended up spending a week and a half there. On our last morning, we were awakened by noise from the porch. Our host had succeeded in dragging ten students back from the housing office to his place. When saying good-bye, I asked him: "Where's Egorovna?"

"She went to the vineyard."

It was the first time she'd gone to work in a week and a half.

We had spent all our time around the house or at the

beach, and it was only when we were leaving that we saw the center of town. In the small square in front of the Town Soviet building, we saw a row of portraits and, above them, the words BEST OF THE TOWN.

The fourth portrait from the left was of Egorovna in all her splendor. Dark suit, white blouse, order of Lenin on a chest held high.

The Chendzher
from Kherson

Here's another story. One evening, my wife and I were sitting with a woman friend in our kitchen in Moscow. The woman was a well-known actress. We drank tea, talked, and the actress began speaking of telekinesis and people able to move heavy objects merely by fixing a gaze on them. Telekinesis, spiritualist séances, and telepathic healing had become all the rage in Moscow.

When there is no public life, when criticizing the authorities or even telling jokes becomes somewhat frightening, when entertainment (theater, movies, television) is permeated with propaganda, and when the bookstores have nothing but volumes of boring speeches in an inhuman language by the General Secretary and other Politburo members, that's the time to get hooked on mysticism. Not a particularly Soviet thing to do, it would seem, but—unlike, say, distributing or even just reading samizdat—it's safe.

Anyway, we were sitting there talking when all of a

sudden the doorbell rang. I went to the door, cursing on the way: Who the hell could it be at this time of night? I opened the door and saw a stranger wearing the uniform of the merchant marine. "Hello there!" It turned out that this merchant marine was on his way from Murmansk to Kherson and had decided to stop over in Moscow. His brother was an old classmate of mine, who, a few years back, had spent the night at my apartment and had had a very good time. He had given our address to his brother, the merchant marine. It should be said that to have guests from the provinces spend the night is nothing unusual in Moscow. The reason for this is not so much nerve . . . or stinginess on the part of the provincials as the absolute impossibility for an ordinary person to get a room in a Moscow hotel. I took a look at the merchant marine, then another good look. I didn't especially want to let him in, but I couldn't bring myself to turn him away: it was night, the weather was bad, and his brother and I had been classmates, after all. . . .

To make a long story short, I said fine, you're here, come in, just don't give my address to your other brothers and your comrades in the Kherson steamship line.

He sat down at the table with us, withdrew a bottle of Embassy vodka (which he said he'd gotten in Murmansk) and a jar of caviar from his briefcase, and gazed with delight at the actress. He had seen her on television just the day before, so you can imagine how lucky he felt. He'd have plenty to tell his buddies in both Murmansk and Kherson. Not to seem like an utter nobody, he set at once to telling us about his wanderings through the great wide world as a mechanic on board a freighter that hauled dry cargo. He told us how they were caught in fog in the Strait of La Pérouse, how they were tossed by waves off the coast of New Zealand, and how they ran aground on the coast off Marseille, or maybe it was Catania.

And as he tossed off the name of one port after another, we grew more dumbfounded, our mouths hanging open, not only my wife and I, but the actress as well. Although she too had the right to travel abroad, her experience of foreign cities (one trip to Paris, one to Budapest, two to East Berlin, and four to Sofia) now seemed pathetically limited.

Having become the center of attention, the merchant marine let himself go. The Bosporus, the Dardanelles, Georges Bank—names that for us were straight Jules Verne.

He had on a handsome uniform with bright chevrons and gold buttons, and the dial on his wristwatch was clearly digital. He glanced at it quite frequently, not because he was in a hurry to finish the Embassy vodka and go to bed, but because he was fairly sure we'd never seen a watch like that before. So the next time he checked the time, I asked him where he had bought that wonderful contraption. "That? I chendzhed that in Las Palmas." A moment later, he pulled out his cigarette lighter, which had a picture of a girl on it. When he held it straight up, she was in a bathing suit, but when he turned it upside down, she had nothing on. And, without my even asking, he told me: "I chendzhed that in Amsterdam." We were all very interested, of course, but I had never heard that word, *chendzhed*, before, so I asked him what it meant.

"Chendzh!" said the merchant marine confidently, setting his glass back on the table. "Didn't you study English in school? Chendzh is English for swapping. Every time

we're about to go abroad, we go around and buy everything in the stores. Watches, perfume, matryoshkis, soap,
pins, buttons. Anything we can lay our hands on."

"And you mean people will swap you things for Soviet
goods?"

"And how! Of course, you won't get very far with them
in places like Hamburg or Vancouver. But we go to other
places too. We Soviets aid the Third World, after all.
And in those countries . . ."

For some reason, his memory of those countries brought
on such a laughing fit that he would have fallen under
the table if I hadn't grabbed him in time. When he had
calmed down, he continued. His most pleasant memories, it seemed, were of the Suez Canal.

"You see, you go down the Suez Canal and there are
Bedouins on the shore. We call all Arabs Bedouins. You
shout to one of them: "Chendzh!" and he shouts back:
"Chendzh!" You lower your stuff down to him on a rope,
and he lifts his up to you on a stick. Of course, at this
point you've got to be on your toes. If you lower your
stuff down to him first, he'll grab it and run. And that'll
be that. If he raises his stuff up to you first, you'll grab
it and that'll be that too. You need your wits about you
the whole time. I remember one time we were carrying . . ."

And he told us a story about the time they were carrying a shipment of Gazik All-Terrain Vehicles, once
again to aid the countries of the Third World. First, they
took off the wheels and chendzhed them. Then, they
pulled out the speedometers and chendzhed them. Next,
the headlights.

"Hold on," I said. "Weren't there any complaints from
the people you were bringing the vehicles to?"

"What are you talking about? What kind of complaints? That was *aid*! If somebody gives you something for nothing, you take it. Forget the vehicles, that's not the half of it. We'd take things from the ship and chendzh them. We'd take a life preserver, unscrew instruments. And one time, when we couldn't find anything else, we swapped our brass anchor. You think that was easy? You couldn't throw it to the Bedouins in one piece; it was too heavy. We dragged it into our cabin, sawed it up into pieces, oiled the blade so it wouldn't make any noise, then threw the pieces out the porthole. The Bedouins ended up going after them with scuba tanks."

And late into the night he kept telling stories of what he chendzhed for what and where, until we were exhausted and he was getting a little tired himself. He began yawning and glancing at his watch—no longer to impress us with it, but to hint that it was time to sleep. It was when I asked him if he was a member of the Communist Party that he came back to life, straightened his shoulders, puffed out his cheeks and said, with a certain courtliness: "Well, of course I'm a Communist!"

Party Honor

Long ago, back in the time of the old rubles, a certain film director signed up on a waiting list for an apartment. There were practically no dwellings under construction in Moscow at that time, and the waiting list was very slow in moving. But finally the director found himself first on the list. He and his wife began to imagine themselves actually receiving authorization for the apartment, and arranging the furniture—where the bed would go, where the television would go. They let their imagination run free for a month, two months; then it was six months, a year. He was still first on the waiting list, and it wasn't moving at all; that, or it was somehow moving sideways.

Finally, someone cleverer than he told him: "You'll be on that waiting list until the Second Coming or until you grease the right person's palm."

But the director was a man of principle (even though he did not belong to the Party). "No," he said, "no way! I've never given a bribe and I never will. Bribes debase both the person who takes and the person who gives."

"Fine, then keep your dignity *and* your place on the waiting list," he was told.

Which is what he did. He stayed on the list for one year and then a second, until his wife began to nag. She no longer wished to live in a communal apartment, no longer wished to stand in line in the morning for the bathroom or to put the kettle on. And she was tired of keeping watch on the kitchen so that her good neighbors did not spit in her soup or do anything else of the sort. She nagged and nagged until gradually her husband's principles began to vanish into thin air.

All right, he thought, if that's how it is, I'll give a bribe this time, but never again. He was inexperienced in such matters, but good people came to his aid and introduced him to an important person from the Moscow Soviet.

They met at the Aragva Restaurant. The director ordered Georgian cognac, *lobio*, *satsivi*, and shashlik. He and the important person drank, ate, and finally the director said straight out to his guest, now relaxed after the cognac: "You see, art is my life. I'm cut off from the practical world. I've never given anyone a bribe and I don't know how to. But you're a man of experience; couldn't you clue me in on whom I should give it to, how much, when and where?"

The official downed another cognac, took a bite of shashlik, wiped his lips decorously with his napkin, and leaned across the table. "Me," he whispered. " Five thousand. Here and now."

The message was clear and direct. "Fine," said the director, taking his wallet from his pocket. But then he was seized by doubt. "What if I hand you the five thousand and they still don't give me the apartment?"

The official was totally aghast at that monstrous suggestion, and almost choked on his shashlik. Tears appeared in his eyes, and his voice trembled. "What do you mean!" he said. "How can you think that of me? Don't you know I'm a Communist!"

And in fact he proved an honest man. A month did not pass before the director received his authorization. He and his wife were happy as clams in that new apartment of theirs. That is, until they got divorced. The director left the apartment to his old wife and signed up on a coop waiting list with his new wife. That too, of course, required the greasing of a palm, but by then the director was seasoned in Soviet real estate—and he had become a Party man to boot.

Keeping to the
Party Line

Lenin once said that only a very educated man, one who mastered the most advanced knowledge of his era, could be a Communist. Among Communists today there are those who more or less correspond to Lenin's ideal. A rank-and-file Communist can be a worker, a kolkhoznik, an academician. He pays his Party dues, attends meetings, carries out important or unimportant Party assignments, but his main attention goes to his own profession. He may be respected in his specialized field, receive a high salary, and have many privileges, but, all the same, he does not belong to the higher caste. The higher caste, the power elite, is known as the *nomenklatura*. It consists of Party workers from the district level right up to the Politburo, who can be in charge of any branch whatsoever of industry, agriculture, science, or art, regardless of his background or training.

I was twenty-three years old when I attended tenth-grade night-school classes in the Crimea. I was a bit on the old side for a schoolboy, but some of my classmates were even older. The oldest was forty-six, and I saw him as an old man. His name was Eremenko. He always came to school in an austere gray suit—a long jacket, wide pants—and with his tie knotted tightly. He always sat in the back row. When he was called to the board, he would go to the front of the room, but he would never answer a single question. He was as silent as a partisan in an interrogation, as one of our teachers used to say. (Of course, her image of a Communist partisan came to her from literature, not from life.)

Eremenko made a sorry sight up there by the blackboard. No matter if the question was point-blank, he wouldn't say a word. He'd blush, he'd sweat, but not a word came out of him. The teacher would ask: "Didn't you prepare the lesson?" Silence. And if he did open his mouth, he'd blurt out something you couldn't make head or tail of. One time he was unable to show the border between Europe and Asia on the map, and when the teacher asked him where we were, he tensed and said: "Asia."

The teachers had no idea what to do with him. The chemistry teacher was the most aggressive, and said that he absolutely should not be allowed to graduate. The others were more liberal. I don't know whether they were afraid of him or what, but they always seemed embarrassed. He was, after all, a man with power. The teachers would say softly, "Sit down, Eremenko," then shame-facedly give him a D. Sometimes they wouldn't give him any mark at all: "All right then, I won't give you a mark today, but please be ready next time."

Naturally, there's always a variety of students—the brilliant, the good, the fair, and the poor. But students as dull-witted as Eremenko usually don't make it to the tenth grade. They might hang on until the fourth, or even the seventh, but then they're either kicked out or they quit themselves, preferring any form of manual labor to mental work. Had Eremenko been an ordinary student, he would never have made it to the tenth grade; but that was precisely the point, he was no ordinary student. He was a member of the power elite, the *nomenklatura*: he was a department head in the district Party committee, and in order to be promoted he needed at least a high-school education. It is true that he did not attend school in the same district where he held office, but in the next district, an agricultural one. Party ethics, as he himself said, did not permit him to go to school in his own district.

Members of the *nomenklatura* usually keep their distance from ordinary mortals, but Eremenko and I became friendly because I helped him with his chemistry and math. Sometimes, after a few hours of wasted work, we'd even have a drink together. At those times, he would be completely open with me. He'd speak with indignation about his chemistry teacher in particular: "What gives her the right to talk to me like that? She must have no idea who I am. In our district, I can call any school principal into my office, have him stand at attention, and keep him standing there for two hours."

One time, I asked him if having such an important position was difficult. I've never forgotten his answer. "Not at all, not difficult at all. In the work we do, the main thing is not to distort the Party line. But how can you distort it?"

He was equally poor in all his subjects, including history. Our usual history teacher, as it happened, was out on maternity leave, and had been replaced by the woman in charge of the education department in the district where Eremenko held office.

She was a very stout and stupid woman. She didn't know much about the subject she taught and, instead of historical facts, she crammed our heads with political information about the Party's policy. Her regular job was entirely dependent on Eremenko, and for that reason she was always well disposed to him in class. She would call him to the board and ask him questions like this: "Comrade Eremenko, can you tell me when the Fifteenth Party Congress took place?"

Silence.

"In nineteen-twenty-seven. Is that correct?"

"It is," Eremenko would answer. "In nineteen-twenty-seven."

"Look at that," the teacher would say. "Excellent preparation. I'm giving you an A."

He was quite encouraged by her and even became a little conceited.

"Say what you want, I do know my history," he would say to me.

Quite an original relationship sprang up between teacher and pupil. In the evening, she would call him to the board, and during the day, he would call her into his office and probe her knowledge about the educational system in the district he helped run. Those surveys of the educational system would usually conclude with the teacher asking for one small favor or another; the pupil was always glad to take such requests under consideration. He told me himself that one time, in great embarrassment, she asked him to arrange for her to be given a suckling pig from a kolkhoz. He phoned a kolkhoz, and that very day two enormous pigs were delivered to her at a cost of one ruble fifty kopecks apiece, old money—fifteen kopecks, or about twenty-five cents, apiece in new money.

Finally, Eremenko finished school, and his report card showed that he had gotten an A in history and hard-earned C's in his other subjects. All other subjects, including chemistry. Now the way to further special Party training was open to him, and he could rise up the career ladder. Armed with his new knowledge, he could boldly take charge of pig-breeding, sheep-breeding, art, whatever.

A few years later, I found out that Eremenko had indeed risen high. He was transferred to the provincial committee, and today is in charge of industry. *All* industry, including, of course, chemicals.

The New Year's Tree

They say that New Year's tells you what the year'll be like. If it starts good, it'll stay good. But if it starts bad, the whole year'll be screwed up.

This year, right before New Year's, something happened to me, but the only problem is I don't know whether to interpret it as good or bad.

And it all happened because of, well, because of—what should I call her—my wife. Other women do a little thinking in advance, but that one spends all the time until the thirty-first of December fooling with those curlers of hers, and if anything goes on under those curlers on her head, I'm the last to know about it. I'd just come home from my shift on the thirty-first. I had a little bite to eat, lay down on the couch, and started watching a program on TV called "I Serve the Soviet Union." I love seeing all those howitzers and tanks and planes. And it's then she comes in and asks me to go out and buy a tree. Because it is New Year's, after all, and our daughter's coming with that new fancy man she's got, and the champagne's already in the refrigerator and the aspic's on the balcony, and the only thing missing is the tree. I said, Where will I get one now, it's the thirty-first already. People must be out there killing themselves for a tree. There're no children to do any dances around the tree, and we don't have to do anything special for our daughter either. She marries one guy and doesn't even live with him a year before they break up, and now she's bringing a new one here, and nobody knows if anything's going to come of this one, and I'm supposed to go out in the freezing cold and kill myself for a tree? But my wife says whether anything comes of the two of them or not doesn't matter; it's not New Year's without a tree. And she drags me to the door.

Anyway, I go out, and it's already getting dark. I start roaming the streets to see what I can find. I go by one place, and they just sold the last tree; another place, they haven't gotten theirs yet, and the line there looks as long as the one in front of Lenin's tomb. Someone says that the place to go is over by the River Station metro stop. So I go, and ask some people where I can buy a tree. They tell me, Go out of the station, turn right, then right again, and that's where they're selling trees; you can haggle with them there, and the line's not too bad; you won't have to wait more than about three, three and a half hours. Of course, when I get there, the place is packed with people, all excited and shouting, You have to take your turn! One tree to a customer! And they don't let you pick it. I wanted to pick one of the better ones, but the girl selling them was too smart. Citizens, she says, no picking allowed here. These are trees, not candidates for the Supreme Soviet. So I end up with a kind of stunted little thing. The branches on one side are all right, but the other side is bare, and the top is bent over, crooked.

Anyway, I take the tree and get my receipt to prove that I acquired the tree legally. I stick the receipt in my pocket, grab the tree by the butt end, and start dragging it away to the metro station. At the station I run into this dark-haired guy who works with me, a real heavy drinker, but that doesn't matter. He starts asking me where I got the tree, and I start giving him directions. I explain it all to him, but for some reason he can't get it through his head. So I take the receipt out of my pocket and draw him a very precise map of how to go and where to turn. Naturally, I'm not thinking that I might need the receipt and that not having it will get me into all sorts of trouble. But I should have been thinking about that, because I've got a head on my shoulders, and I should use it for something besides putting a hat on.

Anyway, I get out at the Sokol metro stop, and I'm dragging the tree along, and up come a couple of those volunteer police. Both of them are young guys, both of them with faces only a mother could love. They're both wearing red armbands and rabbit-fur hats. Except one's hat is gray and the other's is white. The one in the white asks me politely where I got the tree. And so I tell him. And then he says have I got my receipt. Of course I do, I say, reaching into my pocket, and then I feel my heart sinking to my knees.

I say, Oh, I'm sorry, boys, I don't have the receipt because I gave it to that rummy who works with me, I gave the receipt to him.

Then the one in the gray hat looks over at the one in the white hat because one of them is the other's superior.

The one in the white hat says something like, Listen, citizen, we've heard that same cock-and-bull story a dozen times already today. There are plenty of people at headquarters trying the same baloney. Come with us.

And so I say, What are you guys talking about; is this a joke or what? I didn't steal the tree, I didn't cut it down anywhere, I bought it fair and square. And I *had* a receipt, but I gave it to that rummy I ran into. He asked me how to get there, and like a dope I drew him a little map on the receipt. I can't be wasting my time in headquarters with you. My wife's waiting for me. I've got my daughter coming over with that new guy of hers. They'll all be together. How can I not be there?

But those two don't even want to hear what I have to say and they take me off to their volunteer police headquarters. They ask me to leave the tree outside and take me downstairs to the cellar. There's a police captain sitting at a desk down there, and a bunch of volunteer police, and all the people they pulled in off the street— one for picking pockets, one for bashing somebody in the face, one for something else, and a girl they hauled in for loose—whaddaya call it—morals. And then me. Quite a bunch.

The volunteer, the one in the white hat, says to the captain, I brought this comrade in for transporting a tree without a receipt. All right, says the captain, leave him, we'll straighten it out. But he doesn't question me first, he questions the other guys who were there ahead of me. But I didn't have to wait long. Two hours tops. It would've been nothing if it hadn't been New Year's Eve. Anyway, two hours later, the captain writes up a report on the seizure of illegally acquired goods. I start to argue. I tell him I acquired it legally—*they're* the guys who seized it illegally. So what if I gave the receipt to that guy I work with. You can't drag everybody who hasn't got his receipt down to this basement. Maybe they can do that stuff in America, drag people without receipts down into the cellar, but this isn't America here; this is the Soviet Union. It's not easy convincing them. They let me out at around eleven o'clock and tell me I should thank them for doing it. I leave for home, my nerves shot for having wasted all that time, spent all my money, and come back without a tree. And what'll happen when I get home?

Anyway, I go home and tell my wife what happened. She stands there wringing her hands; then she says, Well, it's all right, anything can happen, and they've got that new—whaddaya call it—anticorruption campaign going, they're grabbing anybody they can get their hands on, they're even going after the ministers. Doesn't matter, she says, because we've got a tree, Kolya brought one over. Who's Kolya, I ask her. She tells me he's our daughter's new boyfriend, they just got here and they brought a tree with them and they're trimming it now. And I can see my daughter's coat with the mink collar hanging on the hook and a man's coat and a white rabbit fur hat beside it. At first I don't think much about it, because there are plenty of people with hats like that. I go in the living room from the hall and see my daughter in there with a young man and they're busy trimming the tree. The tree looks kind of familiar. The branches are only good on one side, and the top is crooked. Then the young man turns around, and, of course, I recognize him at once. I get so furious so fast that I just want to go over and let him have it right in the face. My daughter gets scared, runs over to me, and says, What are you doing, that's my boyfriend, that's Kolya! And I tell him

I'm going to let that Kolya have it. But then Kolya says, Easy does it, attacking a volunteer policeman's serious business. And I tell him, You're no volunteer cop here. Then I tell him what I think of him. My daughter wants to know what's the matter, my wife wants to know what's the matter, and so I tell them everything. Now Kolya's a little scared, he acts a little politer. He says, But why were you taking that tree down the street without a receipt for it? Of course, if I knew it was you, I wouldn't have done it, but I had no idea. And I say, That means if you don't know who I am you can steal my tree, is that it? And then you give it to your girlfriend, is that it? It was *my* tree even though it was all bent out of shape and missing branches. Then my daughter says, Daddy, why make such a big deal of it, it's a present, and you shouldn't look a gift horse in the mouth. Kolya starts calling me Dad too and says, Forgive me, Dad, it'll never happen again. And it's your fault, he says, that you chose a tree like that to bring home. That gets me riled up again, and my wife and daughter drag me out to the kitchen. My wife says, So, what does it matter what happened? That's what happened! Why scare off a man who wants to marry your daughter? He's a responsible guy. Did he take the tree he took from you and sell it to buy himself a few drinks? No, he brought it here to us. And then my daughter says, It's a good thing it was Kolya who took the tree from you and not somebody like Petya or Vasya. What's so good about that, I say, what's so good about having my future son-in-law take my tree away from me on the street. But my daughter says it was a good thing. Thanks to him the tree's here. If somebody else had taken it, he would have given it to *his* girlfriend and then we'd be here without any tree at all.

Anyway, they talk me around. I go back in the other

room and make up with Kolya. And just then they start reading the New Year's greeting to the Soviet people and that means it's time to open the bottle. My wife goes and gets the champagne from the refrigerator, and Kolya does a nice job opening the bottle. The chimes start ringing, we clink glasses, we make toasts to health and friendship—the bad should be forgotten and the good remembered.

So what can I say? That's how the New Year started for me.

Free of Charge

FREE EDUCATION

Soviet citizens traveling abroad for one reason or another are, as I've said, instructed to beware of provocative questions and to make quick-witted replies to them. Sometimes it's very difficult to be that fast on your feet, because any question can be a provocation—on housing, salaries, food supply, human rights, dissidents, Sakharov, Afghanistan. One should avoid answering questions on such subjects or counter them with assertions of the socialist system's advantages, which include free education, free medical care, and apartments that are nearly free.

These assertions are now so widely accepted that, during my lectures in the West, students sympathetic to the Soviet Union often ask the same question again and again, and not without a certain malice: "How much did your education cost you?" I am glad to reply that it cost me nothing, because I received no education. My parents, members of the intelligentsia and people with respect for education, were unable to provide for me, and so, like millions of others, I was forced to leave school in early childhood and go to work to earn my daily bread. I finished only one grade of regular school—the first. I missed the second and the third. I attended fourth grade while working on a kolkhoz. I missed the fifth. I did sixth and seventh in night school after an eight-hour workday. Then I was drafted into the army for four years, where no outside school, either night school or correspondence course, was permitted. All my appeals to my superiors met with the same answer: "You're here to defend the Motherland, not to study." After the army, I finished tenth grade while working—(I missed eighth and ninth)—and I attended a teachers' training college for a year and a half but left for the same reason as before—I had to earn a living.

I belong to a generation whose childhood coincided with the war. Things are easier now, and, as a rule, young people receive a high-school education. But far from every family is able to afford higher education for their children.

Education is free, but food, clothing, briefcases, and textbooks cost money. Regular school instruction is not enough to get one into a more or less decent higher institution, and parents are compelled to hire tutors for their children. Tutors charge up to ten rubles an hour, and many parents do not earn five rubles a day. There are many institutions where enrollment is impossible without giving a bribe, and that's a few hundred rubles right there.

Apart from questions of money, there are other hurdles. Certain institutions of higher learning (Moscow State

University, for example) admit practically no Jews. In certain others (the Institute of International Relations), enrollment is limited mostly to children of Party bureaucrats, diplomats, high military people, and KGB.

The authorities' official attitude toward education is one of contempt. Propaganda even instills that contempt in schoolchildren. The Soviet press is full of indignant articles and satirical pieces about young people who, instead of going right to work in factory or on farm, seek to enter institutes and universities. The law sets obstacles in the way of high-school graduates by imposing what is nearly an obligatory two-year term of work. After those two years in a factory or on a kolkhoz or in the army, a person forgets what he's learned and often loses interest in continuing his education, especially since its rewards are not very promising. The salary of an average engineer, doctor, bookkeeper, or schoolteacher is much lower than what a skilled worker earns.

Naturally, despite all these obstacles, some children of ordinary families without money do receive a higher education, but to do so they must display very great ability, a very strong thirst for knowledge, and a readiness for self-sacrifice. In their five years at an institute, they will be ill fed and ill clothed, and will have to earn a little money to live on by unloading freight cars or sorting rotted vegetables at depots. Only at that cost do they get their higher education. And for the rest of their lives they will be constantly reminded of that privilege and required to be grateful for it

FREE MEDICAL CARE

Any Soviet citizen who falls ill can go to a polyclinic, call a doctor to see him at home, or call an ambulance—

none of which costs him anything. If he has to go to the hospital, he will not be sent a bill for treatment. But . . .

My mother came in from the provinces to see me in Moscow in 1970. She looked terrible: thin, jaundiced, weak. I asked her what was wrong. She didn't know. She had pains in her stomach, had lost her appetite entirely, and kept losing weight.

What had the doctors told her? The doctors had told her that she had a spring vitamin deficiency; they had prescribed vitamins and said: "Eat herring to stimulate your appetite."

I'm no expert on medicine, of course, but I lived in Moscow, was a member of the Writers' Union, and had a great many connections, including some in the world of medicine. I was able to get my mother into Botkinsky Hospital. They x-rayed her and immediately saw something that could not be missed—an enormous tumor in her stomach. Fortunately, the tumor proved to be benign, and she could be treated. My mother lived another eight years before dying of heart failure. But what if she hadn't had a son in Moscow?

All right, let's suppose this was a chance incident. Let's suppose that in her province she'd been seen by a poor, poorly trained, or unconscientious doctor, which is not the usual case. But the same thing happened to my father two years later. My parents had moved from one city to another by that time. My father began having pain in the right side of his neck, where there was also a small swelling. A doctor examined him and diagnosed the problem as a swelling of a lymph node and prescribed a heat treatment. My father applied heat to the swelling, which continued to grow. The pain grew worse, it became difficult for him to swallow, but they went on prescribing heat and more heat. Finally, at the urging of my mother and sister, he went to Moscow. The first doctor he saw said it was cancer. Then he was examined by other doctors, x-rays were taken, biopsies were made. The final diagnosis: cancer at the base of the tongue, stage four—meaning the final stage. I had to get my father into a hospital. Making use of all my connections, I got him admitted to Kashirka, as Moscow's well-known oncological center is popularly known. This is an entire hospital city, with enormous wards; it has a frightening resemblance to a death factory. We went there, and called on a woman professor, bringing her a note from another professor. The woman professor sent us to see another professor, a man this time. He suggested my father sign himself in for tests. My father did, the tests were made, another biopsy was taken, and then I was told to go to a certain office. There was a line there, and people were going in one by one, or by twos, and coming out in tears. A man wearing a Master of Sport pin walked over to me and began complaining. He'd come in from Tashkent, where he'd been refused treatment. Kashirka had been his last hope, but they wouldn't admit him. "When they needed me," he said, "the finest doctors would treat me for a head cold. But now they don't need me. What do you think? If I collapse on the street, shouldn't an ambulance take me to a hospital?"

My turn came. I left my father in the corridor and went into the office. The doctor was in a hurry. "Your father has cancer, in an advanced state from neglect. It's incurable. He has three or four months to live at most. You should prepare yourself, these will be very trying and painful months. We can't admit him here. We don't have enough beds and we only admit patients we can help. We don't admit hopeless cases."

"But what can be done?" I asked. "He still has to have some treatment." The doctor told me that I could try to get him admitted to a hospital in the city where my father lived, but there was little chance of his being admitted. Then he wrote out a paper, which said: "The patient needs symptomatic treatment in his city of residence."

My wife and I went around to several Moscow hospitals, used all our connections, pressed all our friends and acquaintances into service, and finally found a doctor who worked in a suburban hospital. Fortunately, he proved to be a reader of mine and accepted my father for treatment. My father was given radioactive treatments. And miracle of miracles! The tumor began to disappear. Three weeks later, my father was discharged from the hospital under a physician's care.

Three years later, he had a recurrence. The doctor who had treated him was away on vacation. So once again we went around to several hospitals, starting with Kashirka, and once again none of them would admit my father, despite what we told them about the results of the first treatment. Finally, the doctor returned from vacation, and once again we appealed to him. My father underwent a second round of treatment. Nine years have passed since then (twelve since the first treatment), and my father is still alive. He is an old man and is frequently in pain, but his cancer has disappeared. If I hadn't lived in Moscow, if I hadn't had so many connections, and if I hadn't finally met that doctor who was well inclined toward me, my father would have been gone long ago.

Medical care is free, and for that very reason they hold it over everyone's head. But if a person has finished working, retired, and is of no use to the state any more, the state will not be overly concerned about his medical care.

I had an uncle who lived in one of the provincial capitals in the Ukraine. He fell sick one day, and his family called an ambulance. The ambulance service asked how old he was. Seventy. "We don't take people like that," they said. True, they did finally come after the family made a scene, but by then it was too late.

My grandmother was luckier. When she turned ninety, doctors began paying more attention to her. The district physician told her: "Please don't get sick. And if something does happen, call me. I'll come right away. You're one of the oldest living people here, and I need you for our statistics."

Medical care is free, but medicine isn't. And some medicine is very, very expensive.

A poor person is better off not bothering with certain serious operations, because a person in recovery needs many rubles in small denominations under his pillow. As soon as the anesthetic wears off, he should reach under his pillow and hand the nurse a ruble. If he wants to rinse out his mouth, that's a ruble; have his bed straightened, another ruble; needs a bedpan, another.

In some hospitals, where the staff has been spoiled, you have to give three rubles. Otherwise, no one will come to help you. A person who has undergone a serious operation might simply not survive the postoperative stage.

The overwhelming majority of doctors limit themselves to their miserable salaries and to small gifts from their patients (for example, a bottle of cognac for a complicated operation). It is not only the state, but the patients as well, who place an extremely low value on the work of doctors. Here's one example. A popular mechanic who was repairing my car told me that his father was seriously ill in the hospital and facing an operation, but the doctors had little hope of success. The mechanic then spoke with the surgeon and found out that his Zaporozhets needed repairing—the clutch was gone. Without a second's hesitation, the mechanic said to the surgeon: "You cure my father and I'll put in a new clutch at cost."

Some doctors are well aware of the corruption, bribery, and thievery everywhere around them, and, not wishing to live like beggars, begin to accept bribes themselves. Some do so moderately and some very immoderately. I know one professor who will not accept less than five hundred rubles for performing an operation in a state hospital. Soviet citizens have no insurance against bandits like these.

And so, yes, medical care in the Soviet Union is free. When you can get it.

NEARLY FREE APARTMENTS

Everyone knows that apartments are cheap in the Soviet Union. Rents are paltry and have practically never been raised throughout all of Soviet history.

But what kind of apartments are they and are they worth more than what the state charges for them?

Now, the housing situation has improved. It's already been twenty-five years since the state began to display genuine concern about solving the so-called housing crisis. The majority of the people I know in Moscow live in comfortable apartments with all the conveniences.

Nevertheless, there was a time . . . But I should start at the beginning.

I arrived in Moscow in 1956. I was writing poetry and hoped that it would be easier to publish in Moscow than in the provinces. But what does arriving in Moscow mean in Soviet terms? You have to have some place to stay, some place to live. And it's no easy matter to get yourself registered for residence in Moscow. People will resort to any trick to get registered. Some offer bribes, others enter into fictitious marriages. But I had no money for bribing anyone and no one to marry fictitiously, because that costs money too, and no small amount either. I had another trump card, however: my qualifications as a worker, which could gain me employment as a carpenter on a construction project or as a locksmith. But it turned out there was a problem. Just before I arrived, Khrushchev had delivered a panicky speech, saying that Moscow was overpopulated, too many people were coming to the city and staying on whether they had the right or not. The city had to be protected against further invasion. The rules for registering as a resident, strict before, now became brutal.

I started going around from one personnel department to another asking: "Do you need a carpenter or a locksmith?" And they did. Any personnel department head was ready to embrace me like his own brother, but they'd suspect I had an ulterior motive. The question would eventually come: "Are you registered to live in Moscow?" Then it was good-bye. I'd go to the police to register. But they'd only scowl at me and ask: "Do you have a certificate to work? No? Then get out of here."

I would.

At the time, I was living in a rather spacious dwelling,

several thousand square yards in size. I'm referring to the Kursk train station. It didn't cost me a kopeck to live there. True, there were certain inconveniences. You'd find yourself a place against the wall on the granite floor, and no sooner would you fall asleep than a policeman would wake you up and drag you outside. People without train tickets weren't allowed to sleep there. If it wasn't raining, you'd go to some little square to spend the night on a bench, but they'd chase you off the benches too.

After several days of that, I suddenly saw a sign advertising for railroad workers. Single and married people would be provided with lodgings. Registration pass not necessary. Address: Panka Rail Machine Station.

I was there in half an hour, and was hired within the hour. People who were not Moscow residents were taken on because the Rail Machine Station was listed as being in Ryazan Province; the entire staff was on assignment outside Moscow.

But my point is housing. It was very cheap—in today's money, something like seventy kopecks a month. But what did you get for that?

Everyone who worked at the station lived in railroad cars. The workers were assigned to heated cattle cars, and management was given passenger cars, old ones that may even have been prerevolutionary. It should be said that there were very few people in management. Our cars were divided in half, each of which contained a compartment for four people, a two-tiered rack, and a kitchen that had nothing in it but a wood stove. The amenities (a wooden outhouse and water) were all outside. There was a lot of turnover. But management fought that turnover and, wishing to keep people on the job, provided living space not only to single people but to family men as well, and even encouraged people to get married. Families also were given half a car; I remember their living spaces quite well. They were neater than ours, had little curtains and geraniums in the windows, and smelled of diapers. And they were more crowded than ours. All any of us had was a single suitcase which we kept in the cloakroom. But family men strove to acquire possessions like a wardrobe, a cradle, dishes, pots and pans. There was no room for any of this. So the families lived without any furniture, decorating their spaces with little curtains and cheap rugs, depicting swans and large-breasted beauties, manufactured in the countryside. For some people this was the most they could hope for.

I remember there was one girl who very much wanted to get married. One day during a smoke break, she sat down beside one of the unmarried guys and struck up a conversation about how hard it was for a young man to live alone, to take care of himself alone, to cook and clean for himself. And then she gazed into his eyes, smiled, and sighed dreamily: "Besides, married people get half a car!"

I did not work long in that railroad organization. Moscow needed construction workers, and soon the restrictions on residence were eased for them. I moved into Moscow and found lodgings in a hostel. Not a bad place. The rooms were ninety-six square feet, and eight people lived in each room. There was an ample kitchen, gas, civilized toilets. There was, however, no hot water, no bath or shower. But after the conditions in which I had been living, these were entirely decent.

Here, management not only did not encourage marriages among the workers, but, on the contrary, did everything it could to prevent them. In time, a battle broke out. Our supervisors, two hale and hearty older women, would run from floor to floor and around the building, grabbing young lovers in the hallways, on the staircase, in the bushes: sometimes they even dragged them out of bed. The two women would shout at them, shame them at meetings and in issues of the wall newspaper. Nevertheless, instinct won the day, and the two supervisors were unable to catch every manifestation of love. The girls and boys usually entered into temporary relationships, but some of them did get married. The husband would usually move in with the wife. The new family's living space was limited to the size of their bed, which they would screen off from the rest of the room with a sheet. The supervisors, and sometimes even the administrators, would come bursting into the room, rip down the sheet, make a scene, and chase the husband out. When the young couple asked what they were supposed to do, the administrators told them: "Do what you want. But there is no need to get married."

Need or no need, people still got married and brought children into the world. In the end, management gave in, and the model bachelors' hostel was transformed into a so-called family hostel. The rooms were divided in half. Two familes took up residence, one in the window half, the other by the door. Once again they used sheets to separate themselves from each other. People who were complete strangers lived side by side for years on end while having children and raising families.

At that time, I began associating with a literary group, made the acquaintance of many Moscow writers, and visited them to read my poems and to listen to others read theirs. Nearly all my new acquaintances, most of whom were born and grew up in Moscow, lived in communal apartments. Two, three, four families in a single apartment, sometimes even more. My next room was in a railroad apartment, where twenty-five families lived with one kitchen and one bathroom for everyone. I won't describe the life that was lived there, the scandals within families, and the quarrels between neighbors in the kitchen. Everyone who lives in a Soviet city knows all this quite well. The nightmarish housing conditions in which the overwhelming majority of the urban population lives were the result not only of objective problems but also of the authorities' utter indifference. Moreover, it was much easier to control people who lived in communal apartments. If someone was making home-brew or telling political jokes, it was no secret. Someone was bound to inform, whether he lived in the apartment or not.

Lately, the housing situation has eased. The authorities have been working on the crisis for something like twenty-five years, and many buildings have been built and millions of families have received apartments. Millions of others, however, are still waiting their turn in communal apartments. They won't live long enough to be given an apartment of their own, and they can't join a coop because coops aren't cheap and not everyone can afford them. For example, my two-room apartment cost seven thousand rubles. I was able to buy it because I received rather large royalties at one point. But where is the average worker, teacher, or doctor going to get that kind of money?

Needless to say, it's much better to live in your own apartment than in a communal one. But even those apartments are, as a rule, quite modest. In Moscow these days, the normal allotment of space is twenty-seven square feet per person, and the district executive committee checks to make sure no one receives any more than that. This means that it's rare for a family of three to have an apartment with more than two rooms. The majority of Soviet apartments have one, two, or three rooms. I knew one family that had four rooms, but there were thirteen people in the family.

Living room, dining room, bedroom, and nursery are just about nonexistent concepts in the vocabulary of Soviet life.

Some people have houses of their own, but they're beyond the reach of nearly everyone. A house can cost ten, twenty, thirty, three hundred thousand rubles. And the only people with money like that are writers in special favor, academicians, store and restaurant managers, and big shots in the underground economy.

But the average Soviet citizen who does not steal or speculate and who lives on his salary alone does not have that kind of money.

And, of course, it's because in the Soviet Union people work just about free of charge too.

DSS

The main principles of Soviet life are freedom, equality, and brotherhood. Everyone knows this. And if anyone forgets, he can just go outside, where he will recall it at once because there's bound to be a large banner somewhere nearby with large letters spelling out, FREEDOM, for example, or EQUALITY, or BROTHERHOOD. Even if you want to forget, there's always something there to remind you.

All the same, from time to time isolated instances of inequality do occur in our daily life, which, of course, rouses the censure of the working masses. Some people even display their displeasure and grumble, creating an unhealthy atmosphere around themselves: Why does So-and-so have this and So-and-so doesn't? But, in saying this, a person fails to realize that we have not yet achieved full Communism; we are still only at the level of socialism. And, as we know, under socialism there is no egalitarianism, nor should there be. From each according to

109

his abilities, to each according to his rank. Was it Marx who said that? Or Lenin? Or maybe it was I who thought it up. I can't remember exactly any more. In any case, I will say that privileges are a good thing. For those who have them, of course. I'd also say that they're a good thing but not always a good thing. Differences in privileges are sometimes grounds for such problems that you might think better not to have those privileges at all.

Here's something by way of example.

One time, a big-name writer, a very big-name writer, from a not very big Asiatic, or perhaps Caucasian, republic came to Moscow on business. Needless to say, he brought all sorts of presents for his fellow writers in Moscow. His fellow writers were important people. One was the secretary of the Writers' Union, another the editor in chief of a magazine, a third the director of a publishing house, a fourth a big shot on the Lenin Prize Committee. And he'd had to bring each of them some souvenir, something made by local craftsmen, a rug or a silver dish or some other inexpensive item costing somewhere between five and seven hundred rubles. And of course he'd brought all the sweets of the East—raisins, melons, figs, or something of the sort. He'd also brought a case of cognac. Since he was indeed a big-name writer and had just about founded the literature of his nation, he always stayed at the Moscow Hotel, which, by the way, does not give rooms to people who walk in off the street. I won't be going into any details here about his meetings with his fellow writers, whom he visited, or who came to see him at the hotel. I'll say only that a great deal was drunk, a great many appetizers were eaten, and many toasts were made: to friendship among nations, to the flowering of our multinational literature, to the beloved guest and the beloved hosts—to such an extent that the case of cognac he'd brought with him proved insufficient, and a second had to be bought on the spot. By the time the second case was beginning to run out, our hero had drunk and eaten so much that he started to feel sick. He woke up in the middle of the night and heard a sound like *baboom, baboom,* in his chest, and his heart felt like it had a spit through it, like a sheep being roasted. The writer felt that he was turning pale and growing weaker. To make a long story short, he thought he was dying.

Though he was a big-name writer, he was a stupid man. And though he associated with important people in Moscow, there was a lot about life in the capital that he had yet to master. He lay on his bed, clutching his heart with one hand, dragging the telephone over with the other, dialing 0-3 with a trembling finger.

That is the number for Moscow's ambulance service, second to none. The writer had not yet managed to hang up the phone when help arrived.

The door opened. In ran a doctor, carrying his case, followed by an orderly with a box containing a cardiograph machine, followed by another orderly with a canvas stretcher. The hotel corridor attendant kept peeking fearfully into the room. The doctor asked the patient what was bothering him, but the latter just bellowed, jabbing his left side. The doctor didn't waste a minute. He took a cardiogram, blood pressure, pulse rate.

"What is it?" asked the sick man in a barely audible voice, very alarmed, needless to say.

"I can't tell you anything definite yet," said the doctor, "but I think that you've had a small but extensive infarct. No more than that."

Hearing those words, the sick man shut his eyes tight and lay there without breathing. His heart was twitching painfully, his legs were going cold, his mouth was dry. He was becoming agitated, and nothing could be worse for him than that.

"Don't get excited," said the doctor. "We'll get you to the hospital. For now we'll give you a shot." He took a hypodermic with a good-sized needle from his case and put that needle where it belonged, in one of the writer's muscles. Then he shifted the writer from the bed to the canvas stretcher and signaled the orderlies, who lifted the stretcher and began carrying it toward the door.

At that moment, the door was flung open and in burst the hotel manager, followed by the corridor attendant. As soon as the hotel manager saw the orderlies and the doctor, he drew himself up, spreading his hands to the sides. "Who are you and where are you taking him?" he demanded.

The doctor politely explained that they had come with the ambulance and were now taking the sick man out to that ambulance to take him somewhere for treatment.

The hotel manager said: "I can't allow him out! Put the stretcher back on the floor."

The doctor replied that that could not be done because the sick man was in urgent need of help.

"It's not for you to say what he needs or doesn't need," said the manager. "I can't let him out of here because he's a DSS."

"DSS who?" asked the doctor.

"DSS," repeated the manager, and explained to the doctor that this stood for deputy to the Supreme Soviet.

The doctor said: "I don't know whether he's a DSS or anything else. All people are the same for me." He was referring to the Hippocratic Oath, which, by the way, he had not taken. Our doctors have their own Soviet oath.

The hotel manager could not have cared less about the Hippocratic Oath, or the Soviet oath for that matter.

Finally, the doctor phoned his hospital to report that the hotel administration was preventing him from fulfilling his duty as a physician. After taking a moment for consideration, the office said the hell with that hotel manager; if he won't allow the sick man out, he should sign a paper saying that he assumes responsibility for any and all fatal consequences. The manager would not sign anything of the sort, nor would he allow the sick man out, and he made a call of his own. "Send a special ambulance to the hotel," he said, "I've got a DSS doubled up over here."

Time passed. The sick man lay on the stretcher, the manager sat, the doctor stood, the corridor attendant looked out the window, and the orderlies went out to the corridor for a smoke.

After a short time, another doctor came dashing into the room, a Kremlin doctor, followed by a nurse and four orderlies. *Their* stretcher was made out of leather, not canvas.

The Kremlin doctor whispered with the doctor who had arrived first and learned what steps had been taken. Then he drove another needle into the sick man and told the orderlies to shift him from the canvas stretcher to the leather one.

The hotel manager now relented and gave the first doctor a paper saying that there was no need for his assistance. So the doctor and his orderlies, with their stretcher, set off for the elevator.

Now it was the newly arrived doctor who called his office, to find out to which branch of the Kremlin hospital the sick man should be taken.

The office wanted to know the sick man's name. The doctor asked the manager, who told him, and the doctor passed it on to his office. After a short silence, the doctor said: "I understand." Addressing the hotel manager coldly, he said: "What kind of nonsense is this? Why are you creating a panic and wasting busy people's time when this man's not a DSS at all. His name's not on the DSS list."

The hotel manager turned slightly pale and looked over inquiringly at the sick man, who had come to a little and said weakly: "Dessert!"

The Kremlin doctor was now somewhat angry. "You should be thinking about God, not dessert." To the hotel manager, he said: "Where's that doctor who treats regular people? He can deal with this man now. We have no time for him."

The hotel manager sent the corridor attendant after the other doctor, and she flew down the stairs faster than an express elevator. She caught the doctor right at the exit and blocked his way. "Go back," she said. "The sick man isn't a DSS after all."

The doctor refused, because he was fed up, had a paper from the hotel manager, and had not taken the Hippocratic Oath.

But the corridor attendant called the doorman over, and the two of them persuaded the doctor to return by promising him and his orderlies a pound each of hunter sausage from the dining room.

The doctor and the orderlies returned to the hotel room and shifted the sick man from the leather stretcher to the canvas one. By then, he was quite bad—the whites of his eyes were showing, his cheeks were gray and his lips blue, and there was a brown froth that smelled like cognac issuing from his mouth. The sick man's legs twitched and, his voice a faint whisper, he managed to wheeze out: "Dessert! Dessert!"

"What's he saying?" the doctor who treated ordinary people asked the doctor who treated the extraordinary. "What's this about dessert? What's dessert got to do with anything?"

"Eastern people," said the Kremlin doctor, "are used to eating dessert. He doesn't want to die without eating a last dessert."

"Wait a minute," said the hotel manager to both the physicians. "Maybe he's not saying dessert; maybe it's something else." He bent close to the sick man and asked: "DSSR?"

"DSSR, DSSR," wheezed the sick man in agreement.

"There you see," said the hotel manager to the Kremlin doctor. "I told you. He's a deputy to the Supreme Soviet of the Republic. Not a DSS, but a DSSR. Put him back." And he grabbed the sick man's legs himself to shift him from the canvas stretcher to the leather one.

"Stop! Stop! Stop!" said the Kremlin doctor, shoving the hotel manager away from the sick man. "We only take deputies to the Supreme Soviet. There's another service for DSSRs."

At that moment, the first doctor nodded to his orderlies and, without waiting for the hunter sausage they'd been promised, they left with their canvas stretcher and cardiograph machine.

By then, the sick man's eyes had closed entirely, and he was no longer wheezing or twitching. It was the hotel manager who was twitching, having now realized that the sick man was in fact a deputy to the Supreme Soviet, if only that of his republic, and that he would have to answer for whatever happened to him. The hotel manager asked the Kremlin doctor to take the sick man wherever he wanted, just to get him out of the hotel. After putting up some resistance, the doctor phoned his office again. The office in turn called someone else, and came to terms on the problem with some higher-up who worked at night. In a display of humanity, the office said: "All right, we'll make an exception; bring him in."

And so, in the end, they carried the writer out and took him to Kuntsevo. If he had been a DSS, they might have gotten him there in time. And had he been an ordinary person, he might have had an even better chance. But, alas, he was neither one nor the other.

Privileges are a good thing, of course, but it's sometimes better to do without them.

Who's the Slob?

The assertion that human rights are violated in the Soviet Union is not quite correct. You can't violate something that doesn't exist.

All the rights and freedoms proclaimed in the Soviet constitution are fictions. The right to work is in fact a duty. A person who seeks to avoid so-called socially useful labor, meaning work on a kolkhoz, in a factory or a state institution, is subject to criminal punishment and is "to be obliged to perform labor." The authorities apply the law against parasites to cow dissidents in the most cynical manner. First, they deprive them of their jobs; then, they try them for not working. They are crippled in the camps by having to do work beyond their strength and reduced in their places of exile to performing labor beneath their skills. (Yuri Orlov, a world-famous physicist, is working as a watchman; Tatyana Velikanova, a mathematician, is a bathhouse attendant.)

The constitution says that every person of a certain

age has the right to vote and to be elected to office. But only those nominated by the Party are elected to office. The right to vote also turns out to be a duty. Every year the Soviet people take part in national or local "elections." This means you go to a polling place, take a ballot, on which only a single name appears, and place it in the ballot box. The polling places do, however, have booths with blinds that can be closed for casting a "secret" ballot. You can go in there, cross out the one name on the ballot, and write in another name or some obscene expression. But the very fact of entering the booth will be noted in the dossier of the citizen committing that "antisocial" act. Any attempt to avoid exercising the "right" to vote will also be noted and taken into account when prizes, apartments, and vacations are assigned and when questions of traveling abroad are decided. This so-called election procedure might seem absolutely senseless: ninety-nine percent of the citizenry elect not a fourth, not a half, but one hundred percent of all the candidates nominated by the Party. But this is not a senseless procedure at all: it is a regularly conducted general check on Soviet citizens' readiness to play the game. It is a loyalty check.

The same is true of all the other freedoms proclaimed in the constitution: freedom of the press, freedom of assembly, the freedom to demonstrate, and so forth. Assemblies and demonstrations that are genuinely free are punishable as crimes, whereas people are forcibly herded to the assemblies and demonstrations organized by the authorities. Attempting to avoid them is viewed as a sign of disloyalty.

When speaking of human-rights violations, we usually mean the rights of particular religious, ethnic, or social groups, and say that the rights of religious people, workers, or writers have been violated. This too is incorrect. There are many people in the Soviet Union who possess privileges of one sort or another, but no one has any rights, including the highest Soviet leaders. I'd even say that in a certain sense the higher leaders have fewer rights than the average Soviet citizen. They are not only obliged to observe rigorously all the rules and rituals of their milieu, they not only live in constant fear of each other, but also they cannot refuse the privileges that are theirs. If one can even imagine a high party official suddenly wishing to stop making use of the special stores, there can be no doubt that this gesture would be interpreted as a protest against the existing system, and that official would lose his position. And without it, he is a nobody.

Here's a story along those lines.

During my last years in Moscow, I lived near the Airport metro station, on Leningrad Avenue. I strolled that avenue often, and one day was walking down one side when I decided to cross to the other. As I approached the curb, I noticed a policeman I knew standing in the middle of the street. (I'd bumped into him fairly often on my walks.) He had a cigarette in his mouth, a baton in his hand, and a walkie-talkie over his shoulder. I began walking toward him, intending to say hello, when suddenly I saw him undergo a metamorphosis. He brought his walkie-talkie to his right ear, then let it fall as he spat out his cigarette and replaced it with his whistle, which he began blowing like a madman. It was a signal to those who had not yet pulled out onto the avenue to stay put, and to those on the avenue to pull over to the side. He waved his baton, brandished his fist, and blew his whistle. And then I heard the wail of an approaching siren.

A motorcade came racing past. A canary yellow BMW

was in the lead, followed by a black Volga, a long, black Zil, an ambulance, a Chaika, and two more Volgas, all black. The siren wailed, the tires hissed, lights flashed, and a voice barked from a loudspeaker in the BMW: "Keep away from the crosswalk, citizens! Drivers, pull to the side!"

The policeman jumped to one side, drew himself up, and saluted, devouring the cars with his eyes as they flew past one after the other like missiles, traveling no less than eighty miles an hour.

Finally, the policeman relaxed a bit, reached for a cigarette, cast a glance at the intersection, and noticed me. "Oh, hello," he said.

"Who was that?" I asked. "Brezhnev?"

"No, no," he said, "not Brezhnev—Kirilenko. But I couldn't see who else. The curtains were drawn."

He was out of matches. I gave him a light from my cigarette and saw that his hands were trembling.

"Why are you so upset?" I asked. "Is this the first time you've had to deal with anything like that?"

"That's not the point," he said. "It's a horror every time. There was once another policeman here, who forgot to button one of his buttons. And the person in the car behind the curtains going by at eighty noticed the button. And the cars weren't out of sight when the direct line to the chief was ringing: 'Who's the slob you've got standing across from Dynamo Stadium?'

"And the chief of the highway police did not ask what the problem was and why the man was a slob. He was too afraid. He immediately called the chief of our precinct, and he too asked: 'Who's the slob you've got standing across from Dynamo Stadium?' But the good thing was that our chief turned out to be a good guy. He transferred the policeman they were calling a slob from Leningrad Avenue to Maslovka Street, to get him out of sight. But he could have stripped him of his awards and kept him from being promoted. And that policeman could go ahead and complain for all the good it would do him. What rights does a policeman have? It's the man behind the curtains who's got the rights. . . ."

That's what the policeman thought, and that's the way it is. Who was he, that policeman? Nobody. And Kirilenko?

Kirilenko was still at the top when I lived in Moscow. He was second to Brezhnev in the Party. When Brezhnev traveled abroad or received medical treatment, Kirilenko ran the Politburo meetings and the government in general. And as long as he held his high position and traveled in motorcades, Kirilenko wanted for nothing. He had apartments and dachas fenced off from the world by forests, fields, rivers, and miles of ocean front. Once, I was in Sochi and saw a ship at anchor there. It might have been a cruiser or a destroyer; I'm no expert on them. All I remember is that it was a military vessel, bristling with cannon and machine guns. The locals told me it was Kirilenko's pleasure craft and that when he was in Sochi, he would take a cruise in it. Kirilenko did not come there often, but the sailors were seen swabbing the deck frequently. Who knew when Kirilenko might appear and want a taste of salt air? In short, Kirilenko was an important man, not like you and me.

I wouldn't have given a thought to Kirilenko if it were not for a certain incident—a fatal incident, by the way. I'm referring to Brezhnev's death. I saw his funeral on television in the United States. I saw his body borne on a gun carriage, Soviet soldiers goose-stepping. The gun carriage was followed by a procession of Politburo members, candidate Politburo members, Central Committee secretaries, marshals, the widow, the children, relatives, hangers-on, and KGB men. Then suddenly I spotted an odd-looking person sidling along timidly in that throng. He seemed both to be taking part in the procession and not to belong there at all. He was, however, not badly dressed; he was wearing a winter coat with an astrakhan collar and an astrakhan hat. His appearance and manner seemed those of a kolkhoz chairman who had come in from a remote province for the funeral of a distinguished relative. Who's the slob? I wondered. Then I looked closer. That was no slob; that was Comrade Andrei Pavlovich Kirilenko.

I couldn't believe my eyes. How could the number-two man in the government be so democratic, walking neither in the front row nor bringing up the rear, but seeming to be walking along with everyone else and at the same time to be separated from them by some invisible line, like a leper.

The explanation came right away. The announcer confirmed what I'd already guessed: a month or two before, Kirilenko had been on the wrong side in some fight and had lost his place on the Politburo.

I began wondering what Comrade Kirilenko was thinking about now, what sort of anti-Soviet thoughts were buzzing under that fur hat of his. Could he help but feel insulted? After all, he had served the Party for fifty years, out of fear and conviction both. He'd been in the leadership for forty-five years, on the Politburo for more than twenty-five, and on holidays had stood beside Brezhnev on Lenin's tomb, waving to the exultant crowds of demonstrators, endless portraits of him swaying over their heads. The same people who were now walking with him in the funeral procession had greeted his every appearance with applause and smiles of flattery, and had rushed headlong to carry out any wish of his. Now they did not even notice him; even the man bearing an umbrella for Kirilenko was turning up his nose.

If he had died in time, he too would have been laid out on a gun carriage and had funeral orations recited for him. And his relatives would have received special pensions. Now, *he* gets a special pension of course, but they don't get a thing. They are no longer relatives of a leading figure in the Party and the government.

I'd be untrue to myself if I said that I had any special concern for the fate of Kirilenko and his relatives. Something else concerns me here: why is it that in the Soviet Union even leaders have no rights? Of course it's not like it used to be before, when they'd simply be taken out and shot. Now, they're given enough to live on, but they live in obscurity and disgrace.

"The place doesn't make the man; the man makes the place," says a Russian proverb. But that doesn't seem to apply to Soviet life today. Only the place matters now— behind the curtains in a racing motorcade that sows fear in people's hearts, on Lenin's tomb, and, finally, in the Kremlin wall.

The leaders themselves are well aware of this. One time, I heard a story about another member of the Politburo, Comrade Dmitri Stepanovich Polyansky. A friend of his from Krasnodar had come to see him. They may have studied in the higher Party school together or perhaps had performed exploits together in the Komsomol. That I don't know. In any case, he came to see his successful friend with a bottle in hand, but Polyansky was not at home. His wife said: "Mitya's speaking to a group at the Three Mountain textile plant." Finally, Polyansky arrived, carrying a length of cloth under one arm. Seeing the surprise in his guest's eyes, Polyansky said: "The workers at the plant gave it to me as a present." "Mitya," said his friend, "what do you need it for? You're a member of the Politburo. You have everything you want." "Yes," said Polyansky, "as long as I'm a member of the Politburo, I have everything I want. But nobody knows what'll happen when they kick me out. Maybe I'll have to sell this length of cloth to buy food someday." A prophetic remark, because later on he was kicked out of the Politburo. But his was not such a lamentable fate. First, he was sent somewhere as an ambassador; then he retired on special pension. I hope he has enough to live on and doesn't have to sell that length of cloth. Surely he won't be given any more now.

But I'll tell you, here in the West you watch television, you read books, and what do you see? Former President Nixon is either writing his memoirs or, if that's not enough for him, he's giving a press conference on television. Former German chancellor Helmut Schmidt delivers an hour-long speech on television, the time provided by his Party, the Social Democrats, and he is even applauded. What is all this?

It's injustice—that's what it is. Of all our leaders, only Khrushchev could bring himself to write his memoirs. Later on, he renounced them in the newspapers and called what he had written a hostile forgery, or something on that order. But our other leaders remain silent and live out their days in obscurity, afraid to give any sign they're still alive. And we don't always know which are alive and which are dead. We recently found out that V. M. Molotov was still alive and had been reinstated in his Party at the age of ninety-four. But where are his comrades in arms? Where are Malenkov, Kaganovich, Shepilov, Shelepin, Shelest? You won't find any mention of their names in the Soviet press or Soviet encyclopedias.

At one point, Khrushchev tried to democratize the Party and introduced a rule to the effect that top Party people were interchangeable. This was one of the causes of his own downfall. Having overthrown Khrushchev, his successors immediately had that unpleasant rule stricken from the books. In so doing, they doomed themselves to leave the political scene honorably only by dying at their posts.

What kind of human rights are those?

Are there people with less freedom than the leaders of the Soviet government?

A Discovery

A well-known Soviet astronomer told me the following story. At the end of the forties, beginning of the fifties, he had worked in a scientific research institute, run experiments, looked at super novas through a telescope, but could not fathom how they were formed. I may not be stating the problem correctly, and astronomers may make me into a laughing stock. First, I'm hoping that the majority of my readers know no more about astronomy than I do; second, the heart of the matter here is in the fact that for all his expertise this scientist was unable to understand anything fundamental about stars.

Sometimes he would be pulled away from his telescope by a colleague who worked in a neighboring laboratory. He came to see the astronomer and have a private word with him about the troubles people in two fields of science, genetics and cybernetics, were having. After those fields were declared bourgeois pseudo sciences, the geneticists and cyberneticists were hounded in the press

and at meetings, dismissed from work, the more invet-
erate among them simply thrown in jail.

The astronomer would listen to all that news, though
he found it extremely unpleasant, and think: "Thank
God that I'm not a geneticist or a cyberneticist, but that
I deal with astronomy which no one has outlawed since
the time of Galileo and which no one would dare call a
pseudoscience now."

And once again he would glue his eye to his telescope
and look out at the stars, record his observations in a
notebook, but something, the main thing, kept eluding
him.

And his colleague from the neighboring laboratory
would come again and again to tell him about the campaign against the rootless cosmopolitans, the majority of
whom proved to be Jews; later on he told him of the
Doctors' Plot and the arrest of the doctors who were
reported to be a part of the international Jewish bourgeois organization, "Joint," on whose orders they had
intended to assassinate certain Soviet leaders, including
Stalin himself.

Naturally, the astronomer found all this news unpleasant, news which was being confirmed in the radio and
the newspapers. But still he thought he might be spared
by what was happening because personally his only interest was astronomy, nothing else; he was no Jew and
belonged to no international organizations. So far no
one had laid a hand on him, and he kept on going to
work, kept on receiving what was a decent salary for a
young scientist, kept on looking at the stars and thinking
about them, but all the same he could not think his way
through to what mattered most.

Meanwhile, something difficult to fathom happened
on Earth. In March 1953, the immortal Stalin died.

And no sooner did this happen then suddenly a thaw set in, both literally and figuratively.

One fine spring morning, just a month after Stalin's death, the scientist was getting ready to leave for work. He went outside, stepped across the puddles, and had walked part of the way to the streetcar, when he saw a copy of *Pravda* posted on a fence.

He could not believe his eyes: What is this, a publication of the Communist Party or of the bourgeois organization, Joint? The newspaper reported that the accusations against the doctors had been false, and that the prisoners' testimony had been obtained through the use of brutal investigative procedures strictly forbidden by Soviet law.

The scientist read all this with his eyeglasses on. Then he took them off, brought his face up close to the paper, and read the article again.

And then suddenly he felt as if a stone had been taken from his heart. He realized that everything that had happened to the geneticists, cyberneticists, cosmopolitans, and doctors bore a perfectly direct relation to him, even though he was not a geneticist, cyberneticist, Jew, cosmopolitan, doctor, or plotter.

Just then his streetcar pulled up, but the scientist had no desire to squeeze his way in, and so he set off for work on foot. It was spring, the snow was melting into puddles, the sun was shining and eclipsing all the other stars, old, new, and super nova. He began to think about those stars and all of a sudden it dawned on him, or, as people say, he got a bright idea, and he understood the very things that had eluded him for all those years: what sort of stars those were, why they were formed, and why they behaved the way they did. In other words, he made a major discovery in his field. I may not be describing the discovery precisely enough because I don't understand much about it, but those who do hold it in very high esteem.

Because of that discovery the astronomer became a member of the Soviet Academy of Sciences and many foreign academies as well: he also received a good deal of money, but that's not the point.

The story made a great impression on me. I discussed it with many other scientists and they all agreed with me that any improvement in society has a direct and beneficial effect on science, even a branch of science that seems most removed from real life.

The brief period of Khrushchev's halfhearted thaw bore immediate fruit in all spheres of intellectual activity. In science, this was most eloquently attested by the launching of the first sputnik and the sending of the first man into space. (Incidentally, this occurred under the leadership of the rocket designer Sergei Korolyov, a man who had been released from Stalin's prisons.)

The new ideological crackdown that followed the thaw, the persecution of the dissidents (including many scientists), also did not fail to have a telling influence on science. And although many brilliant scientists have never been and do not intend to be dissidents—though they may conscientiously serve the Soviet state—the general psychological climate and air of depression cannot fail but be reflected in their work. By the way, the stunning successes in space ended at the same time the thaw did. For the last fifteen years the USSR has been launching spacecraft with the same design. Now, substituting propaganda for real progress, it takes turns sending up Czechs, Indians, women.

Everybody Understands
Everything

NOTHING HAS TO BE DONE

During my last years in Moscow, a beginning writer would visit me from time to time when he was in town from the provinces. He'd complain of not being published and give me his novels and stories, of which there were a great number, to see what I thought of them. He was certain that his works weren't being published because their content was too critical. And indeed they did contain criticism of the Soviet system. But they had another major flaw as well: they lacked even the merest glimmer of talent. Sometimes he would request, and sometimes demand, that I send his manuscripts abroad and help get them published over there. I refused. Then he decided to go to the KGB and present them with an ultimatum: either they were immediately to issue orders that his works be published in the USSR or he would leave the USSR at once.

Apparently, it went something like this.

As soon as he had entered the KGB building, someone walked over to him and said: "Oh, hello there. So you've finally come to see us!"

"You mean you know me?" asked the writer.

"Is there anyone who doesn't?" said the KGB man, spreading his hands. "Have a seat. What brings you here? Do you want to tell us that you don't like the Soviet system?"

"That's right, I don't," said the writer.

"But what specifically don't you like about it?"

The writer replied that, in his opinion, there was no freedom in the Soviet Union, particularly artistic freedom. Human rights were violated, the standard of living was steadily declining—and he voiced other critical remarks as well. Good for about seven years in a camp.

Having listened politely, the KGB man asked: "But why are you telling me all this?"

"I wanted you to know."

"We know. Everyone knows all that."

"But if everyone knows, something should be done about it!"

"That's where you're wrong. Nothing *has* to be done about it!"

Surprised by that turn in the conversation, the writer fell silent.

"Have you said everything you wanted to?" asked the KGB man politely.

"Yes, everything."

"Then why are you still sitting there?"

"I'm waiting for you to arrest me."

"Aha, I see," said the KGB man. "Unfortunately, there's no way we can arrest you today. We're too busy. If the desire doesn't pass, come see us again, and we'll do everything we can to oblige you." And he showed the writer out.

The writer visited me a few more times before he disappeared. I think he finally may have achieved his goal and gotten someone to give him the full treatment for dissidence.

STEAL, BUT WITHIN LIMITS

One day, I was driving along the highway in my car. It's a long way between gas stations, and they don't always have what you need. I pulled into one, and they were out of gas. I pulled into another, but there was an enormous line. My tank was empty before I made it to the next one. I flagged down a dump truck and asked the driver if he wanted to make a couple of extra rubles. He stretched a long piece of tubing from his tank to my gas can, sucked on it to get it going, and then stood back and watched the pink gas flow.

Just then a policeman drove up on his motorcycle and caught us in the act. I was ready to lie and say I had asked the driver to give me just a liter or two so I could make it to the next gas station, but the policeman wouldn't listen to me and began attacking the driver.

"What are you doing? You could cause an accident here. It's not that I care what you're doing with the state's gas—steal as much as you want—but you're at a curve in the road here. Someone could crash into you."

The driver pulled the tubing from his tank, and I took my gas can and walked away. The driver pulled his truck to one side of the road, the policeman drove off, cursing as he went, and we completed our little transaction in peace. We were no longer a hazard to other drivers and, as we all know, stealing from the state is no sin. Even the police know that.

A DECENT, HONEST YOUNG MAN

I don't know how things are now, but in my time, that is, five years ago, people did not read books published in the West only at home with every lock on every door locked, but indulged wherever they happened to be, even on public transportation. On the metro you'd see one person reading *Nedelya*, another an installment of a novel in a newspaper, and a third person might be reading an ordinary newspaper. But if you looked closely, you'd see that if the car was packed, there'd always be two, three, maybe four people who were reading something else. The book covers are wrapped in newspaper, the paper is thin, the letters small. A person reading that sort of book usually does so with concentration, but will suddenly think of something, cover the book, look closely at the people standing near him, and then go back to his reading. Some people even go so far as not to wrap their books in newspaper.

One day, a friend dropped by to see me and told me the following story.

"I was on the metro, and there was a young man sitting across from me. He opens a book and starts reading. The cover's red and has Lenin's silhouette on it. I took another look at him and started feeling upset. Such a nice, intelligent-looking young person, and he's reading Lenin. Then I looked closer at the cover and saw that it said: *Lenin in Zurich* by Alexander Solzhenitsyn. And I suddenly felt awkward for having thought so badly of that young man."

That story reminded both of us of other times, times when young intellectuals did not read Solzhenitsyn's *Lenin* but went to the source himself. They read Lenin, wrote summaries of his thoughts, learned him by heart, quoted him. Young people certainly don't do that any more.

And they say that nothing ever changes in the Soviet Union.

IT'S NOT THE LAWS ON THE BOOKS

All, or nearly all, Soviet people know that in the Soviet Union it's not the laws on the books, but the unwritten rules of behavior, that matter. I would define the minimum observance of those rules as follows.

You have to go to work, do your job more or less conscientiously but without any unwarranted display of initiative. You should not try to improve anything or stand out too much. From time to time you have to attend meetings, political lectures, or rallies. If something is being voted on, and the presiding officer asks who's in favor, you have to raise your hand. (If it's a very large meeting, you don't even have to raise your hand; no one will notice if you don't.) The important thing is never to vote against anything and not to say that you're abstaining, because to oppose any resolution, even one concerning minor local problems like wastepaper or planting trees, will be viewed as a manifestation of political disloyalty. About once a year you have to take part in national or local elections. You don't have to be at the polling place very early, but you shouldn't be late either (around noon is good). There you take your ballot and, without looking at it, or showing any interest in whose name appears on it, you fold it neatly and drop it in the ballot box. Then you buy half a kilo of sausages at the snack bar (if there is one) and off you go. Orders from higher-ups, no matter how absurd they may seem to you, should be accepted without a murmur, though it's all right to avoid carrying out the orders themselves. In general, it's desirable not to think about politics, not to listen to foreign radio broadcasts or to read Soviet newspapers apart from the satirical pieces and the sports news. All contact with foreigners is to be avoided, including that with citizens of the "fraternal" socialist countries. You should be moderately patriotic and love nature. Display your loyalty by being a hockey or soccer fan, or by gathering mushrooms or going fishing. Even the Chekist heroes in detective novels, when they catch a gang of foreign spies after a long, hard search, usually say: "All right, time for a little fishing!" A Chekist is a simple man, one of the guys. He doesn't spend his free time studying the works of Karl Marx or the publications of the latest history-making Party congress, but pursues a simple pastime that is close to everyone's heart and mind. A loyal citizen can carve things out of wood or on a grain of rice but should avoid such dubious hobbies as stamp or coin collecting and ham radio (all of which entail contact with foreigners and unpredictable consequences).

It is advisable not to evince any untoward interest in Soviet history and to avoid discussions of the October Revolution, Stalin's personality cult, collectivization, and other such things; better to believe that all that belongs to the distant past and bears no relationship to the present.

A significant portion of the Soviet population observes these rules only outwardly, while in fact living a semi-underground life. These people go to work and vote in favor of what is being voted on but, on the sly, they listen to the radio, tell anti-Soviet jokes, and are glad to read forbidden literature if any comes their way.

But there are also people who, without challenging the authorities openly, utterly refuse to observe any of the accepted rituals. If they are not punished, it may only be because they're not considered to be in their right mind. Here's a little story about one such person.

THE PASSIVE RESISTER

For as long as I knew him, he always wore the same fall topcoat and carried the same tattered briefcase.

"Oleg," I asked him, "why didn't you charge your patient something this time?"

"Well, he was so interesting to talk to," said Oleg with an embarrassed smile. "We talked for a whole hour after I examined him, and I would have felt uncomfortable asking him for money."

"But after working a whole day in a hospital, it's uncomfortable to have to take a streetcar then ride in a packed subway to see a patient. You could have taken just ten rubles for the visit, like other doctors do. It is work, you know."

"But what if he didn't have ten rubles?"

His patients always seemed to him either poor or exceptionally good conversationalists—one's wife had just left him, another was having problems at work. How can you take money from people like that?

"If I happen to get a rich patient, of course I'll take money from him."

I told him that he had a rich patient in me, because a film script of mine had just been accepted. Of course, they immediately hacked it to pieces, but I'd already been paid.

"If you won't accept money from me, I won't let you treat me, as a matter of principle. I'll go to a clinic and stand in a long line."

"But you don't need any treatment. You're healthy as a horse."

"If I'm so healthy, why did you just listen to my chest?"

"Because I was given a new stethoscope at work and I wanted to try it out."

"Very clever of you. But when patients ask you to make a house call, they want the benefit of your skill, and they're ready to pay for it."

"And I thought they were interested in having a little talk with an intelligent person."

"If you were intelligent, you wouldn't have remained an ordinary physician for twenty years. You would have defended your dissertation, and now you wouldn't be making a hundred and thirty a month, but at least two hundred and fifty."

"You're well aware that I can't defend any dissertation. For that you need a good character reference from the Party committee and the local hospital committee. And I have the reputation of being a backward and socially passive person. I don't go to meetings and political lectures, I didn't take part in the discussions of Brezhnev's book *A Little Stretch of Ground*, I didn't attend the solidarity rally for the people of Chile, I didn't do any voluntary Saturday labor in honor of Comrade Lenin's birthday. And the hospital's Party committee has information that I attend church regularly, which isn't true, I don't go that regularly."

I understood him well but I still felt bad that such an excellent doctor was vegetating as a general practitioner when, given his abilities, he could have risen much higher. And then I said something he'd already heard a thousand times—that all those meetings, rallies, and political lectures were only an idiotic ritual, which people perform without a second's thought and which would have allowed him to practice medicine on a much higher level. If he was absolutely unable to observe those rituals, then he should concentrate on his private practice and earn his money that way, since our society does provide that sort of loophole for doctors.

He smiled, nodded his head, and even agreed with me in part.

"You could be a little more practical," I told him. "What law is there that you have to wear that ragged coat and have to watch every kopeck and still make house calls?"

"If I should happen to get a rich patient, I'll be glad to take his money." Our conversations usually ended with that promise.

One time, he got a general as a patient. The general fell into none of the nonpaying categories. He was not poor, his wife was not planning on leaving him, and it would have been difficult to call him an especially interesting conversationalist. The general was suffering from an odd case of colic, which neither the military nor the Kremlin doctors had been able to understand. The doctor went to see the general in his apartment, which was stuffed with rugs, crystal, and antique furniture. He determined what the problem was, wrote out a prescription, and was about to leave when the general's wife brought him an envelope containing cash.

"And," Oleg told me later, "I took another look at all those rugs and vases, and I couldn't bring myself to do it. I said to myself, From you, comrades, I won't take money."

And he didn't.

Whenever I think of that doctor, I also remember other people I met in my life—teachers, physicians, archivists in grease-stained jackets, typists, museum workers—who often spend their entire lives working at the lowest positions and at the lowest pay. I recall especially one old woman who had graduated from the Sorbonne and knew six languages and who worked as a cleaning woman in a health resort. By avoiding taking part in the lies and the hypocrisy, they keep their souls from being violated; they radiate goodness, humanity, and spiritual nobility. They are without the vanity, which sometimes motivates people to public action. They are not in the least heroic, but it is difficult to corrupt them with little gifts of money, difficult to intimidate them with threats or to break them in prison. Quiet, shy, inconspicuous, they will never start revolutions, never head movements, never hurl challenges or level accusations. There are not many such people in the Soviet Union, and it's thanks to them that manuscripts are not burned, that the memory of the past is not effaced, and that the concepts of honesty and conscience have not lost all meaning.

An Anti-Soviet
Soviet

Many Soviets who end up in the West may experience difficulties adjusting to their new lives; they may require help, and may need to draw attention to themselves in order to get it. In this situation it's probably handiest to be a former KGB agent. If a person walks into a police station and says that he served on the committee for State Security (KGB) as a captain, major, or colonel (the higher, the better), he can count on a very favorable reception. Intelligence agents and journalists will come running. He will be flown about on military planes, appear on television, and publishers will offer him five- and even six-figure contracts. If a person cannot present sufficiently convincing proof of having served on the committee for State Security, he can at least say he was a stool pigeon, an informer, that he eavesdropped on conversations, met with plainclothes professionals in little parks or private apartments or personnel departments, where he reported this, that, and the other. Anyone not wishing to confess to having been an informer can limit himself to admitting he was a fool—I was a fool; I believed in Marxism-Leninism, in Lenin and Stalin, and so forth and so on. I was a believer, but then I wised up. Some wised up after Khrushchev's speech, some after the events in Hungary or Czechoslovakia; others waited until Afghanistan.

In this regard, I have absolutely nothing to brag about. I may have been a fool, but I hated Stalin more or less from the time I was fourteen, I had my doubts about Lenin, never served in the KGB, and, to tell the truth, never even worked as an informer. But I did have occasion to meet and speak with such folk.

Here is the story of my first meeting with one of them.

On a freezing, misty January morning in 1959, I was awakened by a loud, hysterical knock at my door. Opening the door a crack, I saw my landlady, Ludmilla Alekseevna, a former dancer at the Bolshoi Theater, standing half-dressed in the hallway.

"Volodya," she said, sounding terribly alarmed, "there's some man pounding at the back door who says he's a friend of yours."

I looked at my watch. It was half past eight. I usually got up much later than that, because I went to bed very late.

My two landladies, Olga Leopoldovna Pash-Davidov and her daughter, Ludmilla Alekseevna, had both been Bolshoi dancers and were now retired (the mother was over eighty, the daughter close to sixty). Maintaining their old ways, they never went to bed before three o'clock in the morning. I had grown used to their routine, and if I accidentally fell asleep earlier, Olga Leopoldovna would knock at my door until I answered and would say: "You weren't sleeping, were you, Volodya? I came to say good night."

Olga Leopoldovna's late husband was one of the first national artists of the republic and for that reason was a rarity among Moscow's fortunate few in having a four-room apartment of his own in the center of Moscow. He and his wife had lived in one room, with a large, regal poodle. In the second lived Olga's daughter, her husband, their newly born child, and a sheepdog. One room was empty, if you didn't count the small, ill-tempered dog (a Tibetan terrier) which was always lying in one corner. The fourth room was mine. My room, if it can be called that, was less than twelve feet square. It was furnished only with a large iron bed that went from one wall to the other, and a chair, which could only fit sideways between the bed and the window sill. I used the large window sill as a desk. There I kept my typewriter, which I had picked up dirt cheap, and a disorderly pile of my unpublished collected works. That collection was growing slowly but surely, because I was still young, full of strength and hope, and I worked every day, little by little, but fanatically.

At that time, I had rented that room quite recently. No one knew my address, including my closest friends. There was no one who could just come see me out of the blue like that.

I went with my landlady to the back door. All three dogs burst into the hallway, barking madly.

"Who's there?" I asked.

"Vladimir Nikolaevich, please open up," said someone in an embarrassed voice. "I'll just be a minute."

That was both surprising and fishy. Although I was already twenty-seven, I was still only a student, and peo-

ple weren't addressing me by my first name and patronymic yet.

Instead of inviting this uninvited guest in through the
front door, Ludmilla Alekseevna and I began moving
the tubs, buckets, and cardboard boxes that were block-
ing the back door. Finally we opened that door, to see
a relatively young man wearing glasses, whose first words
were: "Just take away the dogs, please."

"Who are you and what do you want?"

"I'll explain everything in a minute."

Ludmilla Alekseevna withdrew, taking all three dogs
with her, and I was left alone with the stranger in the
living room.

"What do you want?" I asked again.

"One minute, one minute. I'll explain," he said, nodding his balding head up and down. He lowered his voice
and said quickly: "Can anyone hear us?"

"No, no one can hear us."

"And the dogs are gone; they can't come bursting in?"

"No, they can't. They have yet to learn how to open
the door themselves."

"Of course, the door opens out. But can anyone hear
us?"

"I don't know," I said, raising my voice, "if anyone can
hear us or not, but I have no intention of whispering.
What do you want?"

"One minute. I'll explain it all in a minute. So you
think no one can hear us?"

I had never had any run-ins with the KGB, had no
idea what they looked like, and, frankly, at that time,
didn't concern myself much about them. But suddenly
I had doubts as to my visitor's profession.

"Can anyone hear us then, Vladimir Nikolaevich?"

"No, no one can hear us."

"Very good. Good, good. I believe you when you say no one can hear us. I'm here on behalf of the student literary association."

"What kind of association is that?" I asked.

"Just a student group. At . . . at . . . at Moscow University. We have get-togethers, read poetry, discuss things. Can anyone hear us?"

"But what do you want from me?"

"Nothing, nothing. Nothing special. We'd just like you to speak at one of our meetings. We read your poetry in *Evening Moscow* and some of our members also heard you speak at Izmailovsky Park. And so we'd like . . . Can anyone hear us? . . . to invite you to speak."

"When?" I asked.

"Now, right now."

"Right now?" I said. "At eight-thirty in the morning? Don't the students have classes in the morning?"

"Of course they have classes, Vladimir Nikolaevich, of course they do. But there are some people from the association who'd like to speak with you beforehand. . . . Can anyone hear us? . . . Maybe we can go over there; it's quite close."

"Why should I go there?"

"So we can talk things over. You may want to speak at one of our meetings. You're not against the idea, I hope."

He filled me with a strange fear, repulsion, and the intense desire to be rid of him. Then, surprising myself, I suddenly said that I only spoke for money. That was pure baloney, because, even though I had spoken in public a few times, as a member of the literary group Magistral (Mainline), no one had ever offered me any money.

"What do you mean *money*?" he said, taken aback. "We're a student group; we don't have any money."

"Well, if you don't, I can't speak. I don't speak for nothing."

"No, no, no, Vladimir Nikolaevich . . . Can anyone hear us? . . . What's all this about money?"

Then we began a long stretch of pointless haggling, he unable to understand why I, a student, a budding poet, and no professional, was displaying such greediness, and I for some reason sticking to my guns and insisting on money. Seeing that this demand caused him confusion, I became all the more insistent, not out of any mercenary considerations, but in an instinctive effort to elude a danger I did not understand. My passion for money apparently knocked him off track, because he stopped asking if anyone could hear us and spent a good while pointlessly insisting that I speak without being paid, even though he could have agreed to my demand without it costing him anything. I can't say why he was knocked off course, most likely because our conversation had departed from the line that had been worked out for it in advance. Finally, fed up with the conversation, I stood up, rather curtly suggested that he leave, and walked to the door to open it for him.

"Wait a minute, wait a minute, wait a minute," he whispered urgently, almost hysterical. "Vladimir Nikolaevich, can anyone hear us? I hope no one can hear us. I did not introduce myself the way I should. I'll do it differently now."

He was immediately transformed. His face assumed a smug and arrogant expression. With a regal gesture, he stuck his hand into the pocket containing his ID.

"Don't bother," I said. "I don't need that to know who you are."

Pain mingled with disappointment on his face. Clearly, he had thought he'd been playing his role with agility and artistry.

"How did you figure it out?" he asked with a fallen voice.

"It wasn't hard," I said. "I don't read detective novels often, but enough to know that all the detectives are like you."

"Really?"

I could see that he was somewhat stunned and that his feelings were hurt. Later on, when I got to know others of his colleagues in the KGB, I observed that the majority are quick to take offense. That touchiness is all that remains of any humanity with which they were born. No matter what general or personal theories guide them, and no matter how they justify what they do, they still sense their actions are contemptible. Yet the ones who don't take offense are the most dangerous of all.

"All right then, all right," he said disappointedly. "You figured it out, fine. So let's go," he proposed, neither a request nor a command.

"Let's go then," I agreed.

I have to say that even though I spoke offhandedly and sarcastically to him, I was terrified. I probably had never been as scared as I was then. I was just starting out as a poet, thinking that perhaps something would come of me. And at the same time, I lived with the constant feeling that something fatal might prevent this from ever coming true: I could be found to have a progressive, incurable disease, I might be hit by a car, or something else along those lines.

But I was a real Soviet citizen, even though Sovietness did not mean I loved the Soviet authorities or believed in Marxism-Leninism-Communism. I didn't believe in any of that and considered all Soviet propaganda empty words for fools. Like the overwhelming majority of people I'd met in my life, I hated Soviet blather, hated political education, meetings, rallies, demonstrations, elections, and voluntary Saturday labor. I tried to avoid all that, but I did not go against the tide. Many years later, I realized that it was precisely that neutrality that made me Soviet. I was a passive member of society, and the authorities expected nothing of any particular use from me. Wherever I worked or served, the administration and Party higher-ups always knew not to expect any ideological activism from me. I was never invited to join the Party, and nobody ever even tried to enlist me as an informer (even in the incident described here). I was a completely harmless member of society. It is the young people, those who display a serious interest in the theoretical foundations of Communism and begin immersing themselves in Marx, Lenin, and Stalin, who pose a much greater danger to the regime. The Soviet authorities realize this. A person who takes the theory seriously will, sooner or later, begin comparing it with the practice, and will end up rejecting one or the other, and, later on, the two of them together. But a person who has not been seduced by the theory will view the practice as a common and immutable evil—one that can be lived with.

And so I maintain that I was one hundred percent Soviet. My Sovietness also manifested itself in the fact that I fully expected the authorities to do whatever they wished, and for that very reason I was not inclined to protest about what mattered most. My sense of rights and justice was nil. Although I had spoken somewhat ironically and in an unpleasant tone of voice to my visitor, I had immediately entered into unspoken agreement with him on the main thing.

I was frightened and thought it entirely possible that I could be whisked away and vanish from the face of the earth. I had no intention of protesting my arrest, although I had committed no crime. I did not ask to see the man's identification, nor did I contest his right to take me wherever he wished.

My landlady, dressed now, was in the hallway when we entered it.

"Will you be gone long, Volodya?" she asked, trying not to look at the man accompanying me.

I turned to him and said loudly, so that my landlady would know who he was: "Will I be gone long?"

"No, no, no. What do you mean!" he said, returning to his mannered confusion. "He'll be back very, very soon."

At the time, I thought I was quite clever to let my landlady know where I was going.

I expected there to be a Black Maria outside, that my arm would be twisted as I was thrown inside. But there was no police van waiting, and my escort suggested that we go on foot. That surprised me, but I began walking.

On the way, he no longer spoke ingratiatingly to me, but was condescending. He asked me why I wrote such sad poems, and I, realizing that I could be shot for writing sad stuff, began to explain that, even though my poems were sad, they contained elements of optimism. I could tell by his face that he didn't find my argument convincing. He kept glancing over at me as if I were a young man who had lost his way, as if it would be a pity to shoot me, but it had to be done.

We walked for a long time down crooked side streets.

Sarcastically (at least I believed I was being sarcastic), I asked him if he was lost.

"Yes, yes. We might be," he said with obvious anxiety. "We could be lost. . . . No, no we're not."

He pointed to a sign, which read: COMMITTEE FOR STATE SECURITY OF THE COUNCIL OF SOVIET MINISTERS.

"There, you see," he said, as if taking pride in his knowledge of the adjoining side streets. "We weren't lost."

I've totally forgotten the door we entered, whether either he or I was asked to show any identification, and what the elevators and corridors were like. I remember only that we went into an office, where an ordinary-looking man of average height in a gray suit was seated at a large but unpretentious desk. He offered me his hand, told me his name—first name and patronymic—and called me by mine. He invited me to be seated and immediately asked: "Do you consider yourself a good Soviet, Vladimir Nikolaevich?"

My heart lightened a little. If they hadn't decided yet whether I was a good Soviet or not, that meant they might not put me in front of a firing squad right away. I at once assured him hotly that of course I was a good Soviet.

"Right," he said. "I didn't have the slightest doubt of it. You're a good Soviet and you should help us. You'll help us and we'll help you." He rubbed his hands, tasting the pleasure already, and then fixed his eyes on me. "All right, tell us."

"Tell you what?" I asked, genuinely failing to understand.

"Tell us what you know."

"I don't know anything."

149

"Come on now, Vladimir Nikolaevich," said the man at the desk with a smile, exchanging glances with the one who had brought me, now sitting in the corner. "You've got to know something!"

"Maybe I do know a little something, but I don't know what it is that interests you."

"Everything interests us, everything."

"I don't understand," I said.

"Vladimir Nikolaevich," he said, clasping his hands in what seemed despair. "Are you a good Soviet or aren't you?"

"Of course I am, but I don't understand what you want from me."

He told me that he wanted me to be open (you help us and we'll help you) in telling him with whom I associated and where I went.

I did not doubt that he had the right to ask me this, but I was also well aware that I had to avoid answering any questions. I said that I didn't associate with anyone and didn't go anywhere.

"What do you mean, what do you mean?" said the man in the corner, coming to life. "You've been to an art exhibit, and you looked at abstract paintings."

Oh, so that was it! Even though that exhibit had been entirely official, and no one had warned me not to go there, as a good Soviet I should have known that, no matter what, it's best to avoid looking at abstract paintings. I didn't ask them how they knew that I'd been to that exhibit and hadn't turned away from the abstract paintings, but the completeness of their information led me to hope they also knew that I'd been unequivocal in my dislike of those paintings. As I remember, I was glad to tell them that I didn't like those paintings.

"Yes. No normal person could like them," said the senior man, with an air of profundity, a view the junior man seconded at once:

"Yes, yes, yes, they profane art."

"And what do you think of Pasternak?" asked the man at the desk.

I said that I had no thoughts on Pasternak, which was nothing but the truth; it was only much later that I read Pasternak and began thinking about him. At that time, Konstantin Simonov and Aleksander Tvardovsky were the main Soviet poets for me, and Mikhail Sholokhov the main prose writer. All this corresponded to their notion of healthy taste in a normal Soviet.

But something was causing them displeasure, and the man at the desk made what seemed a casual remark, but one that he began repeating as time went on: "Just watch out, or you'll have only yourself to blame."

At one point he suddenly broke off the conversation and dashed out of his office. As soon as he was gone, the junior man walked over to his desk, picked up an ordinary wooden ruler, and walked back to his place. Then, holding the ruler like a pistol, he began aiming it at me, grinning mysteriously but not saying a word.

The senior man returned and started in again. "You help us and we'll help you, but if you don't help us, you'll have only yourself to blame."

Once again nothing concrete was said.

"All right, then, who are your friends?"

"I don't have any friends."

"What about Litovtsev and Polsky?"

They were colleagues at the institute; we would read our poetry to one another. It would have been foolish to deny knowing them.

151

I said: "Oh, yes, Litovtsev and Polsky. We go to school together, all three of us write poetry, and we do get together."

"And what do you talk about?"

"Well, poetry, for example."

"What else?"

"Nothing else."

"What do you mean, nothing else?" he said, raising his voice more often now. "You don't talk about girls?"

"No, we don't," I said angrily. "I'm a married man, I have a daughter, and I don't talk about girls."

"Well, well, well," said the man in the corner ironically.

"All right," said the senior man, "girls aside, do you talk about politics?"

"We don't," I said.

"What do you mean, you don't? Aren't you interested in politics?"

"No, I'm not," I said. It happened to be the unadulterated truth at the time.

"How can you be a good Soviet and not be interested in politics?"

"That's just how it is," I said, losing more of my self-control. "I'm a good Soviet, but politics doesn't interest me."

"Well, all right, you're not interested in girls, you're not interested in politics. What about your relationships with foreigners?"

I lost all control and shouted: "What foreigners? What kind of nonsense is that? I don't know a single foreigner."

"What do you mean, what do you mean?" muttered the junior man. "What about the Israeli diplomat?"

At that point, I spat, out of sheer irritation, or at least it seems that way to me now.

This was the story.

One day, Igor Litovtsev and I crossed Kuznetsky Bridge and dropped by a bookstore, where Litovtsev discovered that a collection of Avrosh Gontar's poetry was on sale.

"Who's Gontar?" I asked.

"You don't know him? He's a very good Jewish poet. We should buy his book."

We stood in line at the cashier's and got receipts for two copies. But when we took our receipts to the counter, it turned out that the book had sold out, the curly-haired man in line ahead of us having bought the last four copies.

Overhearing our conversation with the salesgirl, the curly-haired man turned around at once and said that if we were interested in Gontar, he'd be glad to give us each a copy as a present, and he handed us the books then and there. We refused, he insisted, and the five of us (he had two small boys with him, between four and six years old, curly-headed too) went outside together. We accepted the books, but then he immediately began attacking Litovtsev, asking him why the Soviet Union had a policy of anti-Semitism. Litovtsev began muttering. I, as a true Soviet and as someone with no sense of politics, rushed to Litovtsev's aid and said that the Soviet Union had no such policy. The curly-haired man said that as the secretary of the Israeli Embassy he knew what he was talking about, and he continued to attack Litovtsev, ignoring me entirely. He put Litovtsev to shame for not knowing Yiddish or Jewish culture. I told him that Litovtsev was not a Jew, but a pure Russian, and for a Russian he knew plenty about Jewish culture.

I don't know who that Israeli took me for, perhaps some commissar assigned to Litovtsev, but it was obvious that he had no desire to speak with me and kept turning his back to me while, despite my assurances, he continued to berate Litovtsev for not admitting he was a Jew. Litovtsev mumbled something in reply that made it clear he did in fact feel ashamed. The diplomat's children were tugging at his hand. After resisting them for quite some time, he finally gave in, got into his car, and drove away. Litovtsev and I continued on our way.

And now they were beating me over the head with that Israeli, asking what Litovtsev and I had discussed with him.

Becoming increasingly unhinged, I said to the senior man: "Why are you asking when you eavesdropped and know everything anyway?"

"Why do you say that? So you think we were eavesdropping?" said the man in the corner.

"How else could you know about that Israeli?"

The senior man said irritably: "How we know things is our business. But why didn't you come to us and tell us about it yourself?"

"Why should I have?"

"What do you mean? Aren't you a good Soviet?"

"Yes," I said with pride, "I am a good Soviet. But I didn't think if I bumped into someone on the street, I had to come running to you."

"What do you mean? You could see that was provocational Zionist propaganda. Oh, that's right, you're not interested in politics. You're only interested in poetry. And what kind of poetry do they read in the Wellspring literary group?"

"What literary group?" I asked.

"Isn't the name of your group at the institute Wellspring?" asked the senior man, looking over at the man in the corner.

"That's right, Wellspring," said the junior man authoritatively.

I felt a great sense of relief. I had thought that they really did know everything about me, but it turned out there were some things they didn't know.

"You know," I said with malicious pleasure, "I have never had anything to do with that group."

I noticed that my reply took the wind out of their sails. The senior man cast a severe glance at the junior man, who cringed with what I thought was a guilty look.

"Do you know who the leader of that group is?" asked the senior man.

"I have no idea," I replied with utter sincerity.

"All right," said the senior man, in some confusion. "Then tell me what your professors say during their lectures."

"That's a question," I said acridly (and it still gives me pleasure to recall my reply), "I have trouble answering even on my exams."

"Why's that?" asked the senior man, who had not gotten the joke.

"Because," I said spitefully, "if you've been following me, you would have noticed that I'm rarely at the institute. I mostly go to pick up my scholarship funds. If you've checked with my group leader, you've seen my name on the absentee list all the time."

That was the end of the questioning, or almost the end. The senior man said to me that, on the one hand, he believed that I was a good Soviet, but, on the other hand, he had his doubts. If there was anything I hadn't told them or if I had told them anything that wasn't so, I'd have only myself to blame. He said I should go and think about it and come back to see them next Tuesday.

"Bring your poems when you come," he said. "We'll

read them and we'll help you. You help us and we'll help
you. And if you don't help us, you'll have only yourself
to blame."

They proposed that I sign a promise not to divulge
the contents of this meeting, which, like a good Soviet,
I did without making a peep. Once I was outside the
KGB building, I ran right to my friends and, like a good
Soviet, told them everything. Then they told me what
was really going on.

It turned out that I had missed a sensational development in my absence from the institute. The leader of
Wellspring had been arrested for writing an anti-Soviet
poem. I had known him, though I didn't know he was
the group's leader. I even knew a few of his poems. One
time, he had cornered me and recited some of his poems
to me, of which I remember these two lines:

> . . . *And those whom we extol today*
> *will dangle on the lampposts tomorrow.*

I didn't like the poem.

As a Soviet, I did not like that sort of poetry. And as
a non-Soviet I don't like it either.

Now when I recall that first encounter with the KGB,
I can see how ignorant I was. Anyone with the merest
sense of his rights and the law will tell me that I made
a great number of elementary blunders. In the first place,
back at the apartment I should have asked to see the
man's identification as soon as I was sure he was KGB.
In the second place, I should have refused to go to the
KGB without a summons. In the third place, when being
questioned, I should have demanded to be informed why
I had been called in and insisted that a written record

be made. As for my signature, I'm not sure, but I think it wasn't legal to demand it of me.

But if I had been clever and had demonstrated my knowledge of the law and my highly developed sense of justice, they would have taken note of me at the time, and my life would have become more complicated. But I was a real Soviet, who did not believe in Marxism-Leninism or laws or truth or rights. The way I chose to relate to the KGB at the time could not have been more idiotic, and yet it proved to have been entirely right.

Several years passed, and my position changed greatly. I had gone from the lowest level of society to one which, if not the highest, was quite high: I had become a member of the privileged caste of Soviet writers. My view of the world began gradually changing. I came to realize that, as a person and a member of society, I had certain obligations and certain rights. By then I had a better sense of Soviet law and made use of that knowledge in my practical affairs. But, the more scrupulously I observed those laws, the more trouble I encountered. In the end, when I was expelled from the Writers' Union, stripped of Soviet rank, and declared an enemy of the Soviet system, I realized intellectually what I had known instinctively before—that there is no such thing as law in the Soviet Union. It's the unwritten law of behavior that really counts.

Expulsion

I was probably expelled from the Soviet Writers' Union on February 20, 1974. I say probably because a session of the secretariat of the Moscow Writers' Union was scheduled for that date. But to this day I have no idea whether it was held on that day or another, who spoke, what was said, and what the wording of the decision against me was.

Not only did the leaders of the Writers' Union fail to report my expulsion in the press, as they had in similar cases before, but they created a new precedent: they never informed the expelled person of his expulsion. They did not even demand that I hand in my member's card, as they usually do, and that precious document remains among my papers to this day. Somewhat later, I learned that my name had also disappeared from the Literary Fund's* membership list, but who expelled me,

*An organization for the distribution of privileges for writers: medical care, vacations, housing, etc. ————Ed.

when, and on what level the decision was made have also remained a mystery.

Over the course of time, I realized that the authorities had adopted a tactic of complete silence toward me: from the moment I was expelled until I left the country, in December 1980, my name was not mentioned in a single Soviet newspaper. Moreover, the officials in the Writers' Union pretended not to have ever heard of a writer named Voinovich and would answer questions from foreign guests about me with a "Who's he?" Then they would thumb through their reference books on Soviet writers and say they couldn't find my name there.

If a Soviet asked about me at a meeting or a so-called lecture on the international situation, he'd usually be told that I had left the Soviet Union a long time ago and was now living in—here, a great variety of countries would be named—Israel, the USA, even Yugoslavia, where my ancestors on my father's side had originally been from. They were so persistent in repeating that information that when a well-known Soviet critic who lived in the building next to mine ran into me on the street, he went pale, having taken me for an apparition. Then he went on and on, questioning me about when and by what means I had managed to return from abroad. When I replied that I had never been abroad, he grinned in disbelief, as if to say that he understood the serious reasons preventing me from confiding that important secret to him.

However it was, one fine day (I still think it was the twentieth of February), the secretaries of the Moscow branch of the Russian Writers' Union met in a room on the second floor of the Central Writers' Building, unplugged the telephones, and, in an atmosphere of the strictest secrecy, which the Pentagon can only envy, they delivered angry speeches, called on each other to be more vigilant, voted (unanimously), and drew up a top-secret document depriving me once and for all of the high calling of Soviet writer.

This last act in the drama, or, if you prefer, the comedy, which Lydia Chukovsky has called the expulsion process, had been preceded by three acts or, to be more precise, two acts and one interlude.

The first act began six years before, in the spring of 1968, after I had signed letters in defense of several writers, as I said earlier. A Central Committee plenum passed a secret resolution on questions of ideology, one that everyone knew about soon enough, and instructed all editors and censors in the Soviet Union not only immediately to cancel all books, articles, and poems by the offending writers, but also not to allow any mention whatsoever of their names in print, as if they had ceased to exist. No easy matter, of course, but doable in a totalitarian state with experience of such matters. Withdraw a writer's old books from the libraries, don't publish his new ones, don't mention his name in print, and he will have ceased to exist. In that regard, my case seems to have been a fairly easy one. To seize one slender volume published several years earlier in a small printing did not require much effort. And nothing could have been simpler than stopping the two books in manuscript I had at a publisher's. It was even easier to prohibit the six screenplays of mine that were being worked on by directors. But I had written in two other genres as well, and dealing with them proved much more of a problem.

A few songs by well-known composers with lyrics by me had become so popular that they were to be heard every day on radio and television, in the repertoire of thousands of variety shows, and over the sound systems of restaurants or trains. Moreover, one of those songs had virtually become the Soviet cosmonauts' anthem, and not a single space flight was celebrated without it. For a long time, the authorities could not decide what to do about the song. Sometimes it was performed with no mention of the lyricist's name, and sometimes without the lyrics themselves. But they were unable to repudiate it entirely.

My two plays, "I Want to Be Honest" and "Two Comrades" (which I had adapted to the stage from my novellas), proved no less a problem. Those plays were being staged by fifty professional companies and innumerable people's theaters. To ban all those performances would punish not only the author, but also the several thousand people who had some part in staging them and who were not guilty of anything in the Soviet authorities' eyes.

This problem proved quite complicated for the Soviet authorities. The simplest and most convenient way out for them would have been for me to renounce my signature on the letters in defense of the condemned. They demanded this from the other signers as well, but probably the most powerful and massive attacks were aimed at me. I was summoned by officials in the Writers' Union, the Ministry of Culture, the Moscow City Soviet, the political administration of the Soviet Army, the Moscow City Committee, and the Central Committee. In an endless succession of offices I was urged and entreated to withdraw my signature. I was flattered, threatened—they promised to grind me to dust. Alla Shaposhnikov, the secretary of the Moscow City Committee, an ill-tempered woman whose ignorance was legendary, was especially zealous in her efforts. In her eyes, I was the devil incarnate. "Do you know who you're standing up for?" she said to one of the film directors who had spoken up for me. "Do you know what he does? He refers to us as 'them.' " She was personally in charge of keeping a watch on all my efforts to find a loophole and earn a little money. She referred to herself as "we." "We'll get him out of the Writers' Union. We won't let him earn a single kopeck. We know that he writes under other people's names, but we'll get to the bottom of that too." I don't know how I'd incurred that predator's wrath, but her persecution of me went beyond the call of duty and included many personal feelings. I can't say if she had access to my dossier at the KGB or had agents of her own, but everything I said, not only on the phone, but also at home, was known to her immediately, and she made no secret of that either. For the sake of fairness, I should say that my remarks about her were really so unflattering that I cannot bring myself to repeat them here. She persecuted me constantly and unflaggingly until she was transferred to another job. (She now holds the post of deputy minister of higher education.)

At the beginning of 1969, the authorities apparently decided that the signers of the letters had been punished enough, and they unclenched their fists a little. The forbidden names began to appear once again in the pages of newspapers and magazines. The Soviet Writer publishing house began talking about publishing my book again. My plays went back on stage in several theaters (though not fifty now). I was given a severe reprimand by the Writers' Union. Thus ended the first act in the process of my expulsion.

The intermission was a short one, lasting a month and

a half or two. In the spring of 1969, somewhat to my surprise, a German emigré magazine *Grani* [Facets] published the first part of my novel *The Life and Extraordinary Adventures of Private Ivan Chonkin*, which had appeared only in *samizdat* until then. Shaposhnikov and her assistants couldn't let a chance like that pass, and a new act began, one whose complications went on for about four years. During the first half of this period, I was dealt with by the secretaries of the Moscow branch of the Writers' Union, as a group and also one by one, by a special commission created for that purpose, by two officials of the Central Committee, and by some volunteers, who supposedly were acting privately and out of "friendly" feelings. They demanded that I "honestly and openly" admit that the book I had written was not only anti-Soviet but, even worse (and strange that this was worse in their eyes), anti the people, and slanderous, a book that could have almost been written on CIA orders.

The secretariat of the Moscow Writers' Union held two sessions on my case. At the first, which was run by Victor Ilin—the investigator assigned permanently to my case, who was also the secretary of the Moscow branch and a KGB general—the writer Victor Telpugov said that it didn't matter that my novella (despite my protests, they kept calling the first part of my novel a novella, so that it could be considered a complete anti-Soviet work) had ended up abroad, it didn't matter who'd published it; what mattered was that it had been written in the first place. "Even if I knew," said Telpugov, "that this novella had never been printed, and was just lying in the author's desk drawer or was only in the planning stage, I still would have thought that the author should not be dealt with by us but by those whose profession it is to combat the enemies of our system. And I myself would petition the pertinent agencies of government to give the author the punishment he deserves."

Telpugov was followed by the writer Mikhail Bragin, a colonel. (The Writers' Union has as many colonels and generals as the General Staff. They often say of themselves: "I'm a general" or "I'm a colonel"; they never say "retired" or mention to what branch of the service they belong. I suspect they're KGB.) Very wrought up, the colonel said he had never encountered anyone so horrible, anyone who had so insulted his beloved army, and he asked if I had really seen anything in his beloved army like the stuff I described.

I said: "Yes, and worse than that."

These words so offended the colonel that he jumped up, got red in the face, began shifting his weight from one foot to the other and shouting: "It's a lie! A lie! A barefaced lie!"

In deference to the man's age and rank, I replied that if he was subject to fits, he should see a doctor as often as he could and take part in anxiety-producing procedures like this as seldom as possible.

"You tell lies!" said Bragin, unable to calm down.

"I'm warning you," I said, "and I'm warning everyone here, that if I hear the word *lie* once more, I'm leaving immediately."

The word was used again, and I left, accompanied by passionate appeals of "Comrade Voinovich, come back!"

A top-secret communiqué issued after this meeting said that the Secretariat and activists had held a special session out of concern for their comrade and in friendly fashion had pointed out to him the shortcomings in his behavior, which had in fact put him in our enemies' camp. But the comrade had acted provocatively and arrogantly, denying that his so-called work was in essence ideologically harmful, and he had then created a situation of conflict, which he made use of to leave. Then came the concluding line, which I believe I am quoting verbatim here: "Only the lack of a quorum prevented the members of the secretariat from making a final decision on V. N. Voinovich's continued membership in the Soviet Writers' Union."

Pure baloney. If they need a quorum, they never have any problem creating one, whether they have enough members present or not. They did not expel me because they intended to work on me a little more. Destroying a writer's spirit is always more appealing to them than just destroying his career.

In December 1970, the secretariat met in session on my case a second time, and I was given another severe reprimand and a "final" warning. After this, there was no change in my situation. The leaders of the Writers' Union thought that a protest to *Grani* alone was insufficient and called on me to find a "suitable form" in which to condemn my unworthy behavior and my ideologically harmful novella. Since I found no form suitable for this, they stopped publishing me and kept me from earning a living for another two years, until the end of 1972. Then, assuming that they had me on my knees, the authorities decided to forgive me, and even published two of my books at the same time. That was a major ideological mistake on their part, because in those two years I had gotten off my knees and back onto my feet. I did not forgive the authorities for anything they'd done, and I intended to undertake new actions, entirely "incompatible with the high calling of Soviet writer."

On life's stage, however, things do not always develop according to plan. Just as I began casting about for a way to inflict a blow I'd had in mind for quite some time, KGB Colonel Ivanko popped into my life. He had no idea of my hostile intentions; all he wanted was to take my apartment from me so he'd have a place for the toilet he'd brought with him from abroad. (I suspect that Ivanko had not been very conscientious in carrying out his tasks when on assignment, bringing back toilets and not technological secrets from America.)

This began the third act, or an interlude—one which I have described in detail in my book *The Ivankiad.*

I had no desire to have anything to do with Ivanko and would have preferred never to have known he existed. But he persisted in the vicious error of his ways, and I was compelled to bring the full weight of my accumulated fury down on him. Bringing overwhelming forces to bear on me, Ivanko claimed that in acting against him, I was acting against the Soviet authorities. I should point out that he was absolutely right. Ivanko and the Soviet authorities are one and the same. Nevertheless, at this stage of the game Ivanko suffered a shattering defeat, and, cloaking himself in diplomatic immunity, ran shamefully off to the United States. (He came back later on, having been exposed by a former Soviet agent.)

I was on the move. In that same year, 1973, I myself sent *Grani* my novella *By Means of Mutual Correspondence.* Then, along with Sakharov, Maximov, and Galich, I signed a letter in defense of Solzhenitsyn, and later I sent the continuation of *Chonkin* to the West. Then I began following the Soviet authorities' actions, looking for something to find fault with. And I found that something in the creation of VAAP, the All-Union Authors' Rights

Agency. When my satirical letter to the head of that organization was broadcast by Western radio stations, General Ilin phoned my wife and cautiously inquired if I was suffering from a mental disorder.

I was summoned by another secretary of the Writers' Union, Yuri Strekhnin, just a colonel. He asked me if I knew what I was doing.

A session of the prose writers board was called to examine my "personal case" in December 1973, but it did not take place. Various board members called in sick, fled Moscow, or simply did not answer their telephone. Finally, they got a few of them to meet. That happened in January 1974, between the time Lydia Chukovsky was expelled from the Writers' Union and Solzhenitsyn was expelled from the Soviet Union. The large room where this event occurred was packed with people, three-quarters of whom I knew neither by face nor by name. The meeting was chaired by a certain Georgy Radov, who, for some reason, had hated me from the day I'd made my first appearance in literature.

I have to say that I went to that session with very aggressive intentions. I was planning to tell "them," meaning the menacing representatives of a menacing government, what I thought of them. And what I saw before me were pitiful, intimidated little people. One of them, a Hero of the Soviet Union, and a man who had been ingratiating with me not that long ago, was now in the back row, cringing in fear that I might notice him. Another, who only a few days before had run over to me in the metro, and, looking all around, shook my hand and whispered quickly: "I admire your courage." There was an old, pitiable critic, who at one point had been wrung through the grinder himself. His son had just been run over by a car, and they hadn't buried him yet, but still the old man scurried in to the meeting. What brought them all? Well, some wanted to look good to the higher-ups. Others weren't even trying to look good; all they wanted was to avoid the higher-ups' wrath and displeasure. They didn't want them to think they couldn't be counted on. Only Radov made no secret of the pleasure he took in the forthcoming reprisal. (Radov died a short time after this. Three years later, his son said to me: "My father was an honest man; I'm sorry that he did such a bad thing just before he died.")

Radov reported that hostile radio stations were broadcasting a letter whose author was there with them today. "What are your thoughts on the subject?" he asked me.

"It's not an interesting question," I said. "Let's go on to something else."

"When you're asked a question, you should answer it," said Radov in a teacherly tone of voice.

"I don't have to do anything of the sort," I said. "I would if I were here trying to join the Writers' Union, but I'm here to say good-bye."

Somehow that knocked them off course, because they were ready to drive me into a corner, and I seemed to have done it for them. Radov read a passage from the rules of the Writers' Union saying that only people who shared the union's views could be members. I said that when I joined the union, no one had read that rule to me, and, had they, I might not have joined. Then, obviously expecting me to raise objections, Radov repeated several times that the board, the activists, and the members were present in sufficient numbers for a quorum. I said that I had no interest in procedural matters and could not care less whether they stifled me while fully observing the formal rules, or observing them only in part. Then they all began shouting.

"Voinovich, you shouldn't have written that terrible *Chonkin*. It's a very bad book."

"I don't understand why you're talking about your rights, Voinovich. What do you need rights for? Take me, I don't need any."

"We should realize that this man [me] is an ideological enemy of ours. And we should speak with him as an enemy. You're a pup that barks from behind the fence. You're contemptuous of us, and you underrate our talent."

Here I could not resist saying that in fact I had overestimated this speaker's talent.

"Why are you insulting him?" Radov asked.

"Do you think I'm the only one who can be insulted here?" I put in.

"No one's insulting you."

"Oh, sure! He calls me a pup and that's not an insult?"

"He's angry at me because I criticized him once," the insulter said.

"You have delusions of grandeur," I told him. "Do you really think I ever read a word of the junk you write?"

Another began on a lyrical note: "I thought I knew Volodya as a good writer. But now my eyes have been opened. I can't understand what happened to him. We must figure out how he ended up on the other side."

Three people began their speeches with nearly the same words: "Because of the nature of my work, I have to read anti-Soviet literature all the time . . ." but, they said, even in that literature it was rare for them to read such malicious attacks as the ones in my letter.

That gave me grounds for sarcasm. "I thought I'd come to a meeting of my colleagues—who are all these strange people who read anti-Soviet literature all the time and get away with it?"

This circus ended with a vote, unanimous, of course, recommending to the secretariat that I be expelled from the Writers' Union.

The meeting of the secretariat was scheduled for February 20. However, I came down with pneumonia a few days before the meeting. Ilin phoned me on the morning of the twentieth. "I'd like you to come to the meeting. You have to say something. We still know that you're a good writer; we don't want to part company with you. No one wants your blood. Please come. I urge you to."

That was a new tone. He hadn't spoken to me like this before.

I said: "We won't be able to meet before the session. I can't see you, for two reasons. The first reason's not important—I'm sick . . ."

"Very good," interrupted Ilin, sounding happy. "In that case, I'll call off the meeting."

"You don't have to do that," I said. "I won't come when I'm well again either. I have another unimportant little reason—we have nothing to talk about."

Ilin continued trying to persuade me to come. They'll have a talk with you, he said; they won't expel you. At the worst, there'll be another reprimand.

I asked what kind of reprimand that would be when I already had been given two severe reprimands and a final warning.

"Don't worry about it. It's a procedural question. We'll find a way of dealing with it."

"I'm not interested in your procedures any more," I

said. "And I don't acknowledge your reprimands any more. I'm going to reprimand *you*."

"That's just fine," said Ilin. "Come and do it. You criticize us and we'll criticize you."

I said once again that I wouldn't come and that I would send in my criticism in written form that same day.

Just before the session, my wife took my letter to the secretariat. The letter began: "I'm not coming to your meeting because it will be held behind closed doors, in secret, out of public view, which is illegal, and I have no desire to take part in any illegal activity."

My life changed drastically that day. I had a physical sense that I had become free. I could be killed, crushed, but my soul had escaped their clutches.

At two o'clock that night I was awakened by a call from Reuter's Moscow correspondent. He'd just gotten a call from London asking him to check the report that I was under arrest. I said I might be, but I didn't know anything about it yet. Then I turned over and went peacefully back to sleep.

Rabbit Mask

During my last years in the Soviet Union, I lived a rather odd life. Expelled from the Writers' Union, I had been declared something of an outcast. People who used to associate quite willingly with me, now not only forgot my telephone number, but during chance meetings on the street would flee me as if I had the plague. Not everyone, of course. Far from everyone. I had friends who did not abandon me in the most difficult days, even though some did hint that they might get into serious trouble if they continued their old relationship with me. They ignored those threats not because they were trying to be heroes, but simply because they were decent people.

But it was also my lot to encounter people who, as soon as I fell into disfavor with the Soviet authorities, immediately began pretending they did not know who I was. Some were survivors of Stalin's time, when even a nodding acquaintance with someone could cost you your head. They may have survived precisely because they had it in them to turn away from friends and acquaintances in time, from fathers and mothers, if they had to. Those people can be understood and pitied, but it's difficult to respect them.

I remember one. I was at the Writers' Polyclinic, on Chernyakhovsky Street; for some reason, they had not taken away my privileges at the polyclinic. The doctors even insisted that I have a complete physical. I put it off for a long time, and finally gave in.

So there I was, sitting in front of a doctor's office.

The writer L. walked by, and slowed his pace when he saw me. I may not be a good engineer of human souls, but I sensed he was in the grip of doubt: should he walk over and say hello, or should he suddenly remember that he'd left something behind and go running back for it? But while he was thinking it through, his legs automatically continued moving, and before he knew it, he was quite close to me. Now it would be stupid to pretend not to have noticed me. New doubts rippled across his face. What kind of hello? Previously, he would have stopped and asked how things were going, even though the things I was doing were of no interest to him. Now they were, but he could see the critic Z. approaching and the playwright I. sitting there waiting. As he walked past me, L. nodded and even flashed me an almost imperceptible *non passaran* sign, as if giving a brave display of solidarity with me. But he made that gesture so that the critic Z. and the playwright I. could have no doubt that it was any more than a conventional sign of politeness, of a sort which can exist even between people whose views vary. No more than that.

The translator D., an older woman, now walked by in

the other direction. She and I had met in 1960, when I was still under thirty and she was already past sixty. I had just finished writing my first novella, and she had read some of the chapters. Later on, she would say in jest that we'd started out in literature together.

"Hello!" I said to her.

"Hello," she replied as if I were someone she barely knew. Then she took a few more steps, stopped, and came back. "Oh, Volodichka, my dear, hello, hello. My eyes are so bad I didn't recognize you." Then she added, in the hope that talking to me wasn't dangerous: "So they didn't expel you from the Lit Fund?"

"They did. But they left me on at the clinic. I even have to take a complete physical, though it's the last thing I want to do."

This nearly horrified her. "You're not coming out against physicals, are you? There are no politics here. Just doctors. They'll check you, take a cardiogram, run tests. I know you're fighting for some kind of rights, but certainly not against physicals!"

"Don't worry," I said. "I haven't gone so far as to start attacking physicals. It's just that I don't feel like having one."

"Volodichka, I'm seventy-six years old and I want an easy death. I was just invited to America. I'd like to fly there and then on the way back . . ." She made the motion of a plane falling with her hand.

"Don't hope for that. It's not so easy," I said. "Planes fly at high altitudes and it's a long way to fall."

"Volodichka, don't try to talk me out of it. I've thought it all through. You lose consciousness immediately and don't feel a thing. You know, I think about you a lot but I never call, not because I've forgotten about you, but because I have to be protected now. Yes, yes, Volodichka, I have to be protected, because I'm publishing a very important translation from English."

The humorist E. walked by, said hello to the translator, then, noticing me, said hello to me too.

"Hello, Tolya," said the translator. "It's very nice to see you. Volodya and I were just talking about life in general. No politics, none at all. He and I started out together, you know."

"But you'll end up differently," cracked the humorist, and went on his way.

His hurried footsteps seemed to remind the old woman that it wasn't quite safe to sit with me, but she had no excuse to get up and leave, and to do that without an excuse would have been uncomfortable.

"You know, Volodichka, I'm seventy-six, but I'm not senile. I remember everything. I remember when we lived in Peredelkino, how you and I used to sit on the little terrace, and how you brought me the first copies of my book. How come you never call? My number is easy to remember. [She told me it.] But please understand I have to be protected. I'm afraid of them, you know. I've lived through it all, famine, chaos. I don't understand a thing about politics, and I never read Marx, Lenin, or Stalin."

"Me either."

"At your age? Oh, Volodichka, if you only knew how much I'm afraid of them! Once I had to wait out in the corridor there, and they brought a man by; they were holding a revolver on him! It was so horrible!"

"That really is horrible," I agreed, "but no more horrible than being in a falling plane."

"No, no, Volodya, don't tell me. As I said, in a plane

you lose consciousness right away, and then it's all very simple."

"The effect's the same with a revolver. They aim it at you, you lose consciousness, and then it's all very simple."

"Oh, Volodya, you're always joking. Do you really still have the strength left to joke?"

"I wasn't joking. As soon as they aim the revolver at you, you . . ."

"All right, enough, Volodya. You must give me a call. A crazy American is coming to see me soon. He wants to translate you. But don't forget, I have to be protected."

"Maybe it's best if I don't call you then."

"Yes, that might be best." Then, shifting to a whisper, she said: "Just come, don't call. Although . . . we do have elevator operators."

"Don't worry about the elevator operators. I'll come in a mask."

Alarmed, she said: "What kind of mask?"

"Do you remember Vysotsky's line 'They handed out masks of rabbits, elephants, alcoholics'? Well, I happen to have a rabbit mask. I bought it for my daughter for New Year's. It's got great big ears. I'll put it on when I come to see you. If the elevator operator is asked who came to see you, she'll say: 'A rabbit.' "

"Don't make fun of me, Volodya. I'm an old woman. You know, the American I'm translating wrote me that he's always having to speak out in defense of Russians who are being persecuted. And I wrote back to him: 'For God's sake, don't defend anybody; that only makes things worse.' "

"Worse for whom?"

"For everybody, everybody."

"Yes, but there are people who already have it so bad it couldn't get much worse."

"It'll be worse for everybody, Volodya, believe me. And don't forget, they've got their army, their navy, and those . . . what do you call them? . . . nuclear warheads."

"But why should we worry about the warheads? All you and I need is one revolver, one plane crash . . ."

I didn't have a chance to finish my sentence, because I was called in to see the doctor. When I came out, the old woman was no longer there.

I lived another few years in Moscow after that, but never ran into her again. They finally expelled me from the polyclinic too, and I somehow couldn't bring myself to go see the old woman or even give her a call, given her nervousness about being protected. I did not drop by to see her on her eightieth birthday, and when I was leaving the country, I did not go see her to say goodbye.

She is still alive, and I've heard that she's been to America. Her plane did not crash. Either on the way over or on the way back. Personally, I'm very glad, because I know that not all the passengers on her plane could possibly have lived their eight decades yet. Funny she didn't think of that.

Parasites Never

During my final years in the Soviet Union, I had a variety of problems, all connected with my expulsion from the Writers' Union for actions incompatible with the high calling of a Soviet writer. My actions had proven incompatible with that high calling because, first, I did not write quite what the Party and government expected of me and, second, I spoke out in defense of people who, as we usually say, were imprisoned for their convictions, or, to put it another way, for nothing at all. Needless to say, the Soviet authorities could not forgive me for such crimes; not only did they expel me from the Writers' Union, but they also threatened me with all sorts of punishments for my offenses. One of the charges against me was parasitism. Meaning I was accused of not working anywhere and living at the expense of the people.

A policeman in our district, Ivan Sergeyevich Strelnikov, got into the habit of coming by to see me. A tall, gray-haired man, he was, in every way, very polite. He'd come to see me, and—no, he wouldn't break down the door—just ring the doorbell politely and just as politely ask: "May I come in, Vladimir Nikolaevich?"

"Of course, you can," I'd say. "I might not let somebody else in, but you're always welcome."

He was not only polite, but also bashful. He'd come in and take off his hat.

"Sit down, Ivan Sergeyevich," I'd say.

"It's all right," he'd say, "I'll stand."

But I'm a polite person too; I'd insist, and Ivan Sergeyevich would sit on the edge of a chair, and our foolish conversation would begin, something like this.

"Here's the thing, Vladimir Nikolaevich," the policeman would say. "You must forgive me, I'm not here on my own. They sent me . . . but it would be good to know if you're working anywhere?"

"Right here at home," I'd tell him.

"And what is it you're doing here? What kind of work, that is, if it isn't a secret."

"It's no secret, Ivan Sergeyevich, not for you, or for anyone else. I'm a writer and I work here."

"Oh, so you're a writer? Forgive me for saying so, Vladimir Nikolaevich, but did I hear that you were expelled from the Writers' Union?"

"Yes, I was, but in his time Leo Tolstoy was excommunicated from the church. What of it?"

"Well, Vladimir Nikolaevich, I don't know why Tolstoy got himself expelled, but you've *got* to be employed."

"Well, I am for the most part. The constitution says that everyone has the right to work in his chosen specialty. I've chosen my specialty and I'm working in it now."

"That's all well and good, but if you're working, you should have some proof of it."

"I've got as much proof as you could want. See those

books over there? My name's on them, and you don't write books without working."

He looked at the books, respectfully, it must be said, in his heart probably agreeing with me that parasites don't write books. He may even have been embarrassed, but he went ahead in any case and said: "Vladimir Nikolaevich, the books are fine, of course, but what I need is something official."

I explained some more about our much too democratic constitution, which didn't have a word to say about needing "anything official"; it just said that a person has the right to work, and, by the way, if we're going to split hairs, that's a right, not a duty (and there's a big difference between rights and duties), and as far as every person needing some piece of paper to make it official, well, there isn't a word about that. . . .

These conversations with the policeman went on for about four years, though there were long gaps between them. And they did not always run as smoothly as the one I've described. Sometimes I would become extremely irritated and say, "Ivan Sergeyevich, aren't you ashamed to come here? Aren't you ashamed to accuse me of parasitism when my books have had printings in the hundreds of thousands and have been translated into thirty-some languages? And if books don't mean anything to you, then maybe you'll take into consideration that I wrote songs, which you, your children, and nearly the entire population of the Soviet Union have sung. If even that work doesn't count, then maybe you'll be swayed by the fact that I started working at the age of eleven— on kolkhozes, in factories, at construction sites, and I served four years in the Soviet Army. Perhaps that is still not enough for you?"

Embarrassed, the policeman started becoming nervous himself. "But, Vladimir Nikolaevich, personally I have great respect for you. But what can I do? They sent me here."

In the end, all these conversations could be said to have had no consequences for me, in the sense that the authorities did not move to officially declare me a parasite. But unofficially I had entered the ranks of the parasites long before I lost my working papers.

We were fed badly when I was a soldier. But if we complained, we were told that we were parasites, producing nothing of material value; that we did not even deserve the eight rubles (eighty kopecks in today's money) a day that the people were spending on us. And, being politically conscious soldiers, we agreed with that point of view, though today it all seems quite idiotic. If the nation needs soldiers to defend it, it should support them so that they can live like normal members of society. If it doesn't need them, then why have them at all?

As for writers, what's there to say? Writers are always reproached for being parasites, for living at the nation's expense—they should be grateful to the people and should serve them; they should write books for the people and about the people, workers and peasants first and foremost.

Nonsense. I've written about both workers and peasants, but I know that the reader does not form his opinion of a book's heroes because of their social class. He finds them either interesting or not.

A normal reader, regardless of whether he's a worker, a kolkhoznik, or an academician, is better off reading an entertaining novel about the Count of Monte Cristo or Queen Margot than some boring stuff about a fellow member of his own social class. If the logic of those who instruct writers on how and for whom to write, what to write and who should write, were followed literally, then only spies would read spy novels, and Chekhov's story "Kashtanka" would be read only by dogs.

But what I'd like to say is this: Of course a normal writer has a sense of duty toward the people, society, and country. That is a duty he assumes voluntarily. A writer who performs duties that are sent down to him through Party channels is not a writer, but a clerk. When performing his duties, a writer need not feel continually grateful to anyone for the food on his table. The writer creates the spiritual values society needs, and the worth of those values cannot be measured in rubles—though, in a sense, they are. All else aside, a book is a real product, one you can hold in your hand, one that can be bought and sold, one that may even achieve success. Many books are given enormous printings and bring their publishers enormous profits. The works of certain "parasites" exiled from the Soviet Union could have made enormous profits for the country. But then, obviously, it would have been other people who would have had to be called parasites.

Modern society is complex. It needs peasants, workers, engineers, doctors, teachers, students, artists, writers—everyone. Life shows us curious correlations: the more people in one country directly engaged in the production of food, the less food there is in that country. And the more the government of that country fights against its people's art, the less food there is again.

Yes, modern society needs everyone. No one is feeding anyone else in a one-way relationship. Everyone is feeding everyone. With one exception. The Soviet Union does have that one class of people who produce neither material goods nor spiritual values, but sit on committees, clap their hands, and issue instructions as to how peasants should sow their grain and writers write their books.

These are the true parasites.

Domestic Currency

Saying good-bye took a few days, and the feeling never left me that I was attending my own funeral.

Friends came, acquaintances, people I hardly knew, and people I didn't know at all. Of the latter category, I recall two young people who looked like terrorists. They didn't speak, obviously assuming my apartment was bugged. They handed me a note that said their underground organization urgently needed to send a man to the West, and they asked me to find a foreign woman to marry that man. Whether they actually thought themselves terrorists, whether they had an original slant on the marriage business, or whether this was one of the KGB's last provocations, I'll never know. Whoever they were, I was unable to help them because I didn't happen to have an extra foreign bride on hand at the moment. I told them this, and they left very disappointed—not believing me, I think.

The body was decked out, and the stream of visitors

began at dawn and ended only late into the night. The morning visitors came alone or in small groups; they were subdued and sat with sorrowful faces, speaking in whispers, as is only fitting in the presence of the dear departed. But the stream grew greater toward evening, the elevator door banging against the wall more and more often, the doorbell ringing more and more all the time, until finally the apartment was so packed you could barely elbow your way through. The evening visitors also came with sorrowful faces, but the crush of people and the vodka had its effect. People began to get noisy, act like typical guests, and the wake livened up.

Soon that was all over. The stream of guests was gone, the farewell party given by Bella Akhmadulina and Boris Messerer in his enormous studio in the Arbat was over, and the last day had come.

In the darkness of a December Moscow morning, exhausted by the endless farewells of the previous sleepless night, Ira, little Olya, and I went downstairs to a crowd that had been waiting for us, much as people wait for the coffin to proceed to the burial place. The crowd, as befits those circumstances, was composed of people who had been close to us and those who had not, some whom we saw nearly every day and some who hadn't been around for years.

They all stood in silence, watching us come out of our doorway for the last time.

My neighbors also stood in silence, some secretly my fans, some open about it, but all participants in an absurd competition known as "the Ivankiad" which had taken place there in that courtyard seven years before and which has since become known far beyond its confines.

Ira's former pupils also stood in silence, all university

185

students now, some even graduates of institutes, grown-ups now.

For some reason, the fact that an actor at the Contemporary Theater, emerged from the darkness and approached us sticks in my memory. Seven years before, when I had been expelled from the Writers' Union, he had called to say he would come see me as soon as he could, absolutely. He never had (and neither was he obligated to; ours was only a nodding acquaintance). Now, there he was, and we gave each other a hurried hug.

Then there was no time left for hugging. The car doors slammed, and our strange cortege, made up of Zhigulis and foreign cars, sped off to Sheremetyevo Airport. Yet another strange, unnatural confrontation between an individual and the state had come to an end, a struggle the state had waged without stinting on time, effort, or the salaries of secret-service people drawn into that battle.

It was the last act. Our modest belongings (all told, we had four suitcases, one of which contained our daughter's toys) were examined by an entire brigade of customs officials. They checked every item, every shoe, and x-rayed every one of Olya's dolls. They found nothing except, perhaps, a last occasion to attempt to humiliate us. But they let everything through. They took an interest in my medal from the Bavarian Academy of Fine Arts, on whose invitation I was leaving for Munich. Then they thought about it, consulted someone, and let it through too. I assumed an indifferent air, and, in fact, it was all the same to me. The examination was coming to an end, and two of our suitcases were already on the conveyor belt, when all of a sudden they called out to

me and requested my signature on a form. I asked what
kind of form it was.

"A form saying that your manuscript's been confiscated."

That surprised me. "What manuscript?" They showed
me a pile of faded yellow paper—a chapter that had
been left out of a book of mine published long before,
and which I had certainly sent abroad by one means or
another some time ago. I could not have been at my
calmest at that moment, because I flung the form back
at them and, without thinking, said: "Fine. In that case,
I'm going home."

I grabbed our third suitcase from a porter who was
dragging it toward the belt and headed for the partition
that separated us from the people seeing us off.

A plainclothesman stretched out his hands and said:
"Stop, wait!"

I strode over to the senior customs official and barked,
"Aren't you ashamed to disgrace yourself in front of all
those people? Over a couple pieces of paper. Do you
really think I would risk carrying anything of value
through customs?"

I couldn't believe my eyes. The customs official blushed,
lowered his eyes, and syllable by syllable, said: "You're
done with customs. Customs has no claims against you."

I was at a loss. I had thought they were all KGB, some
in customs uniforms, some in plain clothes. Clearly, he
was ashamed and did not want me to think he was one
of them. I walked away. A KGB man in a raincoat ran
to a distant corner with a walkie-talkie in hand, muttering excitedly. Who was he contacting? Lubyanka? Early
on a Sunday morning?

Eventually, he came back in our direction, and I stood

up to confront him. "What are you running around with that thing for? What are you mumbling into it? Aren't you ashamed of yourself?"

"I've got nothing to do with it!" he shouted, sounding edgy.

"That's a lie," I said, and pointed to the customs official. "He may not have anything to do with it, but you certainly do."

"No, I don't," he repeated and darted away.

His seeming lack of ease had a sobering effect on me, and I calmed down. Why had I made such a scene? Our first two suitcases were coming back on the conveyor now. An airport worker walked over and said, with what seemed malicious pleasure, that the plane's engines had been started and it was about to leave—without us. From the crowd that had come to see us off came the voice of a friend: "Volodya, don't do it. You won't get another chance."

I knew that I wouldn't. I began regretting what had happened; I had acted against my own rules. On the whole, I don't have a lot of rules, but one is very firm and considered. I try not to say that I'll do or not do something if I'm not certain that I will do just what I'm about to say I will. A second rule stems from the first. If I've said I'll do something, I should do it. Especially in the case at hand: I had said I was going home, foolishly perhaps, and I ought to keep my word. Now, with hindsight, I think the KGB had no choice but to give in. The question of my leaving the country had been decided high up, on levels to which these men had no access. It was not in their power to violate such a decision. But I didn't know that for certain at the time and, to tell the truth, I felt I was exposing myself to great risk over a trifle. But there was nowhere to turn now.

They had nowhere to turn either, and handed the manuscript back to me. To be honest, I experienced a certain perverse pleasure in that. They had wanted to humiliate me, and I had humiliated them, but I had no idea that there would be yet another trial ahead.

As soon as we were out of view of our friends and the foreign correspondents seeing us off, our way was blocked in a small corridor by customs officials and police. It turned out that, in addition to the examination of our bags, we were also to undergo a strip search. A woman customs officer took my wife and daughter into a booth and let them back out right away. Then it was my turn. Three of us went into the booth: a fat customs official with a large star in his lapel, a police captain who, unlike the customs official, was thin, with a dark tanned face, and me.

"Everything out of your pockets!" ordered the customs official.

I decided to comply. I took everything out—my passport and some money, which I made no attempt to hide and had simply forgotten during the initial inspection. But my money could not have been of less interest to the customs official; the goal he had been set was not to find me guilty of currency dealings, but to humiliate me. I understood that. But I also knew that he couldn't really humiliate me, because I related to him more or less as I would to a cow. I could show resistance, possibly even without any great risk, but I could also submit fully and not feel in the least insulted. I chose to submit. He ordered me to take off my shoes. I took one off. Squatting down, he put his hand inside the shoe and fumbled about. All of a sudden the person in front of me was no menacing guard, but a fat middle-aged man suffering from shortness of breath.

189

"Hey, listen," I said, "what are you looking for, a bomb?"

"No, not a bomb," he said sullenly.

"So what then, your conscience?"

"Take off your other shoe," he said, and extended his hand.

I took off my other shoe and threw it past his hand to the floor. In a tone of command, I said, "Pick it up!" He picked it up and thrust his hand inside. Suddenly enraged, and even prepared to lose my flight (even though that would have been stupid, no question about it), I said: "Aren't you ashamed to be searching me? I'm a writer, not a criminal."

"I haven't read your books," he said; aggressively, it seemed to me.

"It's a shame you haven't," I said. "And just look at you. What are you doing crawling around the floor? You've lost your humanity. If I were you, I'd shoot myself first. What else do you need from me?"

"Nothing! Nothing!" he shouted all of a sudden and darted out of the booth.

At first I thought he had run for help, but soon I realized he had just run. He was ashamed.

I started putting my shoes back on and found myself eye to eye with the policeman. He looked disoriented and seemed not to understand what was happening.

"Where's he gone?" asked the policeman suddenly, addressing me ingratiatingly, as if I were his superior.

"I don't know. Off to shoot himself, probably. You go shoot yourself too."

I thought this would anger him, but instead a pitiable smile appeared on his face and he asked: "Are you going away for long?"

"Not for long," I said. "I'll be back soon."

Then the three of us ran for the plane. I shouted out a few last curses, because a woman airport employee was running after us, exclaiming hysterically: "It's all for your own safety! For your own safety!" She was justifying herself. She was ashamed too.

We proved to be the last passengers to board the plane. As soon as we were seated, the doors closed, and the plane taxied out to the runway. When we were airborne, the stewardess came around with her cart, with its beer, vodka, cognac, whiskey, gin. I took a little bottle of vodka and asked how much it cost. She quoted the price in dollars, then in Deutschmarks.

"What about rubles?" I asked.

"We don't accept domestic currency," she said with a blush.

There's a saying that shame's not smoke; it won't burn your eyes. I think it does. People are alive and human as long as they have their sense of shame. All is not yet lost.

2

Shut Up and Eat!

Literature and Writers in the Soviet Union

Shut Up and Eat!

Near the heart of Moscow, close to the Airport metro station, there are several eight- to ten-story buildings of a better than usual sort, that is, not made of reinforced concrete slabs, but of brick. And the apartments within them aren't cramped little Khrushchev-era slums, but spacious quarters with large rooms and kitchens, wide halls, and high ceilings. By every entryway a woman elevator operator sits and knits socks. She never fails to stop a stranger with the question: "Who do you want to see?" And then she checks to make sure that the caller visits the person whose name is mentioned and not someone else.

The people who live in these buildings can be seen after lunchtime or in the early afternoon. Here come two pudgy elderly citizens wearing blue jeans, light blue turtlenecks, and sunglasses—the kind foreign spies used to be depicted wearing. They walk leisurely, their hands clasped behind their backs, glancing condescendingly at the surroundings, which would seem to exist because of them.

"You haven't read my latest novel?" one citizen asks the other.

"No. I haven't had the time."

"Too bad. Read it. It'll give you enormous pleasure. By the way, I smash them to smithereens in that book, I say everything I think of them."

"About whom? Them?" whispers the first man.

"That's right, them," the second man insists loudly. "The American imperialists."

And, judging by his look of self-satisfaction, once they read his novel, the American imperialists will be thrown into terrible disarray.

Their conversation would suggest they are writers. But an experienced eye can identify a writer without the benefit of one word of conversation. By their expressions, simultaneously self-satisfied and scared, by their sunglasses, jeans, turtleneck sweaters, their wives, dogs, automobiles. There are thousands of subtle signs by which a Soviet writer can be distinguished from a Soviet of any other profession.

The Soviet Writers' Union has eight thousand members. Half of them live in Moscow. Three-quarters of those are registered in the coops near the Airport metro station. Mostly, the rank-and-file writers live there. Not the poorest, though. The ones who never had any money live in state apartments somewhat worse than these. Eminent writers, meaning the secretaries of the Writers' Union, live in state apartments somewhat better. I suppose important people do end up here, people who ride to work in government Volgas or even Chaikas, but they are a great rarity. For the most part, it's the rank and file, people who either ride in their own Zhigulis or just use the metro.

Take those two old men sitting on the bench in front of the building. What are they talking about? Their novels? Their poems? No. They don't write novels or poems. They're retired, living on their pension of one hundred twenty rubles a month and earning a little pocket money by doing in-house reviews for publishers or magazines and—who doesn't these days?—writing their memoirs, describing encounters with prominent people. Even so, they're not overworked in the writing of those memoirs; they have been sitting on that bench since noon, speaking in low tones, peering around for suspicious-looking types with sharp ears.

They're talking about what they heard yesterday from people they know or the BBC. They're saying that the new Party committee secretary went and did the same thing the last one did, meaning he embezzled Party funds. And now the new one is in for the same sort of trouble that caught up with the old one, meaning he'll be reprimanded. He'll be replaced by the old one, whose reprimand has been withdrawn in the meantime. The first secretary of the Writer's Union Comrade Markov tried to have his niece buried at Lit Fund's expense, but he was prevented by some stickler. After the Metropol scandal, Andrei Voznesensky flew to the United States again. The two men say that the Writers' Union was against his going, and Comrade Verchenko hit the ceiling, but Voznesensky went anyway. Because Senator Kennedy is a personal friend of his. And so is Arthur Miller. But neither Kennedy nor Miller can order Verchenko not to hit the ceiling. This means that in Moscow as well Voz-

197

nesensky has an influential friend who is more important and perhaps even more terrifying than Verchenko.

The old men sit there, letting their tongues wag, shooting the breeze about whatever comes to mind, and it would seem that there is no subject too important or too unimportant for them. They speak of Poland, the dissidents, the Jews who are leaving the country and the anti-Semites who are staying and who are so much in fashion that a woman poet once asked a well-known poet at the Writers' Building: "Evgeny Mikhailovich, why are you against anti-Semitism?"

And hats were being distributed yesterday at the Lit Fund. Eminent writers were given hats of young deerskin, well-known writers received muskrat, noted writers got fox, and the rank and file got rabbit. One person considered himself well known and demanded a muskrat hat. He was told: "Comrade, your place in literature is determined not by you but by the secretariat. Go complain to them if you want." He went to the secretariat and was told: "We don't begrudge you the muskrat, of course, but you're not active enough in public life." He was about to object when he suddenly felt ill and was taken to the hospital. Hats aren't his main concern now. The two men say that in a radio broadcast Solzhenitsyn said that there were seven writers in the Soviet Union who write about village life as well as Turgenev or even Tolstoy. Who did he mean? "What do you think?" they ask an approaching drunk. "Who did Solzhenitsyn mean?"

The drunk regards them with sad eyes; their quarrel couldn't interest him less. He's had a bad piece of luck. He had been hoping that for his sixtieth birthday *Literaturnaya Gazeta* would give him fifty lines and a picture, and he's learned that the only piece will be in *The Moscow*

Writer, and not fifty lines, but eight, and no picture. And he was offered a rabbit-fur hat by the Lit Fund. He refused it.

Without answering the question, he continues on his way home and there he writes a statement to "Markov himself": "As of this date, I no longer wish to be considered a member of the Writers' Union. . . ."

His wife is horrified. "Think what you're doing! You've got a daughter. She'll be thrown out of the institute. You've got a book you've been working on four years. They won't publish it now."

"I don't care. I'll send it abroad, to Ardis or Possev. They'll publish it." He pushes his wife from his room, calls a friend on the phone, and reads him the statement with great feeling: "As of this date, I no longer wish . . ."

His wife bursts back into the room. "Petya, what are you doing? You know the phone is bugged!"

He brandishes the receiver at her. "Get out of here! Don't you dare enter this room. My beautiful heroes live here!" As his wife runs from the room crying, he cuts the conversation short. "All right, I'll give you a call tomorrow."

The next day he wakes up with a headache and can't find his statement. His wife tore it to pieces and flushed it down the toilet hours ago. Well, maybe she is right, after all. My daughter hasn't graduated yet, he thinks. And he *has* been working on his book for four years. Possev might publish it, and they might not. If they did, what then? And *The Moscow Writer* was noting his birthday, wasn't it? And Comrade Kobenko, whom some writers called KGBenko, did send him a personal telegram. All in all, it's a life. Of course, he blabbed more than he should have on the phone yesterday, but he didn't say it at a meeting or to any foreign correspondents. In the old days, that would have cost him his head, but it's nothing now; these are liberal times, and everyone understands everything. So a person's feelings were hurt, he had too much to drink, hit his wife, said more than he should have, and doesn't like the Soviet system. Who does?

There's a story that Mussolini's little son once asked his father at dinner: "Daddy, what's fascism?" Frowning, Mussolini growled: "Shut up and eat!"

Shut up and eat! Why it's liberalism run wild!

In the old days, a person would sit at a meeting and keep his mouth shut, not doing anyone any harm. All of a sudden the chairman would call his name. "Now let's hear what Comrade So-and-so is being so quiet about." Comrade So-and-so mounts the podium with trembling legs and mumbles stiffly about his devotion to the Party, the government, and the person of Comrade Stalin. But they say, "No, somehow we don't believe you, you sound reluctant, as if you were being forced to speak, but we're not forcing you. If you don't like the Soviet system, say so. The Soviet system can get along without you; we'll throw you out and your corpse can rot on the garbage dump of history."

Before leaving Moscow, I somehow went to Novodevichy Cemetery. First, I walked through the old half, where Gogol, Chekhov, and Bulgakov are buried; then I walked over to the new section, where, as the poet Vladimir Kornilov put it, "the marshals are lined up like parrots on a turret." I, however, saw them more as a petrified honorary presidium, headed personally by our dear comrade Nikita Sergeevich Khrushchev. One tasteless monument towers over another, their details cast or chiseled naturalistically—wrinkles, eyebrows, eyelashes, decorations, epaulettes, ribbons, and inscriptions that list the deceased's rank and position. There are writers here who have found a place in literature and in our memory—Tvardovsky, Ilya Ehrenburg, Smelyakov . . . But, for the most part . . .

Beneath a cumbersome statue of himself reposes a former field marshal of literature who for a time after his death had been reduced to the rank of unknown soldier. At one time, he had presided over presidiums, thundered against his hapless fellow writers, demanded their blood. His books were printed in enormous editions, a golden rain of prizes, money, and privileges fell upon him, and surely he believed he'd earned it all.

A couple of idlers stop by his tombstone.

"Who's that?"

"Some writer."

"Uh-huh."

If his books weren't forced on schoolchildren as part of their required reading, who would read him now?

No one apart from a few connoisseurs like me.

As I walked around, I thought: Now this is the garbage dump of history.

Nowadays the meetings at the Writers' Union are as quiet and boring as the cemetery. The rank-and-file writers take their places in the auditorium, the generals of literature sit at the speakers' table, Comrade Kuznetsov takes the podium and begins to drone: In the period being reported on, the writers were inspired by the decisions of the such-and-such Party Congress and the instructions of Comrade So-and-so and labored fruitfully and with inspiration. This period saw the publication of

. . . (Here he lists the books, whose quality is judged in accordance with the position their authors occupy.) There have been significant additions to our Leniniana, and our image of the Communist has been developed further, a subject to which, unfortunately, our writers are paying insufficient attention. There have, however, been major accomplishments in this area as well. The union's leadership is constantly concerned with strengthening the writers' connection to real life. Brigades of writers have visited the workers building the Baikal-Amur railway, have read from their works in the tents of reindeer breeders, and have done voluntary Saturday labor at the Likhachev plant.

And then the meetings starts straying from literature, with more and more talk about traveling, rallies, the struggle for peace, and other such nonsense that has nothing to do with most of the people there. The majority of the writers are not allowed to take part in the struggle for peace which involves trips abroad or the clothes, tape recorders, and kitchens brought back from those trips. But Comrade Kuznetsov has a word of consolation for that majority. The writers' daily life and health is a constant concern of the secretariat and the Party organization. During the period being reported on, a new writers' studio building has been constructed, medical services have been improved, a dacha coop is in the works, war veterans' privileges have been expanded, and a number of writers have been granted cash bonuses.

You sit there and listen to all that, thinking, It may not be a cemetery, but it's no writers' union. More like a charitable institution.

The subtext of the speech is clear to everyone. Be

quiet, lie low, obey your superiors. If you can't write about the secretaries of the district or provincial committees, factory managers or kolkhoz chairmen, then write about Young Communists, Pioneers, nature, the police, the working class, and write in the proper spirit; be boring and optimistic, and everything will go well for you: we'll publish your book, give you a free vacation, pay your hospital costs, and, before you know it, you'll have made it to your pension!

"Shut up and eat!

Genius and Crime
On the 90th anniversary of the birth of Mikhail Zoshchenko

Mikhail Mikhailovich Zoshchenko would have been ninety years old today, a jubilee that will most likely be marked officially in the Soviet Union. There may not be any conferences in honor of Zoshchenko, but some articles will probably appear. As well they should! He was a major Soviet writer, a classic, the scourge of the bourgeoisie. Something will probably be said about his humor, his inimitable style, and someone will recall what Gorky said of him.

But if there's going to be a jubilee, and if people are going to reminisce, why not recollect another anniversary as well? Thirty-eight years ago, during another August, Zoshchenko's merits were given extensive and stormy acknowledgment—at sessions of the Leningrad Party activists, at meetings of Leningrad writers, and at many other sessions, gatherings, and emergency meetings. The speeches delivered were passionate. Zoshchenko was a slanderer. Zoshchenko was a mocker. "Zoshchenko turns his low and vulgar little soul inside out and does so with delight, with gusto, wishing to show the world: See what a hooligan I am! It would be hard to find in our literature anything more repulsive than the 'moral' Zoshchenko parades in his novel *Before the Sunrise*, in which he depicts himself and all humans as vile, lascivious animals without shame or conscience."

Those words about shame and conscience were spoken by a man after whom Soviet streets, avenues, factories, and ships have been named: even the city of Mariupole was a given his loathsome name—Zhdanov. He was one of Stalin's henchmen, who, during the siege of Leningrad, while thousands died of hunger, played tennis to burn off the fat he'd put on. This brazen nonentity, devoid of shame and conscience, took charge of literature and art—this monster who, word has it, used only one finger on the piano when he instructed Shostakovich and Prokofiev how to compose music.

He hadn't made his way to music yet in August 1946; he was still busy making short shrift of literature. He was busy calling Zoshchenko a hooligan and slanderer, and Anna Akhmatova half nun, half slut.

Andrei Zhdanov spoke twice and then, as was his custom, he unleashed a pack of writers. Of course, it's crude to compare writers to a pack of dogs, but the analogy is fair. To what else but dogs can we compare people who, sicced on by their masters, attack one of their own and tear him to pieces. They told Zoshchenko that he had no talent, that he was a nonentity, that he was a swine, that he hated the Soviet people, who in turn would reject him and his work.

The meeting of the Leningrad writers was run by Konstantin Simonov, who had come from Moscow. He was handsome, still rather young (he had barely turned forty), and a little gray at the temples. He was at the height of his fame, the author of famous poems, plays, film scripts, and the novel *Days and Nights*. The darling of the public as well as of Stalin, he had been heaped with prizes and decorations. And, on top of that, he was something of a war hero.

He ran the meeting, spoke, gave the floor to others, and when someone in the gallery peeped up in Zoshchenko's defense, he allowed as he saw no difference between defenders of Zoshchenko and defenders of the Anglo-American imperialists.

For reasons of age and geography, I did not attend that meeting, but I did see Simonov at other times and at other meetings and have retained clear image of how he spoke, purring his *r*'s, restrained, calm, merciless. I think he saw himself as a colonel on the battlefield, a sort of ideological Marshal Zhukov, and, supported by the entire might of the Soviet state, he dealt a final blow to the enemy.

What was said in Leningrad was echoed everywhere else.

I was living in Zaporozhe at that time and had just enrolled in a trade school to study carpentry. Our first lessons were not on how to hold a plane or make casein glue, but on how we should understand the unideological, untalented, vulgar, slanderous, and unintelligible works of Zoshchenko and Akhmatova. We didn't know the difference between one chisel and another, but were told the fine points of all there was to know about Zoshchenko and Akhmatova.

We were told of their pernicious activities and their exposure as if nothing more important were happening in the world. Just one year earlier, the Soviet Union had conquered Germany, taken part in the defeat of Japan; now here it was smashing Zoshchenko and Akhmatova.

To be frank, when I think about Zoshchenko's fate, what surprises me is not that the authorities came down on him so heavily, but that they didn't do so earlier.

After all, his heroes never fitted in with Soviet literature. They mined no coal, did not produce great increases in the Motherland's milk, did not run district or provincial committees, did not do their fighting on the battlefields of war, but in communal kitchens.

And the views he expressed were quite out of step for a Soviet writer. He wrote: "Tell me, what 'exactly my ideology' could be if on the whole I'm not attracted by any party? . . . From the point of view of people in the Party, I am a man without principles. So be it. I would say of myself that I am no Communist, no social revolutionary, no monarchist. I am just a Russian. I don't hate anybody, and it is that which is my ideology.' "

Not bad! Of course, he said it in 1922. Afterward, he said nothing of the sort, but he did not renounce what he'd said in the past.

Needless to say, he was attacked viciously. But his books continued to come out. In the thirties, there appeared a six-volume collected works, a selected works, and books of short stories. And that at a time when some colleagues were all but prohibited.

I think this is to be explained by the fact that, unlike the others, Zoshchenko accepted the October Revolution and paid it its due. He was not haughty toward the people he wrote about, those "tenants," as Mikhail Bulgakov, for example was; Zoshchenko had compassion for them as if he were one of them. The moralizing to which he was inclined was not civic in nature; he called on people to live in peace in their communal apartments, without discussing whether it was right or wrong that such apartments existed. Yet he wrote stories, satirical articles, and novellas that described incidents that could not be called typical. The authorities woke up only when they saw the picture those separate pieces formed. They saw that, unlike the others, Zoshchenko had in fact achieved what was officially required by the ideologists of socialist realism. It was Zoshchenko who had created an image of the new man. And that new man was not a representative of the bourgeoisie, which hinders "our" forward progress, but of those who were going forward and dragging us along by force.

The official reason for the state's anger at Zoshchenko was his story "The Adventures of a Monkey" and the novella *Before the Sunrise*. But it's said that there was another and perhaps most significant reason: finding a mustached character in one of Zoshchenko's old stories, Stalin decided that it must of course have been modeled after him. As we know, the Generalissimo was a mistrustful man and saw himself in every character who sported a mustache, including Kornei Chukovsky's "The Cockroach." All the same, I don't think that was the only reason.

At one point, Zoshchenko was offered the podium to express his feelings about his comrades' solicitous criticism. He went to the podium and said: "Why are you hounding me?"

The people hounding Zoshchenko probably didn't know exactly why they were doing it. They had devised a suitable approach and combed his works for lines that could be used against him, but neither those lines nor any individual act or statement by him was the real point. The real point was that the people hounding him instinctively felt he was only pretending to be one of them, but in fact belonged to a completely different breed. The difference between them and him was, let's say, that between dogs and a wolf.

I do not make this analogy in order to call Zoshchenko's enemies dogs once again or to compare Zoshchenko to a predator. What's important to me in that comparison is that a wolf has a true nature, whereas a dog is a corrupt wolf—a wolf which has changed its nature, gone into service, and hates the real wolf, which has remained true to itself.

And just as pseudo wolves hound real wolves, pseudo writers hound real writers.

Here someone might ask: but what about Simonov? Are you saying that he was a pseudo writer?

I have to say that I still hadn't read Zoshchenko at the time he was being hounded. I read him for the first time in about 1956 and was not greatly impressed by his stories. I knew he had been terribly popular at one time and that even in the twenties, when printings were, as a rule, miserably small, his books were printed in the hundreds of thousands. Zoshchenko himself was embarrassed by that. He thought that readers weren't looking for anything but laughs in his satire.

On the other hand, I'd been reading Simonov since my childhood. I loved his poetry, his plays, and the films for which he wrote the script, though I was cool toward his prose.

But time has passed, and I can't read Simonov at all now. All his poems strike me as ungenuine, unoriginal; even his famous "Wait for Me," which people copied out and learned by heart during the war, no longer has any effect on me whatsoever. The same goes for his plays and scripts. His prose I find hopeless, with its cardboard heroes, and premises that are not quite false, but have no resemblance to truth.

Pushkin once said: "Genius and crime are incompatible." Perhaps I am abusing the reader's patience by resorting to Pushkin's authority once again, but this idea seems unusually important to me. The more I think about literature and the fates of various writers, the more I am convinced that Pushkin did not make that statement for its eloquence alone. That line contains an indisputable truth.

Simonov was not an utter villain. There were people whom he helped, books that he saved, situations in which he strove to do good. But he could also be cold and cruel, revealing the inauthenticity of his nature and his talent. He hounded Zoshchenko not only because he was instructed to, but also because he was profoundly hostile to Zoshchenko's authenticity.

My attitude toward Zoshchenko changed, and went in the opposite direction. At first I was not especially interested in him, but now I feel an increasing need to read him. I am rereading his "Sentimental Tales" and his remarkable book *Before the Sunrise*, which Zhdanov so viciously attacked—a book in which he truly does turn his soul inside out.

They say a writer should write for the people. By and large, this is utter nonsense. A writer can write for whomever he wishes. For the masses or for a small circle, for his wife or for himself. If people can't understand what a writer writes, or find it alien, they can, if they live in normal circumstances, punish him by not reading his books. There is no need for hangmen like Zhdanov or Simonov.

Zoshchenko is very much a writer for the people, and in that sense he was fortunate. Readers immediately noticed him, took a liking to him. He was not, however, fortunate as a person. He who made millions of readers laugh suffered from a terrible melancholy he had borne ever since youth; he was morose, gloomy, and locked within himself. He tried to find the reasons for his suffering in his novella *Before the Sunrise*. In it, he tried to find a prescription for happiness. And it seemed to him that he had found it in that book. But right after it appeared, the attacks on him grew even more fierce.

He was expelled from the Writers' Union, his books were no longer printed. In order to earn a living somehow, he reverted to one of his earlier specialties—he began repairing shoes. By nature he was utterly genuine, and he preserved that characteristic in all circumstances. He was always gentle, modest, subtle, humane. I am unable, for instance, to imagine Zoshchenko hounding Simonov, or anyone else, for that matter. His authenticity would never have allowed him to do anything of the sort.

It was precisely that authenticity that Simonov was unable to forgive. In 1953, the question of reinstating Zoshchenko into the Writers' Union was raised. Once again, Simonov spoke. He did not feel constrained, made no effort to avoid speaking, did not call in sick. No. This time he was not against Zoshchenko becoming a member of the Writers' Union again. This time he spoke out against the wording of the resolution, which, it seemed, was meaningless as far as principles were concerned. To rehabilitate Zoshchenko is to admit that we were in the wrong, said Simonov. And for that reason he should not be reinstated, but admitted anew, as a beginning writer—that is, to accept him only for the things written since 1946. Everything written before the Party's censure should continue to be considered literary trash. However, Simonov was not particularly fond of what Zoshchenko had written after 1946 either, and so proposed that his victim be admitted to the Writers' Union, not as a prose writer, but as a translator. Think of it! Simonov, the author of long, boring, sloppily written novels, not recognizing Zoshchenko as a prose writer.

After Zoshchenko's return to the Writers' Union, the hounding stopped. But not for long. A delegation of English students that came to Leningrad in 1954 wished to meet with Zoshchenko and Akhmatova. During that meeting, the students asked both writers about their attitude toward the Central Committee resolution to readmit Zoshchenko, and Zhdanov's speech. Akhmatova said that she thought both were correct. Zoshchenko said that the resolution was not entirely fair. This event occasioned a great deal of argument. Some people berated the students—how could they ask such a question; didn't they have any idea where they were? Others said that Zoshchenko should have been cleverer and said the same thing Akhmatova had. A third group said that Akhmatova should not have misled the students and that her duty as a citizen required her to tell the truth. I think all three groups were right. The English students need not have been sensitive to all the subtleties, which can be known only after one has mastered Soviet psychology. Akhmatova was aware that not only the students but also her enemies would hear her reply; she had contempt for her enemies and had no desire to provide them with an opportunity to turn carelessness to their advantage. Zoshchenko displayed his typical simplicity; had he been able to rid himself of that simplicity, he would not have been Zoshchenko.

He was not forgiven for that impertinence.

So they hounded him to his death. And, to use Akhmatova's expression, he couldn't take the second round. Lidya Chukovsky has spoken of her conversation with Akhmatova three months before Zoshchenko's death. Akhmatova reported that his mind had deteriorated, and he suffered from both paranoia and delusions of grandeur. Focused on himself, he couldn't hear what someone else was saying. To a question about the weather or his summer plans, he would reply: "Gorky says that I'm a great writer." I'm no psychiatrist (neither is Akhmatova), but all I see in that remark is depression, not any kind of psychosis. It was objectively true that he was being persecuted. And the fact that he kept repeating what Gorky had said about him was a last attempt at both telling the truth and saving his own dignity. Furthermore, he attributed the compliment to Gorky; he didn't call himself great.

They hounded Zoshchenko like a wolf for twelve years straight and they hounded him to his death. Later, they recognized him. In the end, they recognize everyone after they're dead: Bunin, Bulgakov, Mandelstam, Tsvetaeva, Pasternak, Akhmatova . . .

Strangulation

There are rumors about afoot that *Doctor Zhivago* will finally be published in Moscow. A correspondent for the London *Times* has termed these rumors sensational. If rumors can be termed sensational, then we never had any shortage of them—the less trustworthy news there is, the more utterly fantastic rumors are.

People say either that a flying saucer hovered over Petrozavodsk for a few hours or that some miracle healer has appeared who can telepathically cure someone ill with cancer thousands of miles away. Or that a foreigner has come to Moscow and is giving unsuspecting Muscovites poisoned T shirts that, once on, can't be pulled off. Unfortunately, or fortunately, the distance between rumor and news is immense.

Rumors about a possible publication of Boris Pasternak's *Doctor Zhivago* have also been in circulation before. They've been flaring up and dying down for some twenty years now, if not more.

A brief reminder of the history of that novel on which Pasternak worked for many years: when he finished it in the fifties, he offered the manuscript to *Novy Mir*. It was rejected by the editorial board, which was headed by Konstantin Simonov at the time. In 1957, the novel was published in Russian by Feltrinelli, an Italian Communist publisher. In 1958, that is, just over a quarter of a century ago, the author of *Doctor Zhivago* was awarded the Nobel Prize. And that truly made for a sensation, which caught everyone by surprise, including the laureate himself. Pasternak sent a telegram to the Swedish Academy that had awarded him the prize and expressed his feelings as follows: "I am infinitely grateful, touched, surprised, embarrassed."

The Soviet authorities could have subscribed to the latter points, for they too were surprised and embarrassed. Who's this Pasternak? Why wasn't Mikhail Sholokhov given the prize, or Konstantin Fedin, or Mikhail Alekseev? Why some Pasternak, whom the Soviet people have never even heard of?

Then all hell broke loose. The Soviet newspapers began to assail the gray-haired laureate with a stream of invective and mudslinging. Writers and so-called simple working people inveighed against Pasternak. They called him anti-Soviet and an enemy of the people. The author of one letter wrote that he knew only Sholokhov and Fedin, good writers, but had no idea who this Pasternak was. Another expressed his feelings in verse:

Pasternak
is as dark and slack
as an empty sack.

The students of the Literary Institute walked past Pasternak's dacha shouting curses Chinese-style and smashing bottles of ink, issued to them beforehand, on his fence. The secretary of the Komsomol Central Committee and future chairman of the KGB, V. Y. Semichastny, called Pasternak a pig and declared that the Soviet government would have no objections if Pasternak left the country.

The meeting held by the Writers' Union was a shameful, pogromlike affair. One after the other, those engineers of human souls mounted the podium to shout hysterically that Pasternak hated the Soviet people, was a lackey of international imperialism, that to speak his name was like making an indecent noise in public, and that Pasternak's place was on the garbage heap.

What motivated those writers? Hatred, spite, envy, and fear. The belief that if they didn't trample him today, they'd be trampled themselves tomorrow.

Two elderly and still more or less respected writers, the poet Ilya Selvinsky, and the literary critic Victor Shklovsky, were in Yalta at the time. Why didn't they use that opportunity to avoid taking part in the general persecution of the man? They were well aware of who Pasternak was as a poet. Selvinsky, after all, had called Pasternak his teacher. But the fear that had eaten away at their souls during the years of Stalin's terror gave them no peace. They were afraid of being accused of hiding behind the Crimean mountains at a key moment in history. They weren't, however, afraid of disgracing their names forever. And so, panting from the heat and the steep incline, gulping heart medicine on the way, they dragged themselves up the mountain to the post office to send a telegram condemning their colleague.

216

Selvinsky's exploit did not pass unnoticed. He who had written: "I have not hammered a single nail in my life" became the subject of one of the most brilliant epigrams in Russian literature:

All's behind you now, the glory and disgrace,
Envy and dull malice remain.
When they crucified your teacher,
You walked over to hammer in the first nail.

The writers who spoke out at the meeting in 1958 promised the author of *Doctor Zhivago* a place on the garbage dump of history. Since then, twenty-six years have passed, and the creator of the novel died quite some time ago. Many of his persecutors have gone to the next world as well. But *Doctor Zhivago* continues to be published and republished in many languages. Even now it is one of the most popular books in the world. It is published in Russian, and despite the vigilance of the border guards, copies end up in the Soviet Union and are distributed by those who speculate in books and by unselfish lovers of literature.

All right, let's assume that it'll be published now even in the Soviet Union. What would that bear comparison to as an event? Perhaps the publication of the serialized version of Bulgakov's the *Master and Margarita* in 1967. But there's an essential difference. Bulgakov's novel seemed to return from oblivion, to rise from the ashes, thereby confirming the author's principal hope—that manuscripts don't burn. *Doctor Zhivago* would not cause a sensation like that. That novel is alive and has been read by millions. And, no matter what, it would be published in the Soviet Union in a paltry edition, of which most would be sent abroad. And those who are destroying literature today would keep some of the copies for themselves. An even smaller number would be sent to the Writers' Union bookstore and allocated to those with membership cards as a reward for good behavior. And a very few would be sent to the bookstores in Moscow and a couple of other cities.

At one point a collection of poems by Osip Mandelstam, who had been martyred in prison, was also published. Speaking to a group of intellectuals in Leningrad, a Party lecturer explained that the volume had been published to demonstrate our freedom of the press to the West. "You should understand," he confided to the audience, "that we have published Mandelstam in order to shut their mouths." "Shut ours too!" came a voice from the audience.

The same thing is happening now. A chosen few will receive the legal edition of Pasternak. And, as before, the general reader will have his mouth shut with volumes by third-rate writers. If any outstanding talent should appear today, he will also be persecuted, stifled, and left to rot by so-called literary public opinion, front-rank workers, and specialists from the KGB. And, at some point, some twenty or thirty years after his death, they'll forgive him for having lived on earth and publish the books they're spitting on today.

All the same, I'd like to end on an optimistic note. The self-assured Soviet authorities think that they control everything, including literature. But the literature they control, encourage, favor, and reward has no greater success than the agriculture they also control. There are many heroes of socialist labor in both fields, but the actual results are deplorable. Nevertheless, the situation in literature is better than in agriculture.

From time to time, not very often, despite everything, writers do appear who can be stifled, left to rot, and killed but who cannot be governed because they are ungovernable. And it is those writers who create the books that must not be destroyed. Writers die as do their oppressors, and states fall, but the books remain. And those who govern literature, no matter what ranks they may hold, should remember that true literature is beyond their control, that anyone encroaching on its sovereignty will suffer inevitable defeat. The case of *Doctor Zhivago* demonstrates this with utter clarity.

The Life and Fate
of Vasily Grossman and His
Life and Fate

People who follow Soviet literature know that the flood of books published every year by thousands of Soviet writers can contain an occasional few deserving of attention. These are books in which the author actually says something, slips something past the merciless Soviet censorship. Some books may even be quite good. But to those better books published by Soviet publishers, I prefer a few—they can be counted on the fingers of one hand—that failed to slip past the censorship.

Vasily Grossman's novel *Life and Fate* is one such book. Had it been published when it was finished, that is, in 1960, I have no doubt that it would have been a literary sensation of world importance.

But that was not to be. Something else happened. Vadim Kozhevnikov, the editor in chief of the magazine *Znamya* (The Banner), to which the author had submitted his novel, read it. Then, as fast as his feet could carry him, took it to the Central Committee, or perhaps the

KGB. But that was not the important thing. The important thing was that the people to whom Kozhevnikov gave the novel read it through and, unlike certain publishers, editors, critics, and literary scholars, saw its true worth right away. Reaction was immediate. The KGB appeared at Grossman's home, seized the manuscript, the drafts, his notes, everything that bore the slightest relation to the novel. Another copy, which Grossman had given to Alexander Tvardovsky, the editor in chief of *Novy Mir*, to read, was removed from his office safe. Not only were all copies seized from the typists who had typed the novel, but the carbon paper they had used was also confiscated, and people say that the ribbons were torn out of the typewriters.

All this material was placed in a canvas bag, sealed, and disappeared forever. Or so it seemed at the time.

This was an absolutely unique case in the history of long-suffering Soviet literature. Before this, authors had been arrested and all their papers seized indiscriminately, or discriminately. This time it was not the author who was arrested, but the novel. That's the word for it— not taken, not seized, not confiscated, but arrested, like a live human being.

That had never happened before. For the sake of comparison, Pasternak never concealed his novel *Doctor Zhivago* from anyone. He gave it to friends and editors to read, using the mails, but it never occurred to anyone to arrest him at that time. The scandal broke only after the book had been published.

The most contradictory rumors circulated for many years after the arrest of Grossman's novel. No one, or next to no one, knew what the book was like and why that fate had befallen it. Now that this book has returned from oblivion and we have had the chance to read it, we can say why the novel was arrested.

Grossman's novel is written in the classic tradition of realism—critical realism, that is. In any case, the novel bears no relation to socialist pseudo realism and is as different from the classical models of that school as a live person is from a plaster cast.

Reading Grossman's novel, one automatically compares it to *War and Peace*. And indeed, like Tolstoy's novel, Grossman's *Life and Fate* is an epic novel painted on a vast historical canvas. As in Tolstoy, both the war scenes and the scenes of peace are of identical importance. The action takes place in Moscow and deep in the provinces, at the front and in the rear, in Stalin's headquarters and in Hitler's. One of the novel's heroines is killed in a German gas chamber, and one of its heroes is broken by inhuman torture in Lubyanka.

Grossman is a chronicler of his times. One may speak of this novel's uncommon humanism, of the author's incorrigible and indestructible faith in the good and in all the better qualities that reside in man. One is struck by his profound insight into his characters: people are shown in all their shabbiness and grandeur. A husband suspects that his wife has denounced him to the NKVD, and the wife suspects her lover of the same. Risking his own neck, the commander of a tank corps delays executing an order from Stalin to avoid unnecessary loss of life. A character will display unusual strength of spirit when facing death, yet commit shameful acts out of fear of losing some petty privileges.

No, this book is not the least like those in which the authors have managed to say a little something about one thing or another and have succeeded in slipping the bits past the censor. Not a single page in this book could have slipped past the censor, because truth cries out on every page.

In comparison with the better books written in the tradition of the epic novel in the entire Soviet period, Grossman's *Life and Fate* strikes me as the most major, the most significant.

Soviet literature is run by incompetents, some of whom are even near illiterates. But even these have a certain unfailing animal instinct that allows them to tell what is alive from what is dead, what is genuine from what is fake. And it's not in the least surprising that after reading *Life and Fate* they realized it could not be brushed into shape and corrected by removing something here and adding something there or by artificially attaching a happy ending. They could find no better solution than to seize and conceal the book.

Grossman left no stone unturned in his efforts to win the return of his manuscript, and was finally seen by the Party's chief ideologist, Mikhail Suslov. Suslov told Grossman that his ideologically harmful novel would not be printed for two hundred years at the very least.

One of Grossman's friends, Boris Yampolsky, characterized this statement as the monstrous arrogance of a court favorite who thought he had power over time itself. But what I read into Suslov's words is that he had no doubt (and here that animal instinct was at work again) that Grossman's novel would live a very long time.

When making predictions about time, Party ideologists often fall flat on their faces. Nikita Khrushchev promised that Communism would be built in twenty years, but now it's clear that it can scarcely be built in two hundred.

Suslov was wrong about Grossman's novel by exactly 180 years, that is, by ninety percent. The novel was set free and published, not in two hundred years, but in twenty. Perhaps, just before his own death, Suslov learned that time was not quite in his power. But Grossman was never to see his novel in print. Unable to stand the blow that had befallen him, he became ill with cancer and died four years later, before the age of sixty. He worked until the end. Mortally ill, he completed an astonishing novella, *Forever Flowing*, which I think many have underrated.

Grossman suffered more than physical pain at the end. For a writer, there is nothing more terrible than to die without having seen his main work in print and without the confidence that it would someday reach the world of readers.

In that sense, Pasternak, whose novel was also ultimately his undoing, seems to have had a much happier fate than Grossman. Hounded and spurned, he at least saw his novel in print and knew that it enjoyed a great measure of success. But Grossman, like Bulgakov before him, died virtually unknown. His tragedy was eclipsed by other events. Some of those events were significant, like Solzhenitsyn's appearance in literature, and some were trivial. For example, I recall that at one point the West kicked up a great ruckus because the Soviet authorities had refused one of the more fashionable poets a trip abroad. (That poet had been abroad before and would go again; in fact, these days he's in the West more often than he is under the shade of his native aspens.) But the arrest of a great novel and the death of its creator went nearly unnoticed. "They strangled me out of sight," said Grossman before his death.

The more I think about the title, *Life and Fate*, the more prophetic and precise it seems to me. Life and fate are by no means the same thing. And it's no easy matter at all to remain true to one's fate in the life Grossman describes. The author's life was reflected in the novel's fate, and—before its posthumous publication—the novel's fate was reflected tragically in the author's life.

The Head Censor

In the summer of 1980, shortly before I emigrated, there was a rumor going around Moscow that a new feature film about Sherlock Holmes would soon be appearing on Soviet television. But another rumor was circulating at the same time to the effect that the film had been banned and was "shelved," and that the film makers had been reprimanded for attempting to put such an ideologically harmful work on the air. That was strange because the book on which it was based had been printed and reprinted dozens of times in the Soviet Union, and it was difficult to imagine how any fault could be found with it. Soon, however, the whole mystery was cleared up.

The sedition was to be found in the first shots of the film, when Sherlock Holmes and Doctor Watson meet for the first time.

"Oh, I see you've been in Afghanistan," says Sherlock Holmes in the film.

And to the stunned doctor's question as to how he guessed, the famous detective replies:

"My thoughts went like this: This doctor has a military bearing about him. Judging by his tan, he's just back from the tropics. He's been through some major experiences and an illness as is clearly visible from his exhausted face. His left arm's been injured and he's holding it in an unnatural position. Where could an English doctor have been wounded like that in a tropical country? In Afghanistan, of course."

And so, a classic by a long-dead English writer had suddenly become topical and absolutely unpassable in the eyes of Soviet censorship.

After a while, however, the higher-ups' anger cooled and they allowed the film makers to redo the sound track. Sherlock Holmes could now be heard to say, "I can see you've just come from a certain Eastern country."

But this purely political alteration also had an effect on the work's artistic level. Sherlock Holmes is supposed to stagger us with the accuracy of his deductions. But an approximation such as "a certain Eastern country," we would have been able to duplicate ourselves with the feeblest mental effort. This is a small but typical example of how censorship destroys artistic form when it excises information that it finds inconvenient.

When people speak of censorship, they're primarily referring to a special institution, Glavlit, whose tasks include preventing the disclosure of military and state secrets in the press and on radio and television, or in literature, film, and the theater. The censors at Glavlit have a long list, one that grows longer every year, of military units, geographic points, industrial installations, natural disasters in the territory of the USSR, catastrophes and accidents in the territory of the USSR, scientific discoveries, and also last names that are either entirely forbidden to be mentioned in print or allowed to be mentioned in part, on special instructions from governmental or penal agencies. These last include figures belonging to the Communist Party (from Trotsky to Khrushchev) and certain writers, dissidents, and scientists engaged in highly classified work. For example, it was forbidden to mention Andrei Sakharov's name in print when he was active in Soviet science and receiving the highest Soviet awards. Then his name was prohibited because he had become a dissident. Now, his name is mentioned quite often but always and only with approval from the highest levels of the Party. The list of forbidden names has reached such disastrous proportions that the censors have increasing trouble in coping with their work. This was recently demonstrated when they allowed the publication of a science-fiction novel by Arthur C. Clarke in which all the Soviet astronauts have the same names as Soviet dissidents, mention of whom is forbidden.

In Soviet editorial slang, the errors committed by censors or editors are known as blunders, and those blunders, I hope, have not crept into the pages of the Soviet press for the last time. About ten years ago, the mathematician Yuri Gastev published a "hooliganish" book on mathematical logic. In the foreword, he expressed his special gratitude to doctors Chain and Stocks for their help. Chain and Stocks were not mathematicians, not logicians, and could not possibly have helped Gastev with his book. They *are* doctors, and their names are to be found in the expression "Chain-Stocks breathing," which occurs in the agony before death. Stalin experienced that sort of breathing before his death, which fact Gastev was acknowledging in his foreword. Gastev had been arrested in the Stalin years, and it was only the leader's death that had allowed him to continue and complete his education. Gastev went even further and, in his bibliography, listed at least ten works by dissidents that for the most part had no relation to his subject.

At about that same time, a similar blunder was made by the censors with the magazine *Aurora*. One of the articles contained a favorable mention of Sakharov, for which, as always in such cases, the blame fell on the head censor first.

It should be said that Glavlit is only one of the agencies that make up the censorship, and it exists only to check publications, films, and performances in their final stage. The first censor of any work, operating while the work is in progress, is, as we know, the author himself. At the next stage, the work is sent out to readers. Next, it is edited by a few people—a junior editor, a regular editor, a senior editor, and the editor in chief. Their task is to bring the manuscript to a point where it corresponds to certain definite ideological and artistic requirements, even though those ideological and artistic requirements nearly always run counter to each other.

Here is a rough outline of the duties of the first editor of a manuscript that has been accepted for publication and will appear on the publisher's list:

1. To make the manuscript more or less legible; to improve, if necessary, the structure, the style, the language; to correct grammatical errors (acknowledged Soviet writers include a large percentage of the functionally illiterate), and, in some cases, to rewrite the manuscript entirely.

2. To check that the manuscript is in keeping with the

basic canons of socialist realism, that is, that it contains the obligatory positive hero, that good (from the Communist point of view) conquers evil, and that the work's overall tone is unfailingly optimistic.

3. To allow no criticism of the existing system, nor hint of such criticism. Soviet reality as a whole is to be described in bright colors, whereas capitalist reality is to be painted in the darkest hues. This requirement is even more strictly observed than the others. For that reason, all travel notes written by people who have been abroad that do not mention unemployment, drugs, crime, and the other flaws of capitalism are, as a rule, subjected to withering criticism.

Moreover, the editor doubles as a censor and, like the censor, is obliged to ensure that a book contains no mention whatsoever of any secrets that are not to be divulged or any names that are prohibited. Needless to say, if the author himself is one of those whose names are on the forbidden list, the publication of his book, no matter what its contents, is entirely out of the question.

The editor is the first to be held responsible for any mistakes that slip through in a published book. In the majority of cases, when a book incurs the Party's displeasure, the author is simply criticized in the press or at meetings (usually closed), but the editor pays a stiffer price—he is reprimanded or loses his position.

Of course, the most horrible error is a political error, a term that can include nearly anything: the positive depiction of a person or thing that has incurred the Party's displeasure, references to certain events (e.g., the war in Afghanistan), and even praise or insufficient criticism for one movement or another in art.

Sometimes a common grammatical, spelling, or typographical mistake becomes a political error. During and after the war, all Soviet newspapers printed the orders given by Stalin as those of the supreme commander in chief. In doing this, there were a few instances in which, by oversight, the letter *l* was left out of Stalin's title, *glavnokomanduyushchi*, so that the word read something like "shit commander." Such spelling errors, under Stalin, were equated with sabotage. I know of a case where, after allowing just such a typo to get past, the editor in chief was immediately taken before a firing squad. Lidya Chukovsky told me about a newspaper editor who had nightmares all through the war; he kept dreaming that the latest edition of his paper had mixed up Lenin's and Stalin's initials, printing them as I. V. Lenin and V. I. Stalin.

The fear of making this sort of mistake is so great that the editorial staffs of the large newspapers have a special employee, known as the "fresh eye," who, when all the editors and proofreaders are finished, gives the entire paper a very close reading.

As I've said, in Stalin's time, the punishments were particularly drastic, but similar errors are punished severely even now. For example, when we were still friends with China, Sergei Ivanko, the hero of my novel *The Ivankiad*, worked as the fresh eye for the newspaper *Literature and Life* and was dismissed when the paper reported to its readers that the "economies of the USA and China have shown great increases." (I hope it's clear that the "USA" should have read "USSR.")

The main worry for editors of magazines and books is the subtext, that is, the allusions the author has consciously worked in and associations the author did not foresee. Even German concentration camps are nearly a forbidden subject (some books have been published on them, but only with special permission), because they invariably remind the reader of the camps in his own country. For much the same reason, the subjects of fascism and Nazism are under a nearly complete ban. In the sixties, Mikhail Romm's documentary film *Ordinary Fascism* met with strong criticism from the Party because the art of the Third Reich shown in that film was too reminiscent of Soviet art.

As people who are intimidated and without rights, editors look for allusions even where they don't exist. At one point, accusations were made against the director Andrei Tarkovsky's film *Andrei Rublev* because the peasants were too poorly dressed and looked like Soviet kolkhozniks. How in the world *should* Russian peasants of the fourteenth century have been dressed?

A rather foolish children's film, *Look Out, Turtle Ahead*, was made. A turtle that is the pet of students in a Soviet school escapes and ends up on a road just as a column of tanks is approaching. Seeing the turtle, the lead tank comes to a halt, causing the rest of the column to halt as well. The commander, who is somewhere in the rear, radios to the lead tank to find out what the problem is. The lead tank radios back that there is a turtle on the road. After a lot of back and forth on the radio, the commmander issues a noble order: the tanks are to go off the road and around the turtle (instead of having one of the tankmen jump out and toss the turtle aside). When discussing the film, one of the editors cast a wily glance at the screenwriters and the director and said: "So what you mean here is a turtle, a che?" "A che?" said one of the screenwriters. "Yes, a little che and a large Soviet tank." That is, he saw the film makers as using the Russian word for turtle, *cherepaxha*, to stand for Czechoslovakia, even though in the film the tanks went around that little che, whereas in real life, as we know, quite the opposite occurred.

Oral and written instructions direct editors and censors to seek out not only ordinary subtexts but also "uncontrollable subtexts."

Moreover, they are supposed to combat what are called "allusions," that is, thoughts connected with neither the text nor the subtext, but that may arise in the reader's mind. In answering the question of what an allusion is, a well-known Soviet director said: "For instance, you're in a movie theater, watching a travelogue, and they show, let's say, the Caucasus Mountains, the snow-covered peaks and clouds, and you think: Even so, Brezhnev is a bastard."

Apart from the professional censors and the editors, the censor's function is fulfilled by a great variety of agencies, no matter how removed they might be from literature and art.

Before a book about geologists, even if it's a novel, can see the light of day, the publisher sends it to the Department of Geology; if it's about border guards, to the KGB; if it's about revolutionaries, to the Institute of Marxism-Leninism, and so forth. All these institutions check that there are no factual errors and also make remarks (often crude and ignorant) about the work's artistic qualities, which the author has to accept, or pretend to accept.

Needless to say, the role of censor is played by the administrative wings of the Writers' Union, the Party (from the district committee to the Central Committee), district, municipal, and provincial cultural agencies, the

Soviet Ministry of Culture and those of the republics, and many other organizations, and, in certain instances, by "worthy" individuals, meaning leading workers, cosmonauts, generals, among others. I have been "edited" by all three of these last categories.

But fear is the head censor in the Soviet Union.

When beginning a new work, every Soviet writer is always aware that his recompense might be not only fame and fortune but also a prohibition on part of his book, on the whole, on all of his books, expulsion from the Writers' Union, or, in the extreme, prison.

If the Enemy Does
Not Surrender . . .
Observations on Fifty Years
of Socialist Realism

Fifty years ago, in August 1934, the Hall of Columns
in the Unions' Building in Moscow was the site of a
grandiose two-week-long performance known as the First
All-Union Congress of Soviet Writers. With solemn ceremony, the congress announced the unification of all
writers who "support the platform of the Soviet system
and who seek to take part in the building of socialism."
One after the other, the representatives of a literature
unprecedented in the world mounted the podium. Writers assumed the role of a collective god and promised
to create a new man in the shortest possible time. Every
so often, to the roll of drums, delegations of leading
workers, kolkhozniks, Red Army soldiers, and Pioneers
would come bursting into the conference hall. With great
ceremony, they reported on their unprecedented successes on the labor front and called on the writers to
reflect these heroic feats immediately, creating a great
literature whose achievements could be comparable to

235

those of the workers and the peasants. (Skipping ahead, I'll say that, all those superlatives aside, Soviet literature indeed performed that task, and its achievements are entirely on a par with those of Soviet industry and Soviet agriculture.)

Praise was heaped on all the chiefs of the ruling Party, headed by the great leader of the entire Soviet people, of the entire world proletariat, of all progressive humanity, the best friend of Soviet writers, Comrade Stalin. Using the most exalted and poetic turns of phrase, the writers extolled their now legitimate status and, long before George Orwell, declared slavery the highest level of creative freedom.

The congress made many remarkable decisions, one of which was that now and forevermore all writers, without exception, were to use the method known as socialist realism in their work.

The official line has it that socialist realism is the truthful and historically concrete depiction of life in its revolutionary development.

There were other definitions. One of the organizers of the congress said more or less the following: Socialist realism is Shakespeare, Rembrandt, and Beethoven in the service of the proletariat. Somewhat later, Alexander Fadeyev, a theorist and classic example of socialist realism, said, when asked what it was: "Who the hell knows!" In our time, a new, unofficial, but exhaustive formulation has appeared: Socialist realism means extolling the top leadership in a form that's accessible to them.

The congress was chaired by the founder of the new realism, Maxim Gorky. The great proletarian writer wept with emotion on seeing all those writers assembled peaceably under one roof—proletarian writers, fellow travelers, representatives of the smaller nations, and Asiatic bards who had not yet mastered grammar but who had already learned how to put their thumbprints on their royalty receipts.

But while Gorky was wiping away his tears and asking in embarrassment not to be called great too often, Genrikh Yagoda, a former pharmacist, had already prepared a compound of lethal poisons for Gorky; had already tested it on laboratory rats, and perhaps even on lesser writers selected to serve the aims of science.

Gorky was playing his final role on the stage in the Hall of Columns. History had no more need of him. He had already accomplished all he was capable of. He had already written *Mother*, the novel that would serve as the model for coming generations of socialist realists. He had sung the praises of Lenin and Stalin. And his famous phrase "If the enemy does not surrender, he is wiped out" was already in circulation. What else could be gotten from the man? The living person who could travel around visiting canal construction sites, kolkhozes, reform schools, deliver speeches, and weep an old man's tears of emotion was no longer of any use. His name was needed for signs. Streets, kolkhozes, factories, theaters, steamships were named after Gorky, and the city of Nizhni Novgorod had its name changed to Gorky. (Ironically, it is there today that Andrei Sakharov has been exiled as a pernicious enemy who must be wiped out.)

The congress finished its work, and, bearing presents, the delegates left to return to their cities and mountain villages, where they began the painstaking daily labor of wiping out literature and the people who create it.

When speaking of the writers who fell victim to the Soviet regime, we usually list the same people time and again: Babel, Mandelstam, Bulgakov, Platonov, Zosh-chenko, Tsvetaeva, Akhmatova, Pasternak.

Some people pronounce those names with bitterness, and some with pride. They say that real Russian literature lived on and developed in spite of everything. In fact, it did not develop in spite of everything but due to the Party, and to Comrade Stalin personally. Because Comrade Stalin could have cut that development short in a day's time and, at one fell stroke, have been done with all the writers mentioned above. But Stalin displayed tolerance, an approach all his own—his famous delicate touch. Even Mandelstam, who wrote that Stalin's thick fingers were like fat worms, was not dispatched to certain death immediately. Stalin gave him the opportunity to live a while in exile and do a little more writing. He gave Mandelstam a chance to reform. But neither he, nor the writers mentioned above, reformed, and, to the very end, none of them had any liking for the Soviet system. No, of course they did not speak out against it, and they agreed to be considered socialist realists. In the more trying times, they even attempted to compose panegyrics to Lenin and Stalin. But, for the sake of fairness, it must be said that they did this unwillingly, clumsily, and halfheartedly. In fact, in their hearts, they did not accept the new system, had nothing but contempt for Party and government policy in the arts and literature, and continued to write for the desk drawer or to memorize their works. Never surrendering fully, they pretended that they had. And for that reason they were hounded, refused publication, starved, imprisoned; some were driven mad, others to suicide. If the enemy will not surrender, he must be wiped out.

But what if he does surrender?

There is no simple answer to that rhetorical question. First, you have to define the meaning of surrender.

Vladimir Mayakovsky began surrendering long before he committed suicide, when he stepped "on the throat of his own song." When accepting the Soviet system, Gorky had not yet realized that the new rules of behavior also had to be accepted fully, not just in part. He still wasn't minding his own business—he was still defending certain books, helping people to get out of prison, others to find an apartment, medicine, firewood, and he was still writing. In other words, he had surrendered ninety-nine percent, but was trying to hide one percent of his soul from the Party. For that very reason, he proved worth destroying. They say that after Gorky's death some of his notes were found and when Stalin, or maybe it was someone else read them, he said: "No matter how often you feed a wolf, he's always got an eye on the forest." As a matter of fact, the wolf in question no longer had his eye on the forest; he would merely squint over at it from time to time.

I think that the Soviet authorities did not set certain of their goals immediately and with sinister intent, but, instead, came to them instinctively. The authorities did not immediately realize that literature as a whole and every individual of talent were their enemies, but came to this knowledge after a long period of trial and error. For example, in the beginning certain writers (Bunin, Kuprin, Merezhkovsky, Averchenko) did not accept the new system, were contemptuous of it, and cursed it. They clearly were enemies. The system tried to win over those who were vacillating. It hoped to reeducate those who accepted the new system but had not freed themselves of the remnants of the past and who thought that the describable and the real were one and the same. But there were also writers who, without any hesitation, took the side of the new system immediately, and who honestly and selflessly attempted to adapt their books to the new requirements. Yet it turned out that even this sort of writer was an enemy and worthy of destruction as long as there was a drop of talent left in him. It was not in the least obligatory to destroy the man himself; destroying the talent within him was sufficient.

All artistic talent proved to be an enemy of the Soviet system. Some farsighted writers understood this at once. Some simply fell silent. Others took to drink. In my opinion, Valentin Kataev consciously pretended to have no talent for thirty years. Some writers pretended so well, they lost their talent forever.

THE ZOMBIES OF
SOVIET LITERATURE

Alexander Tvardovsky gave an interview to *Literaturnaya Gazeta* just as 1967 was coming to an end. When listing the names of the authors whose works his magazine intended to print in the coming year, he expressed special pleasure that one of the older Soviet writers and a grand master of prose, Konstantin Fedin, had agreed to give *Novy Mir* a few new chapters from his novel *The Bonfire*.

A few days before the issue containing the master's work was to be published, an employee of *Nedelya* (The Week, *Izvestiya*'s weekly supplement) came to *Novy Mir*'s prose section and asked them to recommend a piece of *The Bonfire* to excerpt in the weekly. The people in the prose section exchanged glances and then in embar-

240

rassment admitted that they had not read the novel and for that reason could not recommend any particular passages. The man from *Nedelya* went up to the editorial offices, where Tvardovsky's was located. No one there proved to have read the novel either. The novel had been read only by the copy editors whose job it was to catch grammatical and spelling errors. But even they could not recall what the novel was about, and one of them told the man from *Nedelya* that he could pick something at random, because the entire novel was uniformly meaningless and boring.

Needless to say, as soon as the new chapters were printed, nearly every national newspaper and magazine exploded with enormous articles by leading critics about this major new event in Soviet literature.

Unlike certain of his colleagues, Fedin was not talentless from the start. His novels *Cities and Years* and *The Brothers* had been popular in the twenties. People had read them, argued about them, spurned them or praised them. One way or the other, they had caught the readers' interest. But then, after long hesitation perhaps, he decided to become a model Soviet writer and began writing his books in accordance with the rules prescribed for literature. The longer his books became and the more boring, the more mediocre they were, the more laudatory reviews appeared and the more high state awards he received.

Toward the end of his life, Fedin was a member of the Academy, the chairman of the Soviet Writers' Union, a deputy to the Supreme Soviet of the USSR, the recipient of all the highest literary awards, and a hero of socialist labor. He was presented all those awards only after demonstrating many times over that he was utterly finished as a writer and that a single living line would never issue from his pen.

Soviet literature has not only dead classic writers, but living ones as well, or, to be more precise, writers who seem to be alive. In other words, they exist, they take part in endless ceremonial meetings, they deliver long, boring speeches, and from time to time they publish books thick as bricks. No one reads them—not even the editors, not even the censors. Everyone knows in advance that those books will be utterly bereft of content, that they were written in exact conformity with the existing prescriptions, and that they will not contain a single living word or fresh idea. And it is for those reasons that they can be printed immediately, without any delay whatsoever, that they will be inundated with panegyrics by Soviet critics, and honored with high awards by the Soviet government.

All of the system's acknowledged leading lights, including Alexei Tolstoy, Fadeyev, and Sholokhov, paid for their position with the degradation of their personality and talent. Sholokhov's decline is especially disastrous if one believes that he was in fact the author of *And Quiet Flows the Don*.

Sholokhov made an astounding debut: he published the first volume of his epic in 1923, the second in 1924. When he finished the last volume, he was only thirty-five years old, essentially still a young writer. But it turned out that he had stopped growing and from then on slid steadily downward. The clumsily structured *Virgin Soil Upturned*, the mediocre *Fate of a Man* were followed by absolutely hopeless works. Even in Soviet literature it's no easy task to find anything quite as devoid of talent as Sholokhov's novel *They Did Battle for the Motherland*.

The more he drank and the worse he wrote, the greater the official honor and praise he received. It was only in his later years, when he was not writing at all, that he was twice awarded the title of hero of socialist labor.

Sholokhov's talent was persistently and systematically destroyed over a period of many years. Long before his physical death, he had died inwardly; he had become a drunken, corrupt, malicious, and foolish creature.

If the enemy will not surrender, he will be wiped out. And if he does surrender, he'll be wiped out even more efficiently.

CENSORSHIP AND PRESCRIPTION

Everybody knows that censorship is fierce in the Soviet Union. Any mention of certain facts and events that once played important roles in Soviet history are mercilessly crossed out, whether they be in fiction or nonfiction. The long, long list of forbidden names includes leaders of the October Revolution, the Civil War, the Soviet state, writers, artists, actors, philosophers, and dissidents. But in addition to everything banned, permanently or temporarily, a prescriptive formula has been devised, and by observing it, writers can always count on official favor and success.

The ideal work of socialist realism should bring the reader to the conclusion that the Soviet system is the best in the world.

The book should center around a positive hero. In previous times, he would be a revolutionary fanatic, like Pavel Korchagin, but today all that is required is a total idiot along the lines of Kochetov's secretary of the provincial committee or a politically conscious worker who maintains that a true revolutionary is someone who over-fulfills his production task and obeys his superiors. The positive hero is a well-built man, a Nordic type (blond hair, light blue eyes, simple Russian first and last names). He is always ready to sacrifice himself to save the Motherland, the flag, and socialist property, to forge steel and bring in the harvest. He works a lot, smokes a lot, sleeps a little. His relations with women are something of a puzzle. He reads only Marx, Lenin, and whoever happens to be the general secretary at the time. He is always convinced that his is the right cause; he speaks softly but with confidence, his handshake is firm, and he looks people right in the eye. In his rare free moments, his favorite pastime is fishing.

The positive hero is opposed by a negative figure. Usually, this is a sickly intellectual, and, even if he does no direct harm, he is unwilling to save the Motherland and the flag, and seeks to avoid fulfilling the plan. He has sweaty palms, darting eyes, and the smell of rotting teeth on his breath. He does not fish; instead, he reads abstract poetry. He usually has a Polish-sounding last name, though it is perfectly clear that he's a Jew. It goes without saying that he's temperamentally antipatriotic and has a penchant for everything foreign (whiskey, jeans, jazz). Foreigners and religious people can also play the negative role. (I read one antireligious novel that depicted the life of the Skoptsy sect, which practices self-castration. The author got so carried away in defaming his characters that he portrayed the sect's leader as a very active and successful seducer of women.)

It is the duty of a model socialist-realist novel to contain what are called "signs of the new." Let's say that the positive hero declares his love to the positive heroine.

She will interupt him at the most emotional moment to exclaim: "Look, there goes a sputnik!"

A model Soviet writer should display a special sensitivity to the ethnic question. If there's a Russian and a Tadzhik in a novel, the Tadzhik must be portrayed as good, but the Russian should be just a little bit better.

These primitive prescriptions seem as idiotic as ordering rockets to be built in the shapes of hammers or sickles.

THE TRUTH OF FACT
AND THE TRUTH OF THE TIME

"Write the truth," Stalin said at one point to Soviet writers. Did he mean the truth? . . .

And what is the truth? asks the model Soviet critic. Then he goes on to explain that we don't need every last truth, but only the useful ones. There's the truth of fact and there's the truth of the time. Stalin's camps, the ravaging of the peasants, the workers' meager lives, communal apartments, lines, epidemic drunkenness, contempt for official ideology—all these are the truth of fact. Blossoming kolkhozes, workers who think only of overfulfilling plans, mass-scale heroic labor, fabulous increases in people's well-being, the nation's wholehearted dedication to the ideas of Communism—these are the truth of the times.

Once again, this may appear Orwellian, but in fact it all existed long before Orwell's "The truth is a lie, the lie is the truth."

It is thought that literature should serve the people. But how?

That is defined by the Party—or, to be more precise,

by the top leadership. As a rule, they do not read books themselves and become somewhat tongue-tied when speaking their own native language. And, no matter how they try, they cannot correctly pronounce foreign words like *socialist, communist,* and *imperialist,* even though they say them time and again, day in and day out all their lives. They genuinely do not understand why literature is needed and why state money should be spent on it. Neither do they understand that money need not be spent on literature, that a book not only has spiritual value (which makes no sense to them), but also is a product that can be bought and sold, and sometimes even more profitably than a sack of potatoes. So, in the end, they come to what is for them the natural conclusion that literature exists to sing praises. And whose? First and foremost, that of the rulers themselves, of course. And they say to the writers, in forms that are sometimes more veiled than at others: Praise us and you'll have everything. They simply cannot understand why a writer would seek to avoid praising them and genuinely think that any such person must be either a fool or a madman.

Some people share these sentiments. Learning of my troubles, a relative of mine made a special trip from the provinces to advise me on how to get out of my situation. "Write about Brezhnev," he said, thinking that I lived in some dream world and was unable to come to that clever idea on my own.

Among Party leaders there are also those who are ready to admit that literature is needed, and not only to praise. Literature, they say, should aid our forward progress. For example, it should aid the fulfillment of the production plan for smelting pig iron, manufacturing automobiles, bringing in the harvest. Like the hero of

Mark Twain's *A Connecticut Yankee in King Arthur's Court*, they would like to derive some use from a writer, by attaching a small dynamo to his writing hand in order to produce electricity.

At one time I was acquainted with the secretary of a rural district committee. He had great respect for me and took an interest in what I wrote. One time, I gave him a novella I had written that ended with the hero being burned in a hut accidentally set on fire by a crazy old woman. The secretary liked the novella. He even said he had cried while reading it. But he also had an urge to make it better and adapt it to the needs of the present. He said more or less the following: "It's a good novella, you know. But why's that crazy old woman there? She serves no purpose. Sometimes our kolkhozes get defective radiators, and they sometimes cause fires." Sincerely wishing to help me, he proposed that I rewrite the ending so that the fire breaks out because of a defective radiator. He even gave me the address of the radiator plant and the director's name, so that I could use it in my novella. He was very distressed when I turned down his suggestion. That district committee secretary dealt with agriculture. His advice came from the goodness of his heart and had no practical consequences for me. But he could just as easily be transferred to literature someday, and then that would have been a different sort of conversation.

But people don't have to be transferred to literary positions for that. Anyone who feels like it, regardless of his degree of competence, can intervene in literature, correct writers, improve or even ban their works. One of my plays was banned because it displeased Nikolai Podgorny, the chairman of the Presidium of the Supreme Soviet, who usually preferred dominoes to all other forms of mental diversion. The editor of a newspaper for young people was reprimanded for printing a poem of mine that displeased Marshal Malinovsky, the Soviet defense minister. In a song for which I did the lyrics, one line was corrected on instructions from a cosmonaut. After a house painter wrote an abusive letter to *Izvestiya*, the best story was removed from a book of mine.

OFFICIAL AND MARGINAL LITERATURE

Specialists who study the Russian literature of the Soviet period include some who assess that literature's achievements quite favorably. They point out that even at the most trying times literature never ceased to exist and people continued to write. Then comes the list of names I have already mentioned. This is true, of course. But it also should be remembered that among the writers in the Writers' Union who were published by Soviet publishers, there were always two categories, which resembled each other as much as a wolf resembles a lamb.

Those in the first category can be called "state writers." These are writers who have won the solid confidence of the Soviet authorities and who either hold the higher positions in the Writers' Union or are the editors in chief of the most important magazines. Moreover, they can be deputies to the Supreme Soviet of the USSR or of the Russian Republic, and members or candidate members of the Central Committee. What they write is viewed as a matter of state importance. No editor can reject their manuscripts on his own discretion. If he dislikes something in a manuscript, he can have a little talk with the author or appeal to the Central Committee, where a final decision will be made. When a book by a state writer appears in print, no newspaper has the right to review it negatively unless there are special orders to do so from above. At one time, if a state writer happened to commit an error, he would be corrected either by the Central Committee or by Stalin himself. There can be only one mistake: failure sufficiently to reflect the role of the Party. Fadeev made that mistake in *The Young Guard,* and Sholokhov did the same in *And Quiet Flows the Don.* The Party corrected them, and they rewrote their works (Sholokhov many times), after which the books were accepted, forever to be numbered among the classics.

Now the state writers have fully matured and do not commit that sort of error; their books reflect the role of the Party beyond all measure, and the Central Committee no longer has any need to correct their books or even to read them.

The second category is made up of writers who do not travel the high road of Soviet literature, but are off somewhere to the side. They usually don't write about leading workers, toilers of the fields, or Party committee secretaries, but about demons, prisoners, suicides, drunkards, and people who live in communal apartments and hit each other over the head with frying pans.

Those in power can deal with these "marginal writers" as they please. They can publish them or not, praise or curse them, pay them no notice until someone points out that they have achieved unforeseen popularity with readers, who for some reason prefer demons, drunks, and suicides to Party secretaries and leading workers.

The best writers of the Stalin period are part of what I call "marginal literature." Not one of them lived a life that ended well. They were imprisoned, hounded, castigated, killed, and excommunicated from official Soviet literature. For that reason they cannot be considered a part of it, though sometimes they are published, reluctantly, after their death.

The honors go not to them, but to their hangmen. In the Soviet Union there is a Pavlenko Street, a Serafimovich House of Creative Work, a Fadeev Writers' Building, a Fedin Library, a Nikolai Ostrovsky Museum, and a city named Gorky—all honoring state writers.

But no libraries, museums, streets, or ships have been named for Bulgakov, Platonov, Zoshchenko, Mandelstam, Tsvetaeva , Akhmatova, or Pasternak. And rightly so. I would not like to see the two categories of names lumped together.

True Soviet literature is the literature that has always been encouraged, acknowledged, and rewarded by the Soviet state and that was created in full conformity with the scientifically derived method of socialist realism. In assessing the achievements of that literature, I fully agree with the most orthodox Soviet critics and am glad to give first place to Gorky's *Mother* and Mayakovsky's long poem "Vladimir Ilich Lenin" and would have no regret in including Fadeyev's *The Rout* and Dmitri Furmanov's *Chapayev* among the top works. And though he was paralyzed, Ostrovsky made it to the top of the heap with his novel *How the Steel Was Tempered.* But *And Quiet Flows the Don* cannot be included as part of socialist realism; it is too human a work, and even after several mutilations still did not correspond to the basic requirements. (The savage Cossack Melekhov, who cuts down Bolsheviks with his saber, can hardly serve as a model positive hero for Soviet literature.) On the other hand, Sholokhov's

Virgin Soil Upturned or *They Did Battle for the Motherland* fits naturally with the literature of socialist realism. I gladly cede to socialist realism Alexander Serafimovich's *The Iron Flood,* Feodor Gladkov's *Cement,* Panferov's *Ingots,* Fedin's *The Bonfire,* and all the thousands of other bricklike novels, which individually can be used to prop up a tilty bureau or can be laid end on end to make a tower of Babel, a monument to a stillborn literature.

No tower can be erected with the books written by the marginal writers. There may not even be enough of them to fill a single bookshelf. But they have survived their creators and those who would destroy them. Those books cannot be shot, drowned in slander, abolished by a resolution from the top, or stifled with silence. Gorky was wrong when he said that if the enemy does not surrender, he'll be wiped out. If he does not surrender, he cannot be wiped out.

CHILDREN OF THE THAW

The period of Soviet history known as the Thaw deserves detailed examination; I can treat it here only in passing. Some people claim that in fact no thaw took place. Others have a more favorable opinion of it. All in all, the thaw was a turning point in the history of the Soviet state. No matter how timid and inconsistent Khrushchev's unmasking of Stalin was, and regardless of what Khrushchev's actual intentions were, this process undermined the ideological foundation of the state, producing consequences that have not yet been overcome and that will never be overcome. When the state collapses or undergoes a radical change (and if it proves incapable of change, it will certainly collapse), historians will inevitably go back to the thaw, as the origin and beginning of it all.

A thaw is a thaw, not a spring. But the ice melts, turning into cold water, and life of some sort is reborn in that water.

Things did thaw in the Soviet Union in that period, and the first effects were to be seen in literature. Literature began to revive; old organisms returned to life and new ones appeared. Writers whose very existence would have been unthinkable a short time before now began to make their way into literature. In the end they made for a rather good-sized group, which Felix Kuznetsov, a literary supervisor of the time, called the fourth generation. I would say that all of us writers, regardless of our views, tastes, and abilities, belonged to that generation, and were a sort of new fellow traveler. We gave formal recognition to the Soviet system and to socialist realism. In practice, however, we rejected the entire literature created through the use of that method. We disdained our older colleagues and took our lessons from Bunin or Chekhov or Hemingway or Salinger, but never from Fedin or Gladkov. This process expanded and began attracting writers of the older generation, who came back to life after being frozen and went running in pursuit of the young writers. A literature that, on the basis of early signs, could boldly be called "harshly critical," if not anti-Soviet, came into being, managed somehow to stay alive, and seeped in through every hole there was. From time to time the authorities would wake up and plug some holes. But new ones were always found. This process culminated in the appearance of Solzhenitsyn, who by then made no attempt to pass himself off as a fellow traveler. His novel *One Day in the Life of Ivan*

Denisovich, which has nothing Soviet about it, was not only published, but also nominated for a Lenin prize.

The authorities soon caught on, but by then it was too late—the genie was out of the bottle. (Had it not been for the thaw, Solzhenitsyn would at best be living now in Ryazan, a retired schoolteacher, secretly making copies of his work.)

In brief, the thaw resulted in the birth of a literature that the authorities have been trying to combat ever since.

All of today's writers who have achieved some renown—the "village" writers, the "city" writers, and the émigrés—are children of the thaw.

The Soviet authorities made many mistakes in the process of destroying literature. Wishing to eclipse Shakespeare, the authorities took talented writers and broke them. They made state writers out of those whose spirits they had broken, and those who could not be broken were literally squeezed out of existence. All this large-scale, intensive effort proved quite pointless. Books by writers who were physically destroyed are perfectly alive, while those written by the destroyers are now used for pulp. A writer who had been destroyed spiritually lost his talent and began to write on a level accessible to an average member of the Party power elite. Why expend such effort turning writers into members of the power elite when it's so much simpler to turn members of the power elite into writers? If a member of the power elite can be in charge of literature, why can't he produce it as well?

Literature is always renewing itself. The old generation is replaced by the new. At one point the semiofficial Soviet chronology of the generations went more or less as follows: the first generation was the postrevolutionary one, the second the prewar, the third the postwar, and the fourth the post-Stalin generation of the thaw. A fifth generation has yet to appear in Soviet literature. Instead, a new breed of writers has come out onto the stage of literature.

A MAJOR FIGURE IN

GOVERNMENT AND LITERATURE

At the very end of the sixties, I was a member of the Writers' Union's prose board. One day, the board had a normal meeting—some minor matters were discussed, then we moved on to the question of accepting new members.

At that moment two secretaries of the Moscow branch, Lazar Karelin and Victor Ilin, a former KGB general, entered the room.

"Comrades," announced Karelin, "we have very good news today. We're received word from Nikolai Trofimovich Sizov that he's been accepted as a member of the Writers' Union. Comrade Sizov is a major figure in government and literature. . . ."

Comrade Sizov's literary career had begun before my very eyes. At one time, Sizov was my immediate superior. He was then political information section chief for All-Union Radio. Since he was a member of the power elite, the Party could shift him wherever it wished. So one fine day he was suddenly transferred from radio to the post of chief of Moscow police and was given the rank of major general. Later on he was to become the deputy chairman of the Moscow City Soviet and, finally, the

general director of the Mosfilm studio, where I believe
he still works.

When Sizov was chief of police, Kochetov, the editor
in chief of the magazine "October" and a leading light
of Soviet literature, requested registration for residence
in Moscow for one of his relatives. The chief did not
turn down the request. And the editor published the
chief's novel. That novel was followed into print by other
novels, novellas, and short stories. The hero of one of
Sizov's novels was a provincial committee secretary whose
life story read like Khrushchev's. Thus yet another Soviet
writer was born. For the sake of fairness, it must be said
that Sizov writes no worse than Karelin or most of the
other secretaries of the Writers' Union—simply because
it's impossible to write any worse than that.

Under Stalin, the Party officials assigned to the Writers' Union remained what they were and did not dare
call themselves writers. Stalin, who, by the way, banned
the publication of his own poetry, written in his youth,
would not have been pleased had those officials termed
themselves writers. In the liberal Khrushchev period,
officials began infiltrating literature, and under Brezhnev, they burst into literature en masse. Now corruption
thrives every bit as much in Soviet literature as it does
in the world of commerce.

It's an honor to be a writer, because it immediately
puts a person in the company of Pushkin and Tolstoy.
It's profitable too, because the length of one's book, the
size of the printing, and, especially, the royalties do not
depend on the book's quality or on reader demand, but
entirely on the author's place in the Soviet hierarchy.
It's safe to be a writer, because in literature bribes don't
pass from hand to hand but take the form of favors.

You publish me and I'll publish you, and we'll both receive our advances and royalties by perfectly legal means, and royalties, unlike salaries, have no limits. Corruption evolves and improves. It used to be that one editor would print another and vice versa. But now he has to publish other people, those who have some control over the good life. Millionaires, KGB men, managers of stores and saunas, building managers, and the chairmen of dacha coops have all entered the field of literature.

The corruption of literature has gone so far as to have obliterated all the boundary lines between the professional writer and those who are published because they have pull. A KGB general writes no worse than a professional writer, and the professional writes no better than a store manager.

When Marshal Brezhnev began to publish his three-volume book of mythology, all the leading lights of Soviet literature, the secretaries of the Writers' Union, the heroes of socialist labor, and all the other prize winners were unanimous in declaring, both verbally and in print, that these books were inimitable masterpieces, comparable only to the best (not just any) pages of *War and Peace.*

THE LONGER THE SILENCE ...

Soviet literature has approached the ideal it strove for instinctively from the moment it came into being. Written and unwritten rules for writers' behavior and for the writing of their books have been elaborated to the point of absurdity. There's a rule for everything and there is a hierarchy of positive heroes. Officially speaking, Lenin is, of course, the principal positive hero of Soviet literature. Every year hundreds of Soviet writers add to the store of what is called Leniniana—novels, poems, plays, and film scripts about Lenin and his immediate family, written in all the languages of the peoples of the USSR. Needless to say, in the majority of these works, the leader of the world proletariat seems to have his head in the clouds, as befits an ideal socialist realist hero.

In point of fact, Lenin is not the principal hero of Soviet literature. That hero is whoever happens to be in power. Under Stalin it was Stalin, under Khrushchev it was Khrushchev, and under Brezhnev it was Brezhnev. Andropov did not hold power long enough to become the principal hero of Soviet literature, nor did Chernenko.

But it doesn't take much to foresee the coming of a new principal hero. By background the secretary of a provincial committee in the south, he will be young, vigorous, democratic (he'll mix with people on the street), and educated (with degrees in law and agronomy). At first he will appear in literature under a fictitious name. But when the personality cult around the general secretary has taken final shape, it will then even be possible to portray him under his name.

It is not only heroes, but also writers, who are ranked in strict accordance with their importance. The secretary of the Soviet Writers' Union is considered a better writer than the secretary of the Russian Writers' Union, who in turn enjoys greater esteem than the secretaries of a province or municipal writers' organization.

Epithets—eminent, famous, well known—are dispersed in strict accordance with position. The higher the position, the more lavish the praise on the anniversary of a writer's birth and the more magnificent his funeral.

Burial plots are also apportioned by the writer's rank.

Important writers are, to all intents and purposes, members of the Party power elite. They shop for food in the special Party stores, vacation at Party health resorts, and receive medical treatment in the Kremlin's hospitals. Their books are given enormous printings, and their royalties are astronomical. To criticize these demigods is absolutely forbidden.

Living literature was the enemy of the new system, and now that enemy has been laid low, trampled, and nearly wiped out.

The writers of "marginal literature" have nearly disappeared from Russia now. Some have emigrated; others (Vasily Shushkin, Yuri Kazakov, Yuri Trifonov) have died. The serious writers who still exist on the edge of official literature can be counted on the fingers of a hand. As I have said, they are all the children of the thaw, and the youngest of them are close to fifty. Most have their main work behind them. The future of literature will belong to the young writers. But where are they? They are nowhere to be found in official literature. As a rule, young writers do not manage saunas or stores, and there's nothing to be gotten from them. So who will publish them? What reason is there to publish them?

I was once asked at a U.S. university what a young writer really needed besides paper and pen. My answer was that a young writer also needs a publisher and readers. In order to grow, he needs to be published and hear his readers' responses. He needs the support, approval, and criticism of older writers. Without all this, a young writer will feel that his work is reaching no one.

I am speaking mainly of prose. Poetry is simpler to distribute; a poem can easily be copied or memorized and stay alive under the most difficult conditions. It's tougher with prose. In any case, given the current situation, I do not foresee any new breakthroughs or achievements in prose occurring within the boundaries of official Soviet literature.

Such is the glorious trail that Soviet literature has blazed for itself in the course of its history. All the same, proceeding not only from my faith in prose, but from my innate optimism, I still believe that literature cannot ever be wiped out entirely. Literature amasses energy in periods of enforced silence. When the pressure is removed or slackens (which does happen from time to time), that energy will break through to the surface and give birth to a new, important, and perhaps even great literature.

In the words of Nikolai Ushakov:

I taught myself to hide my words
safely away out of reach.
The longer the silence,
the more astonishing the speech.

3

Abracadabra

Absurdity and
Soviet Life

Zero Solution

As soon as the Soviet people choose me as their leader, I will arrange a meeting with the President of the United States of America. In any suitable or unsuitable place.

"Ronnie," I'll say (or whoever), "come, let's finally talk about disarmament, not for the sake of propaganda, but let's speak openly on questions of substance, no holds barred. You're for the zero solution? So am I. Let's remove all the detonators from the nuclear warheads and beat our missiles into ploughshares. A round zero on your side and one just as round on ours. I'll even agree to let the English and the French keep their missiles. (Though, in the event of a world conflict, if they're decent people they'll rain their nuclear weapons only on each other.)

But, to be honest, in any drawn-out war (a war without nuclear weapons is bound to be drawn out), it's not only a country's military potential that matters. Its economic potential plays a part too. And, in questions of economics, even bourgeois propaganda cannot assert that we took advantage of détente or anything else to achieve superiority over the West.

Quite the contrary. In adhering to a peaceful foreign policy, our country has from its very inception steadily, irreversibly, and single-mindedly been reducing its economic potential, whereas the capitalist countries have been increasing theirs.

By now we have almost reduced our economic potential to a zero solution of its own. I say "almost" because we do have a few odds and ends left. In some stores you can still buy a piece of sausage.

The reason we are able to do this is that we were the first to walk a path never walked before. Unfortunately, we have proved to possess great natural resources that we have still failed to exhaust fully. But even there we have made spectacular achievements. You'll find it easy to agree with me if your advisers present you with an accurate account of how much gold, oil, fur, and caviar we sell abroad each year. And now we're building a gas pipe line so that we can pump all our gas to the West too. As for the hard currency we will receive from the West in exchange, that's not worth worrying about. We'll use it to buy even more complex equipment, which we'll stack in an open field so it can rust freely.

We don't have far to go to reach the zero point. We need only fulfill the Food Programs and exert a bit of discipline and we'll have lost our shirts and our pants.

We have caught up with and overtaken the United States many times already. Now you try to catch up with us. Bring your economy down to our level, so that we will have equality in armaments and in everything else as well.

Make no mistake—I am no Utopian and don't think that the economy of a country as rich as yours can be undermined just like that. But it is possible if one works out an intelligent long-range plan of action. It would be our pleasure to assist you in this. In any case, I have drawn up a list of strictly scientific recommendations, based on our historical experience. If you follow these recommendations, complete success is guaranteed. Needless to say, these recommendations are general in nature and can be supplemented and varied as they are put into practice.

In order to achieve economic parity with the Soviet Union, the following must be done:

1. Carry out a political coup d'état, and declare your party the sole leading and guiding force in U.S. society. Your party must be headed by you personally.

2. Ban all other parties, arrest their most active members, exile their leaders to the Soviet Union, or even execute them.

3. Arrest the members of your own party who will oppose these changes, make an example of them in show trials, and then execute them.

4. Confiscate from private ownership all banks, plants, factories, stores, restaurants, ships, planes, automobiles, horses, cows, goats, sheep, and pigs.

5. Turn all private apartments into communal apartments and turn other buildings into museums, public restrooms, cattle pens, and other things useful to society.

6. Raze Capitol Hill and replace it with a swimming pool for workers, as we did with the Church of Christ the Saviour.

7. Send all farmers to Alaska to do construction work on the Trans-Alaskan strategic railroad, turn their farms

into kolkhozes and local branches of the ruling party and State Security, formerly the FBI and the CIA. Recruit people with no talent for productive labor into those kolkhozes and agencies, thereby solving the problem of unemployment once and for all.

8. Declare some science (for example, botany), a Communist pseudo science.

9. Undertake a gigantic transformation of nature in the United States, and, to that end, divert the Mississippi into the Nevada desert so that you can raise cotton and rice there. The former Mississippi River basin will itself in time become a desert, a good source of sand.

10. Resettle the population of Hawaii to Maine; put them to work there as lumberjacks.

11. Take upon yourself the direct control of all spheres of life—political, economic, and social—and issue constant instructions on the milking of cows, the building of houses, the development of quantum mechanics, the breeding of rabbits, the writing of literature, the composition of music, and so forth.

12. All the means of mass communication, including newspapers, radio, and television, should quote in full your long and boring speeches every day of the week.

13. Name cities after yourself, and also settlements, factories, kolkhozes, various means of conveyance, streets, and buildings.

14. Have sculptures and portraits of you placed in all cities, villages, and settlements.

15. Introduce hundreds of new medals for valor in war and for labor and make sure that you personally are the first to be awarded them. Of course, the award ceremonies are to be given the greatest possible coverage in the press and broadcast on radio and television.

16. Your books, articles, notes—your each and every pronouncement—should cause the workers to respond with a frenzy of approval. They should be studied in all educational institutions, workers' collectives, and military units.

I could, of course, suggest a whole other series of useful measures, but even if you limit yourself to putting the above-mentioned recommendations into practice, your economy will in a very short period of historical time—sixty or seventy years—be close to a zero solution.

Of course there will remain the problem of geo-strategic balance, because, unlike the United States, we are surrounded by hostile fraternal nations, which, in the event of world conflict, might behave in the most treacherous fashion. But that problem can be solved quite simply. To even everything out, we only have to resettle half the Chinese in Mexico and half the Poles, Czechs, Bulgarians, Rumanians, Hungarians, and East Germans in Canada. We can resettle them while they're asleep, so they will continue to think that their older brother, the Soviet Union, is still right alongside them.

When you have done all that, perhaps we can meet again and do some serious negotiating on a zero solution to the question of nuclear missiles.

My Trip to the
United States

A little while back it seemed like a good idea to me to go to the United States for a time—to take care of a little business and for a general look at what was going on. Besides, the route to that citadel of capitalism was familiar; in my three plus years in the West, I'd already flown there five times.

I started getting ready: I bought a ticket from Munich to New York, packed my suitcase, and then it was time to start dealing with the necessary paperwork. My last visa had expired, and I needed a new one. I had, of course, secured visas before. But on each of those five occasions I had had official invitations, with official letterheads, signed by political people. I had been invited this time too, but it had been a verbal invitation, not signed and sealed. I could have asked for a written invitation, but for some reason I didn't think of that in time. "All right," I said to myself, "I'll just go. And if they ask me at the consulate why I want to enter their country . . ." I started doing some thinking, drawing up a list of all my reasons. I'd say I was traveling on invitation from an important person. But how would they view the person who invited me? To me, that person was very important, but he might be no one at all in the consulate's eyes. Suppose this person *is* important to the consulate, even so they might ask me: "If he really invited you, you should have the invitation from him in hand, a paper." I thought of telling them that I hadn't known that it, I mean the paper, was absolutely necessary. But the consulate might be offended: "What's the matter with you? What kind of country do you think we are? You think you can just pick up and go there without any papers at all?"

I got myself very worked up. If they refused me a visa, I was in trouble, because I'd already booked a flight, paid for the ticket, and left absolutely no time to get a written invitation from overseas. I had no idea what to do, so I went to bed, my head teeming with the wildest ideas.

As I was falling asleep, everything began to get mixed up in my mind—I couldn't tell what was real and what was a dream, and I began having the most improbable visions. I thought, Well, I might come to terms with the Americans, but I haven't requested visas from the Germans yet, nor have I applied to a travel committee. I seemed to remember that they did have a travel committee. Go to all four corners of the world if you want, they might say; nobody needs you here. Those were my thoughts as I was falling asleep. But just at that moment the Soviet in me woke up and made an objection: "What's he saying, that no one needs you here? Don't they have any kind of authorities here? And what's this about any-

269

body going where he wants to? What if he doesn't come back?"

Those reflections, which came to me in the night, served as the basis for a dream that might not have been a nightmare, but was about as unpleasant as they come. I dreamed that I was summoned to the local Munich city committee or provincial committee or to some other such body. A group of important persons of some kind were in session with leading workers from the local private sector, all of them well-fed individuals wearing medals pinned to their dark blue suits. I entered just as they were reading the questionnaire I'd filled out. Not a very detailed one, a mile or so long. I'm not about to brag, but the information on my form looked pretty good. I was born, went to school, worked, did not serve in the White Army, had never been on trial, and had never been in occupied territory. Not a bad questionnaire; everyone should have one like that. I could see that for the most part the members of the committee were satisfied with me.

"So you'd like a visa for the United States?" they asked.

"That's right, I feel like going."

"But what for?" they said.

"What do you mean what for? Just out of curiosity, to get to know life there a little."

Once again satisfied, the little old men on the committee nodded their downy heads. "Good, good," they said. "Seeking knowledge is very praiseworthy. But you intend to go there without any guide when the international situation is, as you know, very complicated. You might run into extremists, you might be asked some provocative questions, they might ask you if it's true that we have problems with unemployment, drugs, and crime here."

"Well, as far as provocative questions go, you have no need to worry, I'm a past master at handling them. I'll tell them that we're dealing successfully with the little unemployment there is, and I'll add that instead of asking me questions like that, they should take a walk around Harlem at midnight." I could see that the committee members were very pleased by my level of political consciousness.

"All right then," they said, "we can see you're well prepared for the trip and well versed in politics too. But can you name the General Secretary of the Capitalist Party of America?"

"Why are you asking me such childish questions?" I said. "Every infant knows that the General Secretary of the Capitalist Party of America is that staunch capitalist and leading fighter for peace Comrade Ronald Reagan."

"That's right," they said, "correct."

I was close to telling the committee to go to hell when a big-bosomed woman rose. She was a hero of capitalist labor, and she began taking a hand in the matter, asking me if I had any relatives living abroad. There was a simple answer for that: No. They all exchanged glances. "Are you sure? Think about it."

I thought about it. I said: "I have no relatives abroad."

"You didn't leave anybody in the Soviet Union?"

"I have some in the Soviet Union, of course," I said, "but there's no one at all abroad."

Then, what I would call a rather stupid skirmish broke out among us. They said, "But the Soviet Union is located abroad! That means you have relatives *abroad*."

I wasn't going to argue about the Soviet Union, but as for my relatives, I told the committee quite clearly that on their questionnaires where it asks if you've been abroad, they write no. "So are you calling them liars?"

At that point, one of the old men on the committee jumped to his ailing feet and said: "What do you take us for? What are you trying to pull here?"

I started losing my patience too. The hell with it, I thought, the hell with the United States; it should fall into the sea before I have to suffer such outrages to my human dignity. "Listen, old man, you and your committee are soft in the head. Use your brains, be logical. I've been abroad, but my relatives never left the country. Judge for yourself. After all, even your bourgeois papers write about the fact that Soviet people need to win the right to travel abroad. But if they were already abroad, then why would they have to win the right to travel?"

At that moment someone shook me hard, and I woke up. My wife was bending over me. "What's the matter with you?" she said. "You're shouting and waving your arms around."

"What do you expect when they ask me such stupid questions?" I said. And I told her about the idiots I had been dreaming about.

"Well, calm down," she said. "Those aren't real idiots, just idiots in a dream."

"It doesn't matter to me whether they're real or not. I hate both kinds."

Then I gradually came back to my senses. Of course there are plenty of idiots in Germany too but they don't sit on committees like that and they ask you those idiotic questions only in a dream. And if a person wants to go somewhere, he doesn't need permission of any sort from the local German authorities. He just shows his passport to a policeman on the way to the plane. The policeman looks at the passport, glances through some list to check if the person is a wanted criminal, and, if he isn't, then it's *Bitte*, go."

The country you're headed for may require a visa, as does the United States. But when I went to the consulate, no one asked me anything about an invitation. They just gave me a form with a few questions on it, including: "Were you ever a Communist?" I was pleased to answer that question by saying no. I never had. There was a question about my purpose in visiting the United States. I thought for a minute and then I wrote: "Just for fun!" The U.S. authorities apparently found that answer satisfactory, because fifteen minutes later I was granted a visa good for four years, during which time I could go to the United States and back every day of the week—if I had the money, of course.

Abracadabra

No matter what you say, there's no publication like the *Literaturnaya Gazeta*. If it were in my power, I would print more copies of it and translate it into all foreign languages so that everyone could enjoy its articles, which are often quite exceptional. For example, in the July 4 issue I read an interesting article by Alexander Sabov, "Longo Mai: An Attempt at a New Way of Life." That wasn't just an article; it was a gem. Judge for yourself.

Comrade Sabov notes that in 1972 some young people founded a cooperative farm in the Alps, called it "Longo Mai," and "invited the youth of Europe there for summer conferences. The guests were provided with modest board and unlimited opportunties for work and discussion. Only two types of newcomers were categorically turned down: ideological snivelers and idlers."

I read that paragraph a few times, trying to understand what it meant. Some young people had set up an agricultural cooperative, meaning something on the or-

der of a kolkhoz. They invited the youth of Europe to
come. They provided modest board and unlimited opportunities to work and debate. What kind of work?
Attending conferences or plowing fields? And what do
ideological snivelers have to do with anything? The article informs us that at the very beginning so many people came to that strange kolkhoz that its members had
to make it through the winter on spinach and turnips.
I can't make head or tail of it. If the ideological snivelers
who went there were not idlers and went not only to
debate but to work as well, then why was their harvest
so skimpy that they were forced to live on nothing but
spinach and turnips?

Further on, the article stated that the young kolkhozniks had intended to plant new orchards, but had not
managed anything of the sort and had gathered lavender, which they then sold at markets in Switzerland. By
some miracle, they got hold of a Swiss Army surplus
horse. Each new line added to my confusion. What were
they actually doing? Were they planting orchards or
gathering what grew wild? There's nothing miraculous
about getting a horse in Switzerland or the other Western countries; owning horses isn't prohibited, as it is in
the Soviet Union. Not only can cooperatives buy horses,
but so can ordinary people. And if the horse was some
surplus nag, it could be picked up dirt cheap. No miracle
needed. The article also said that the kolkhozniks hitched
the horse to a wagon on which they wrote: "Pioneer
Village Longo Mai" and set off on what the author called
"their first European voyages." Some kolkhozniks! Instead of laboring on their mountain slopes, they set off
on voyages. The article mentions that, in addition to
bulletins and lavender, their cart contained a guitar, a

fiddle, and an accordion. It wasn't so much the fiddle and the guitar I found surprising, as that modest combination of bulletins and lavender.

What kind of abracadabra is that? If they were selling lavender, what did they need bulletins for? And if they were distributing bulletins, then what were they doing with the lavender?

Then came another series of interesting facts: the reactionary French authorities had not allowed the kolkhozniks' 165 sheep to cross their border. And do you know what the kolkhozniks did? Something very simple. They made passports, with photographs, for each of the 165 sheep and hung them on their collars, and the French border guards had no choice but to allow those passport-bearing sheep across.

Yes, yes. Still, let's focus in on this. A conference, an old horse, new orchards, bulletins and lavender, sheep with passports. Ah, now I see! Some reactionary French prefect deported those kolkhozniks from France and was not ashamed to state publicly that they had settled in an area where national defense interests required increased vigilance. The prefect also expressed his belief that these young people belonged to an "international organization, whose goals and activities pose a threat to the institutions of our country."

I am prepared to be indignant about this reactionary who took the law into his own hands and used it against these young people, innocent as their sheep, and I thought that Alexander Sabov would help convince me that they were truly innocent. But, two paragraphs later, the *Literaturnaya Gazeta*'s correspondent reports some extremely dubious information about those kids. It turns out that one of them, when he was sixteen years old, had intended to go to Latin America, there to . . . here the correspondent used three dots . . . like Che Guevara. But do what like Che Guevara? Live like Che or gather lavender Che style? But to the best of my knowledge Che Guevara was not in the lavender business. An Argentine, he was a participant in the Cuban revolution. Later on he had a falling out with Fidel Castro, formed a guerrilla detachment, and went off to liberate other countries of Latin America. I don't know about bulletins, but Che did not take any lavender with him. He took machine guns and hand grenades; he killed other people and was himself killed in Bolivia. The young Austrian, Willy, had not gone to Latin America because another kolkhoznik, by the name of Ropplan, had convinced him that there was plenty of Che Guevara–type work to be done in Europe and that they'd be starting soon.

Three years later, Willy deserted from the army and reported that fact in a telegram to the Austrian chancellor. By that time, his friend Ropplan was in prison for his part in a mutiny of a paratroop regiment. Sabov says that a third friend "forced a plane full of generals to land in a wilderness area, thereby disrupting an important military operation." Good God! What generals? And how did that kolkhoznik force that plane to land in a wilderness area? Was he a pilot? Or did he shoot it down with some sort of weapon? That doesn't matter. It's not a tradition of the *Gazeta* to coddle its readers with detailed explanations. Needless to say, the reactionary French authorities put the young man on death row, and it took a miracle to save him. Both young men were freed from prison because of a campaign of solidarity that was launched in France. The writer Friedrich Durenmatt spoke in their defense in Switzerland.

Let's imagine for a minute a Soviet soldier deserting and sending a telegram to Gorbachev. Or one forcing down a plane carrying Soviet generals, thereby disrupting an important operation in, let's say, Afghanistan. Soviet law is strict, and it's entirely possible that these soldiers would end up on death row. But then imagine a campaign for their liberation, progressive Soviet writers speaking out in their defense in the *Literaturnaya Gazeta*, the soldiers being freed.

But let's keep going. No matter how perfidious the French authorities were, the Swiss proved even more perfidious. They weren't about to throw the kolkhozniks in prison. On the contrary, they encouraged them to go off to the mountains, so they wouldn't cause trouble in the cities. The Swiss newspapers even started a campaign to collect one hundred thousand francs for Longo Mai. The father of a lanky youth named Nikki came up with enough money from his modest means to buy an entire hectare of land. All the same, Nikki spent days on end in the marketplace playing his fiddle, collecting marks, kroner, and francs for the cause.

The coop Longo Mai flowered from then on, with textile production, various crops, large flocks of sheep. But still, is this a kolkhoz? Longo Mai has affiliates in other countries.

Sabov quotes one of the leaders of Longo Mai as saying that a coop "as a legal formulation, was important to us for the outside world but internally it had little meaning." In other words, the coop was a front; in fact, "it was our alternative to the existing system."

According to Sabov, the West has plenty to say about these splendid young workers. They're called a "sect," the children of May, anarcho-syndicalists, neo-Blankists,

Nechaevists, Kropotkinists, pacifists, and terrorists. Hearing all the names they've been called, the Longo Maiists began laughing so hard that it seemed to Sabov that their laughter made the mountains shake. None of those names fit, of course. They were all only enemies . . . no, listen . . . enemies of militarization, industry, and society. That was all.

It must be said that this sort of material doesn't appear often even in the *Literaturnaya Gazeta*. Still, I would not have written about this article if it had not concluded with a short note from the editor: "Our correspondent informs us that the young people reported on here wish to find like-minded people on Soviet collective or state farms. We invite responses."

That did it for me. A fine thing, a publication of the Writers' Union calling on our kolkhoz youth to organize and recruit deserters, mutineers, and terrorists into their ranks, gather information about where Soviet troops are stationed, invite the youth of Europe to join them, buy old army horses, gather lavender, travel with bulletins, fiddles, and accordions, create an alternative to the existing system, and fight against militarization, industry, and society.

I've seen a great many kolkhozes of all sorts in the Soviet Union, but I've never seen one like that. But now, after the *Gazeta*'s appeal, perhaps I can hope to see one.

A Fourth Aspect
of Humanism

The Soviet propaganda arsenal has one subject it constantly harps on and develops, a subject that never grows old.

Let's take another issue of *Literaturnaya Gazeta*, this time the January 16, 1985, edition. Of course, one could choose any other newspaper, but the *Gazeta* is a bit more expressive than most, because it is the creation of literary artists.

The edition's front page sports a picture of the orders of Lenin and the Friendship Among Nations, which the newspaper received for its contributions to the cause of educating the workers. There are also silhouettes of Pushkin and Gorky, the spiritual fathers of those who publish the paper today. Here's a photograph of a smug-looking candidate for deputy meeting with the electorate, who appear delighted with him. And here are articles with titles like "The People's Trust" and "To Serve the Motherland." On the whole, a pretty typical issue.

On page two, my eye is caught by the title "The Face of Hatred," a short piece in a section with the general heading "Screen Journalism." The piece is devoted to the latest achievement of Soviet documentary film makers: *A Plot Against the Land of the Soviets*. An intriguing title but one that was old long ago. The film's subject, as I understand it, is not distinguished for its originality either. The White Guards, the Entente, the fascist hordes all tried to smash the Soviet state, but they failed. Nevertheless, they haven't given up hope. What had not been achieved by Entente bayonets and fascist machine guns, the dark forces of the present day intend to achieve through lies, slander, and outcries about human rights. It was a short piece, and so I wasn't sure whether the film makers had managed to depict all of international imperialism's insidious methods: the jeans, jazz, T shirts with writing on them, and Coca-Cola. On the other hand, the film makers had lavished attention on the so-called dissidents. "The remnants of the White Guards, fascist stooges, nationalists, all this anti-Soviet riffraff . . . today find confederates in people like the renegade Shcharansky and the literary Vlasovite* Solzhenitsyn," said the article.

The author of the piece found no epithet for Sakharov and simply called him a defender of human rights, putting the words in quotation marks. The film most likely depicted other sinister persons as well, but their names weren't mentioned in the article. All that was said was: "The screen is merciless in tearing off masks of every sort, revealing a single face beneath both the mask of

---

* Andrei Vlasov was a Soviet general during World War II. He was captured by the Germans and subsequently led an army against the Soviet Union. ——Ed.

the 'human rights activist' and the singer of the 'capitalist paradise'—the face of hatred."

I haven't seen the film and don't know whether or not hatred was actually that legible on the faces of the persons listed, but I'm willing to take the author's word for it. Certainly all three of them have sufficient grounds for hatred.

Unfortunately, hatred does exist and has a destructive influence on people's souls and relations. But there's hatred and there's hatred. There's the initial hatred—that of an aggressor for his victim. And there's hatred as response—the victim's hatred for the aggressor. It makes for a vicious circle. Hatred is terrible, surely, but it's a feeling very difficult to guard against.

Personally speaking, I hate some people. For example, I hate the people who make that sort of film and the people who write glowing reviews of those films.

But *Literaturnaya Gazeta* combats hatred. As well it should. It is, after all, the publication of the Writers' Union, and in Russia writers have always preached goodness, not hatred. However, *Gazeta* does depart somewhat from that tradition. It struggles against hatred but it also preaches it. On that very same page, with no space between the two articles, there is a long piece called "The Unforgettable," by literary critic Ivan Kozlov. Its subject is indicated in parentheses: "(Soviet Literature on the Ultimate Boundaries of War.)" The article devotes a very long passage to what the author calls the "sacred" feeling of hatred as depicted by various writers—hatred in the name of love for humanity. Kozlov asserts that during the war Soviet literature educated soldiers in hatred, not against the German people, but against Nazism. And that was true at the beginning of the war. Then came a

shift in mood, and the propaganda machine also underwent a shift. Sholokhov wrote *The Science of Hatred,* and
Ehrenburg, *Kill the German.* The poet Konstantin Simonov developed that theme: "Kill every German you
see." But that was a terrible war of worldwide rage, hatred
upon hatred. Though even then there were people who
made a distinction between Germans and Nazis, just as
now there are people who can distinguish between Russians and Communists. Kozlov supports his idea with a
quotation from well before the war. "The writer A. Surkov, spoke convincingly and well at the First Congress
of Soviet Writers about hatred in the name of love for
man and mankind as a very important integral part of
socialist humanism." Later on, Kozlov quotes the following from Surkov's speech: "In our country the concepts
LOVE, JOY, and PRIDE, the constituents of HUMANISM, are
widely used in poetry, and rightly so." This statement is
written neither convincingly nor well; but plainly, it is
utter nonsense. If, by stretching things, love can be included as one of socialism's components, joy and pride
don't fit in the least. What came next in the speech was
not utter nonsense but something even worse. Listen.
"But some . . . poets somehow or other overlook a fourth
aspect of humanism, one expressed in the severe and
beautiful concept of HATRED." It is obvious that it was
Surkov who had emphasized the word "hatred" and not
the author of the newspaper piece. The fact that these
words were not spoken during the war, but seven years
before, is noted with approval. In other words, there was
no reason for hatred yet, but hatred already existed.

Soviet propaganda has been laboring long and cease-
lessly to pervert human notions of good and evil, but
here it can boast a masterful display of plainly worded

misanthropy. It was not a matter of chance that the author of the article dug up statements made fifty years earlier. He could not have found anything more recent.

At one time, Orwell's slogans "War is Peace" and "Freedom is Slavery" seemed to many a product of an imagination run wild. But even in Orwell's time, these perversions were not fantasy. They were a permanent fixture of reality.

Advocates of so-called socialist humanism always thought that, unlike ordinary humanism, theirs was inseparable from cruelty and hatred—in the name of a higher end, of course. I remember that, many years after the war, a Soviet poet wrote an opus on the subject of socialist humanism: It is during the war, the Soviet soldiers are in their trenches and the Germans in theirs. A minefield stretches between the two lines, but of this the Germans are unaware. Suddenly, out of nowhere, a little girl appears. The author describes her in the most touching way: she is small, thin, wearing a little white dress, and with ribbons in her braids. The soldiers are horrified. Not only because the little girl is sure to be blown up any second, but because the explosion will reveal to the enemy the presence of a minefield. A difficult situation, but the solution is clear. A socialist-humanist machine gunner cuts the girl down with a single burst, and the enemy remains in the dark. Remembering the incident, the poet muses that if the same scene were to be replayed in his lifetime, "I know that I would do the same thing again, I know I would put my unshaven cheek against my machine gun."

"Necessary" cruelty is one of the most popular themes in socialist realism. But the praises of cruelty and hatred, even when they are not necessary, are sung quite often as well. In one of his supposedly humorous poems, Simonov says that if God, when summoning him to the next world, offered to let him bring something he loved with him, he would choose friends, to have someone to be friends with, but he would also take enemies, so that he could have someone to be enemies with. That's the essence of socialist humanism's misanthropy. Even in life after death, an enemy becomes essential. Now that Simonov's up there, in the next world, I hope his enemies there are not the sort of inoffensive ones he found here on this sinful earth—for example, the writer Mikhail Zoshchenko, whom Simonov helped persecute.

But let's go back to our issue of *Literaturnaya Gazeta,* where hatred is a fourth aspect of humanism. I'll skip the international page, which is usually packed with samples of Surkovlike humanism, and move on to page fourteen and Grigory Baklanov's article "At No Risk of Censure." He enjoys the reputation of a writer who writes the truth about the war. He may well write truthfully about the war, but when he turns to the present, he betrays no aversion to lying.

His article was a response to a piece in the American magazine *Esquire,* "Why Do Men Love War?" Here, the lie is contained in the very fact of a response. We are made to believe that Baklanov is a free writer living in a time of freedom, freely leafing through *Esquire,* a magazine to which he has access (like other magazines published in English and other foreign languages outside our country that are so handily available at Moscow's newsstands). The lie would have us believe that he came across that horrible article, read it freely in English, and decided freely to express his indignation in written form.

I know Baklanov. I seriously doubt that he has any

command of the English language and am certain that he has no access to *Esquire* or any other foreign magazine. He was probably given that article in translation; I even suspect it wasn't the whole article, but only certain quotes from it, and I am sure he was told that it might not be a bad idea to respond. He could slip a little something of his own in among the quotes. Even from the quotes included in the article, it is plain to any experienced Soviet reader that the author, a former U.S. officer, is not writing about the love of war but of man's habituation to it. He does not defend that in the least. But Baklanov paraphrases the article, quotes various warmongers, and shares memories of his trips to the United States. He spent three weeks traveling through various states, lectured at various universities, and, it seems, did not once observe any display of hatred for his country and his people. But that guileless line is dwarfed in an article whose title claims that in the United States advocating hatred has become so much a matter of habit that it carries no risk of censure. That is an outright lie and part of the propaganda of hatred: if the Americans hate us, we should hate them in return.

This is only one issue of *Literaturnaya Gazeta,* but, as was said earlier, it differs in no way from others. The entire Soviet propaganda machine is engaged in the production of hatred. Soviet journalists roam the countries of the West, painting their images in the darkest of colors. Judging by their descriptions, there is no good in any of those countries, only unemployment, inflation, crime, decadence, and, needless to say, neo-Nazis, revanchists, and open warmongers. What do Soviet ideologists seek by depicting the rest of humanity in this fashion? What feelings do they wish to inculcate in Soviet people? Love, joy, and pride? No. Only hatred, that fourth aspect of humanism. And how does this square with the Soviet Union's so-called peace initiatives and its efforts to reduce international tension? Can a stable peace be built by advocating hatred?

Hatred is no aspect of humanism. In all its aspects, hatred is hatred, the product of malicious, simple-minded, spiritually crippled people, hostile toward genuine humanism. Soviet propaganda never uses the words "human rights" except in quotation marks. These lessons in hatred are not entirely successful, but, vying for people's minds year in, year out, they do have their effect. Ask any ordinary Soviet intellectual what pity is and he'll tell you that pity is degrading to a person. Utter nonsense! Any person in whom ordinary human feeling has not atrophied feels pity for those who suffer, and he himself may hunger for pity.

I've already mentioned that the *Gazeta*'s front page has a silhouette of Pushkin as its emblem. Pushkin did once publish a paper called the *Literaturnaya Gazeta*, but he would have had nothing to do with today's version. He did not consider hatred an aspect of humanism. In his era, which Pushkin called "cruel," but which witnessed no crimes like ours, he "praised freedom and called for mercy for the fallen." More or less what Sakharov is doing. Mercy, not hatred for the fallen.

As a matter of conscience, Pushkin's silhouette should be removed from the front page of *Literaturnaya Gazeta* and replaced by a portrait of someone like Surkov. But perhaps a more major figure could be found among those who advocate misanthropic humanism. Maybe someone like Hitler, Goebbels, Stalin, Zhdanov . . .

Nostalgia

Every house alien to me,
every temple empty.
It's all one, all the same.
But if there's a bush by the road
Especially a rowan-berry . . .

Marina Tsvetaeva

Lana Peters (also known as Svetlana Alliluyeva Stalin) returned to Moscow. Oleg Bitov, a correspondent for *Literaturnaya Gazeta*, also returned. KGB officer Vitaly Yurchenko redefected. Two Soviet soldiers went back after defecting in Kabul and spending a short time in London. A third soldier returned to Moscow from Washington. The young people could not put down roots in foreign soil, couldn't adapt to customs they could not understand and to a language that forces you to do strange things with your tongue. (The tongue may have no bones, as the proverb says, but it can prove a very clumsy and helpless part of the human body.) It may be that the boys got excited and redeserted prematurely. Perhaps in ten or twenty years they would have adapted to new ways of life, grown used to popcorn and Coca-Cola.

Time cures all, including nostalgia. But the cure is not always complete. Recently, after a sixty-year stay in the United States, a certain Mary Armstrong returned to

England. She was ninety-nine years old at the time. Surrounded by journalists at Heathrow Airport, she told them: "I don't like America and I don't like Americans. British people are much friendlier."

Nostalgia is quite a strange ailment. It afflicts people not only outside the boundaries of their native land, but within them as well. I know an old country woman who was forever longing to go to Moscow, where her daughter lived. Her husband was dead, she had no cows, and there was practically nothing left to do around the house. She dreamed of going to Moscow where she had a daughter and grandchildren, giving her daughter a hand, of being useful. And so she prepared to leave. From a trunk she got out the dress she was married in decades before (even before the dispossession of the kulaks), gathered up some presents (she always took the same presents: a bucketful of slippery salted milk-agaric mushrooms), bought a ticket for an unreserved seat on the train, and left for Moscow. For Moscow!

She arrived, lived in Moscow a while, and at first was as pleased as could be. She cooked, did the washing, outfitted her grandhcildren for school, and went to church to light a candle for her late husband's soul.

But after a couple of weeks, the old woman began to feel homesick, out of place. She would sit by the window and stare with inexpressible melancholy at the little boxes packed with people like bees in a hive. But going outside was even worse—trolley buses, cars, jackhammers. . . . No matter where you went, something was booming, whistling, gnashing, and endless crowds with net shopping bags and briefcases swept by in a hurry, everyone mean, shoving, stomping on your feet, dashing out into traffic. . . . Suddenly, overcome by nostalgia, the woman grabbed her empty bucket and headed for home, her village, the sticks, Saratov . . . If you think about it, Moscow, New York, or Rio de Janeiro would probably all have been the same to that old woman. All equally alien. If it had entered some journalist's mind to hold a press conference for her, she could have said quite a few negative things about our country's capital. But an old woman is an old woman; who cares what she thinks? She was not related to any famous tyrants (though her late husband did have a tyrannical bent), she had not deserted from the Soviet Army, nor had she served in the KGB.

While we're on the subject of the KGB, here in the West some people display such deference to those who work for that establishment that even a minor KGB official like Bitov was treated like a movie star, and people hung on every foolish word he had to say. I don't know how he captured the journalists' attention and what secrets he promised to reveal, but he wrote nothing but fluff for the Western papers and utter nonsense for *Literaturnaya Gazeta*. After he returned to Moscow, many people in the West thought and wrote a lot about him and an entire film was shot, in London, in which people drone on about whether Bitov was abducted or had returned home of his own free will. If it had been of his own free will, then had he actually defected to the West earlier or had he been sent there on assignment? I'm told that his colleagues at *Literaturnaya Gazeta* even called Bitov our man in the West. Perhaps the same can be said of Yurchenko.

Svetlana occasioned an even greater range of opinion. She was no KGB agent, but more on the order of a princess, whose every move can cause a sensation. She defected from the Soviet Union—a sensation. She defected to the Soviet Union—another sensation. And she did not stop there.

She defected the first time seventeen years ago, when the Soviet government allowed her to take the ashes of her recent husband to India. Having dispensed with the ashes, she turned up in the U.S. Embassy, requested political asylum, and caused as much commotion as if Stalin himself had appeared there.

I remember her defection clearly. Like many other people in our country, I listened to her countless interviews on foreign radio, and it must be said that she truly did cause a sensation. After all, it wasn't just anybody who had defected, not just some insignificant journalist, but the daughter of Stalin himself. The world was waiting to hear what she'd say. What sizzling secrets would she reveal? Why had she defected? What was she running from?

Now we all know that she was running from herself, just as we also know that you can't run very far from yourself.

Not long ago, I spent a year at Princeton University, where Einstein lived and worked during the last years of his life. Many well-known scientists, writers, political figures, and diplomats live around there. Svetlana had lived there too and had left it shortly before I arrived. I heard her spoken of often in Princeton as difficult and quarrelsome by nature. They said it was hard for her to get close to people and easy for her to break with them. She avoided associating with Russians. She spoke only English with the daughter of her latest marriage, to an American, and kept her origin a secret from her. She set no roots down, but moved to England, to Cambridge.

I don't know whether it was there or in the States that she became disillusioned with the West; in any case, she had plenty of time to become disenchanted. In that time she could not only have become disenchanted with the West, but also have forgotten a great deal of what she had fled, cursing, seventeen years before.

During those seventeen years, she saw, comprehended, and realized a great deal. She realized that the Western world is not as good as it seems from afar. And the world in which she had grown up was not as bad as it seems close up. Of course, at one time her father had committed a few follies, but those were bends to be expected in the new road he was laying, and it was all in the past now. As far as freedom is concerned, she decided, it doesn't exist in the West either. She, Svetlana Alliluyeva, had not been free for a single day in the West.

When I read these revelations, I think: In what sense wasn't she free? Had she been in prison? Had someone forbidden her to write or publish what she wished? Or to move from one place to another, from one country to another, or even to return to the Soviet Union? I would even say that, judging by Svetlana's behavior, she appears to have felt unusually free of many of the obligations that few people can afford to neglect. She left the children of her first marriage behind and then she took her thirteen-year-old daughter with her to the Soviet Union. That American child had not only to face learning the foreign language from which she had been so jealously guarded, but foreign customs, the history of something called the CPSU, and perhaps even the tedious works of her grandfather's disciples. And when *she* began to feel the pain of nostalgia, it wasn't such a simple matter for her to return to her native sequoias.

The old grandfathers in the Kremlin today don't like to toss foreign visas around. Gorbachev saved the day.

So the prodigal daughter revisited her native aspen trees for a time. They say that the minute Svetlana returned home, she went straight to the Kremlin wall to pay her respects to her father's ashes and to put flowers by his grave. (I understand her daughterly feelings, but I personally would have hoped the grave had been overgrown with tall weeds and its sinister spirit had ceased hanging over Russia.)

After laying the flowers, she called a press conference to vent her grievances against the West. She said that in the West she had been surrounded by lawyers and businessmen, whereas all she had wanted was to associate with writers, artists, and actors. What infantile romanticism! And what if she had moved in the circles she desired? Would she then have been freed of her profound guilt toward the land of her birth? Would she not have returned home? I, for one, think that had writers and artists accepted her into their company, her ravenous nature would have still remained unsatisfied. And perhaps she should not have striven to frequent those circles, but, rather, should have searched for others like herself. People like the children of Hitler, Mussolini, Mao Zedong, and Enver Xoxha (though it is true that some of them left no descendants).

Another of her grievances was that in the West people did not treat her as an individual, but as Stalin's daughter. What had she counted on? How else should she be treated? Her misfortune in being Stalin's daughter can be blamed neither on the West nor on the East, but on Stalin (and this is the sole thing for which I can forgive him) and on his wife, who shot herself (or was shot by him) well after Svetlana was born.

It's understandable that we are interested in Stalin. Like many others, I read Svetlana's books precisely because they were written by Stalin's daughter. For me, and for many other readers, Stalin's personality is more than a matter of idle interest. I want to know what character traits and what circumstances allowed him to commit crimes unprecedented in history. I want to know what made it possible for him to rule the Soviet empire for such a long period. Testimony from a close relative like a daughter could well be of significance. Unfortunately, I must say that both her books disappointed me. They contained no sizzling revelations, no original ideas, and, to be blunt, her language was wanting.

It sometimes happens that when writing about an eminent person, an author proves himself of great stature. That was the case in Nadezhda Mandelstam's book about Osip Mandelstam and Lidya Chukovsky's book about Anna Akhmatova. Svetlana's books reflect her personality, of course, but it must be said that hers is not very interesting. Especially when viewed beside such an exceptional figure as that of Joseph Vissarionovich Stalin.

I'm aware that to be the daughter of such a criminal is no easy lot. But he conferred many privileges on her which she did not refuse, and not only in the West. Too, if she were not Stalin's daughter, she would not have been given a room in the Sovetskaya Hotel upon her return to Moscow. Quite likely she would have drawn a cell in Lefortovo Prison. Incidentally, she herself said that many defectors do not return home only because they fear punishment. I would like to add that, were it not for such punishments, they might not have defected in the first place.

But she of course was received as Stalin's daughter.

Eleven years ago, in an interview, she complained about the press, which had greatly exaggerated the honorariums she was receiving, saying they ran somewhere between four and six million dollars. For her first book she received only the sum of two million, and next to nothing for her second—fifty thousand and ninety thousand for the paperback rights. Besides, most of the money had been spent. She had donated two hundred thousand toward the construction of a hospital, another two hundred had gone into the Svetlana Alliluyeva Fund and fifty thousand to the Tolstoy Fund, and the lawyers had taken two hundred thousand. When she married Wes Peters, all she had left was a million three hundred thousand. And she came out of the marriage with no more than half a million.

So she did not prove to be a very practical woman. But that's not what interests me. Did she really believe that, if she were not Stalin's daughter, her books would have earned millions or even thousands? Emigré writers in the United States who write books of that caliber are better off working as night watchmen, shoemakers (as Stalin's own father once did), or going on welfare. No one's arguing that there are many injustices in the West. But there's plenty of injustice in the Soviet Union too. As the daughter of a tyrant, she inhabited an artificial world, and she will continue to do so. If she really desired to live in the society that, as she put it, she had once again come to love, then she should have accepted the same conditions as ordinary members of that society and moved into a communal apartment with a shared kitchen and a shared bathroom. Her pension (given her years on the job, insufficient by Soviet standards) would have been set at thrity or forty rubles a month, if not less. As for the society in question, it gathers every day in its communal kitchens. That society was, truth to tell, more interesting and livelier in Stalin's time. People spat in each other's pots and whacked each other over the head with frying pans. Now it's the old women on pension who did not earn themselves private apartments from the Soviet authorities who gather in those communal kitchens. Were Svetlana the daughter of some undistinguished man, she too would have ended up by the communal stove.

"Homesickness is a confusion long since exposed for what it is," said the poet Marina Tsvetaeva.

Yes, but not quite.

Here I am living far from the places where I was born and grew up. To be frank, I'm not experiencing any particular financial problems. It is true that I chanced to have quite decent people as parents, and no one has as yet given me a million because of them (Svetlana is right, the West is very unfair). And so I have had to earn my own way. Needless to say, I associate with the local people—lawyers and businessmen, lathe operators and bakers. I may have had more luck than Svetlana—I meet with writers and aritists from time to time.

So what do I lack? The Russian language? I haven't yet forgotten what I love about the language (and I don't think there's any danger of that) and I do not miss in the least the crude language in which the Soviet leaders express themselves and in which the records of interrogations are drawn up. What else is there? Russian birch trees? But I've observed that birches have no nationality. I've seen them in the United States, Switzerland, France. Here in the village of Stockdorf, outside Munich, three splendid birches grow right in front of my window. And they're exactly like those I used to see in the village of Vertoshino, outside Moscow.

I sit here and write, gazing out at those birches. If I get bored, I can buy a ticket and travel wherever I please. To the United States, to Italy, to Spain, to any country I choose. Except for one. One that, despite everything, is still dearer to me than all the rest combined. It doesn't matter that life is poor and squalid there. It doesn't matter that there are shortages of sausages, light bulbs, and detergent there. But there is something lacking there that does matter—freedom, which, despite assertions to the contrary, is not a conscious necessity but a vital need for every person who is aware of himself as an independent individual. I am not referring here to the numerous freedoms that don't exist in the Soviet Union, but are nevertheless proclaimed by the Soviet constitution: freedom of speech, assembly, demonstration. What I mean here is freedom in general. Including the freedom not to attend rallies and assemblies, the freedom to say what you want, to write whatever comes to mind, and if it all comes to nothing, to kiss it good-bye and go off to Princeton, Cambridge, Munich, and then go back home and not have to pay for this with prison or by having to give idiotic press conferences.

By the way, some people return to the Soviet Union without having to give press conferences. Recently, Feodor Chaliapin's remains were returned to Moscow from Paris. Soviet propaganda treated this as a major ideological victory. His remains were placed in the Bolshoi Theater and then a procession of famous singers and actors accompanied Chaliapin to Novodevichy Cemetery. All of this was shown on Soviet television, and the viewers were told that the famous singer's will had been done, his dream had come true. I'm not so sure people dream about their remains being returned to their native land. In any case, Chaliapin doesn't seem to have indulged in that dream. In a letter to Maxim Gorky he expressed himself as follows: "I won't go back to those bastards dead or alive."

That's pretty definite, isn't it?

It must be said that on the whole the Soviet authorities exhibit a pointless inclination to seek out remains and have them brought "home." In 1966, the remains of Nikolai Ogarev were exhumed in London and shipped to Moscow. They have been fighting for many years for Alexander Herzen's remains, which rest in Nice. It's hard to say why they want the remains of all those rebel émigrés. Were they alive, they would be (and of this there is no doubt) open enemies of the current system in Russia. Pushkin was right again: "They are capable only of loving the dead."

Not all the dead. While pursuing remains outside the country, on their own territory they were busy smashing Pasternak's house to smithereens. They threw out the poet's manuscripts and books, and demolished the piano that Henrik and Stanislav Neigauz and Sviatoslav Richter had once played.

Now a similar outrage is in the works for the home of Kornei Chukovsky, on whose books several generations of Soviet people have grown up.

They feel no shame in that. They feel no shame in anything.

And so when you hear of all these things, your nostalgia passes. But the pity for your nation and the outrage grow all the stronger.

What's the Problem?
Who's to Blame?
What's to Be Done?*

The line for beer was horribly long, and like a fool I got into it. An hour passed and I had moved no more than halfway to the beer stand. I stood there, torn by doubt. On the one hand, to hell with the beer; on the other, I've already stood here an hour, why waste it. All the same, I was leaning toward leaving when I noticed a revolt brewing in the line. Not so much a revolt—that's too strong a word—but a definite grumbling. The men were upset: Why isn't the line moving? Probably because some wise guys are slipping in up front or taking ten mugs each or the girl is selling beer through the back door to people she knows. The grumbling began to spread, moving from the tail end of the line to the head. It reached the counter, where it quieted down. A moment later, the explanation went from the head of the line to the tail end.

---

* The eternal Russian questions. *Who's to Blame?* was a book by Alexander Hertzen; *What's to Be Done?* was a title used for a novel by Chernyshevsky and a pamphlet by Lenin. ———Ed.

"Mugs are the problem," I heard the people in front of me say. "The problem is that there are too many people and not enough mugs."

"Mugs are the problem," said the people in front to those behind them. "The problem is mugs."

Everyone nodded in agreement, everyone calmed down. They weren't being cheated, no one was slipping into the front of the line, no one was getting beer through the back door; the only problem was a shortage of mugs. And so, people continued standing in line, inching peacefully forward. And I did too. About an hour and a half later, my wait was over. Even though I'm not a great fan of beer and never drink more than a mug at a time, that day I ordered two. There was something uncomfortable in admitting that I had waited two and a half hours for just one beer.

WHO'S TO BLAME?

The beginning of 1953. I was serving in the army, attending mechanics' school. The usual army schedule: reveille, formation, latrine, formation, calisthenics, wash-up, make the bed, morning roll call, breakfast ("Forward march, singing!"), formation, return to barracks, formation ("Forward march, singing!"), eight hours of classes (drill, engine theory, exercise, topography, rules, theory of flight, political education), lunch, a nap, three hours of homework ("Forward march, singing!"), dinner, forty minutes of personal time (to write letters, polish your buttons, sew your collar), formation, an evening walk ("Forward march, singing!"), five minutes of free time (the sergeant's command would be: "Have a smoke, relax, get ready for lights out . . . Disperse!"), formation, evening roll call, lights out, taps.

There was no time to read papers or magazines, but wherever you looked there were "cosmopolitans," stealing, speculating, kowtowing to the West, "but they eat the fat of the Russian land," according to Mikhalkov. There was the satirical article "Pinia from Zhmerinka," and the long poem "Who Lives Well in Russia?" Answer: the Jews. Then, finally, the campaign culminated in the Doctors' Plot; on orders from the Jewish bourgeois nationalist organization Joint, Jewish physicians had hatched a conspiracy of terrorism. The Jews had murdered Andrei Zhdanov and Alexander Shcherbakov, and had intended to murder a few marshals and Generalissimo Stalin.

I was far from my Motherland at the time and did not see this with my own eyes, but later on I learned that the populace had panicked. People had refused to be treated by Jewish physicians and threw away the medicine they'd prescribed for them; Russian students beat up their Jewish classmates, and the Jews themselves were not only afraid of the people's wrath but were even ashamed of belonging to that "pernicious tribe." Many years later, a friend told me of a letter he had written at the time. "I'm ashamed to be a Jew," he had written to his parents.

Meanwhile, in our school things continued to take their normal course. Then suddenly, one day during a political-education class, cadet Vasilev rose, red-faced with tension, and asked: "Comrade First Lieutenant, why don't we shoot the Jews in the Soviet Union?"

Confusion ensued. The class held its breath. The first lieutenant remained silent. After thinking a while, he smiled at Vasilev and said: "I understand the cause of your concern, but you didn't phrase the question properly. Naturally, the crimes committed by people of Jewish nationality make us indignant and arouse our righteous anger, but we should remember that we are humanists and internationalists, and we know that there are different sorts of Jews. Some Jews are bad and some are good, hard-working people."

"Like Fishman, for example," suggested Ermolenko happily.

"That's right, Fishman, for example," the first lieutenant readily agreed, and he bowed politely to the embarrassed Fishman, who was sitting in the last row.

Vasilev turned even redder, clenched his fists, and said decisively: "Fishman's not a Jew."

Even though Vasilev had no reason to doubt Fishman's origins, he also knew that Fishman, for all his faults, was one of the guys. Vasilev was ready to shoot all the Jews, with one exception—Fishman.

1979. In a certain social circle in Moscow, I made the acquaintance of a psychiatrist, who told me that he had just read a book by the writer F. It was a novel about a middle-aged Jew who finally renounces his Communist illusions, converts to Russian Orthodoxy, is baptized, and reflects a great deal on the Jews' historical guilt toward the Russian people. The author (a Jew) said that it is shameful to compare the stream of blood shed by Jews with the river shed by Russians.

The psychiatrist liked the novel very much.

"What did you like about it?" I asked. "It's a badly written, boring book."

"I'm already past the age when I read books for controversial subjects or stylistic niceties. I'm interested only in ideas."

"So what ideas did you find in that book?"

"It has one main idea, a very true one. It convincingly proves that the Jews are to blame for everything. And Blank is the chief culprit. Did you know that Lenin's real name was Blank?"

"No," I said, "I know that his real name was Ulyanov."

"It's not Ulyanov; it's Blank. His mother's father was a Jew by the name of Blank."

"Fine, but what was your grandfather on your mother's side?"

I was in luck. It turned out that his grandfather had been a Tartar.

"And so that means you're a Tartar?"

"No. I'm a Russian."

Our argument ended there, because once a person gets it into his head that the Jews are to blame for everything, there is no proof that can budge him from that point of view.

1981. Germany. I received an invitation from an elderly woman, a Russian émigré. Her husband, a German businessman, and I were served vodka; she drank tea. She was interested in what was happening in Russia, especially regarding ethnic problems.

"I quarrel with everyone. No one ever agrees with me," she said. "So tell me, is it true that there is no Ukrainian language, only a Little Russian dialect of the Russian language?"

"No," I said, "I don't think that's true. If you heard people speaking Ukrainian and didn't know the language, you wouldn't understand what they were saying.

To me that suggests that there is a Ukrainian language."

She did not respond, but clearly she did not agree. We spoke of other things for a while. Then she said: "Tell me, why are there so many non-Russians among the dissidents and the Soviet rulers?"

"Do you mean why are there so many Jews?"

"Yes, that's right," she said somewhat haltingly.

"As for the dissidents," I said, "some are Jews, of course. And as for the people in power . . . Tell me, do you think Brezhnev is a Jew?"

"You mean he isn't?"

No, Brezhnev is not a Jew. Neither are any of the other members of the Politburo."

"What do you mean?" she said, withdrawing a Soviet newspaper with pictures of the Politburo members, which she'd hidden behind her books. Regarding them with disgust, she said: "You mean these people are Russians?"

"Well, they're not Jews. But if you want to go into details, let's take a closer look. Brezhnev is a Russian, Andropov's a Russian, Gromyko's a Russian," and I continued through the list. "These fourteen men are the real rulers of the Soviet state. Ten are Russian, two are Ukrainian, one is a Kazakh, and one a Latvian."

The old woman folded her newspaper carefully and hid it again behind her books. She raised no objections but did not appear to have changed her opinion.

About thirty years ago an epigram was composed about the well-known Soviet poet and anti-Semite Sergei Smirnov, who suffered from a painful physical handicap and an inferiority complex:

He's a cripple himself
and his verses are lame . . .

Who's fault is that?
The Jews are to blame.

WHAT'S TO BE DONE?

One day at ten-thirty in the morning I was walking through Minaevsky Market with my net shopping bag when suddenly from behind me I heard:

"What's to be done, what's to be done?" It was asked with passionate excitement.

Hearing that question, which at one time had so stirred Russian society, I too grew excited.

That's all we need, I thought. That question! Nikolai Chernyshevsky had asked it in his novel about the crystal palaces and Vera Pavlovna's dreams, and Lenin had asked in his pamphlet on the painful questions of his time. You'd think it would all have been taken care of—the palaces have been built and the problems resolved. But there it was: the question had remained.

I turned around.

Directly behind me, two winos who had long since renounced the vanities of this world were stumbling blindly along the arcades.

One of them, a bit taller than the other, was wearing cotton gloves and holding his head as if his teeth, temples, and both ears were killing him. He was chanting: "What's to be done? What's to be done?"

The other one, unshaven and in a bad way himself, took his friend by the elbow and said persuasively: "Let's kill a little time. They'll lift the blockade in half an hour, and we'll get ourselves two bottles right off."

And I thought of Turgenev's words: "In my days of doubt, my days of painful reflection on the fate of my native land, you alone are my mainstay and support, O great, mighty, truthful, free Russian language! Without you, how not to fall into despair at the sight of everything that is happening at home? But it is unthinkable that a language such as this was not given to a great people!"

And, really, what other word is there apart from *block-ade* for the calamity of having to wait for the liquor store to open, a store that does not open at eight o'clock, like all others (why not?), but at eleven. Doesn't that say it all?

And what better expression than *killing time* for walking wearisomely back and forth in front of the stores, when it's impossible to stand, sit, talk, or think about anything else, when all you can do is wait until you've waited out that last unbearable, endless half hour.

"Let's kill a little time. They'll lift the blockade in half an hour, and we'll get ourselves two bottles right off."

O great, mighty, truthful, free Russian language!

The Only Correct
World View

One day in Moscow I found myself with a group of
intellectuals. They sat in the kitchen, drank tea, and, as
is their custom, discussed all, or nearly all, local and
world problems and events. They spoke of the recent
arrest of two dissidents, the search of another dissident's
apartment, the rising price of gold (which had absolutely
no effect on their lives), Reagan's latest press conference,
Sakharov's latest statement, North Korea, South Africa.
They flew off into the future. They delved back into the
past and began arguing about the assassination of Tsar
Alexander II by the Narodnaya Volya a hundred years
ago.

One of those taking part in this conversation was a
brave and ebullient young woman. She had already served
time for working on a *samizdat* magazine and had apparently come close to prison a second time as well: she'd
been dragged in to the KGB, questioned, but she had

acted boldly, been impertinent to the investigator, and given no testimony.

Now, she spoke of an event that took place a hundred years ago with the same excitement she displayed when describing her interrogation at Lefortovo Prison the day before.

"Oh, those people in the Narodnaya Volya! That Perovskaya! If I'd been alive then, I'd have strangled her with my own hands."

"Nonsense," I said. "You wouldn't have strangled Perovskaya."

The woman grew even more excited. "I wouldn't have? That bastard who killed our Tsar? I would have strangled her without a second's hesitation."

"What are you talking about," I said. "You don't know yourself well enough. Back then you not only wouldn't have strangled Perovskaya, but you'd have been throwing bombs right alongside her."

She was prepared for any objection but that one. "Me? Throw bombs at our Tsar? But I'm a confirmed monarchist!"

"I can see you're a confirmed monarchist. These days it's fashionable to be a confirmed monarchist. But back then it was fashionable to throw bombs at the Tsar. And given your character, there's no question you would have been with the bomb-throwers."

Then again, there's a writer who still lives in Moscow with whom I became friendly about twenty years ago. When we first met, he was a relatively young man, passionate, romantic, and certain that his convictions ran deep. As a matter of fact, he had never had a conviction in his life. His ideas were not based on any direct observation of life, but on quotations from the founders of the dogma he happened to be following at the time.

For him, the world was simple and easily knowable, and he could always find the appropriate quotation to answer any difficult question life might pose.

It's easy enough to figure out that this infallible dogma of his, the only correct world view, was Marxism, although twenty years ago it was already beginning to be out of fashion. By the time we first came to know each other, my friend was already disenchanted with Stalin and had "returned" to Lenin. There was a small, framed portrait of Lenin on his desk, a portrait of Mayakovsky on the wall, and a large bust of Garibaldi on a flower stand.

My friend considered me a cynic because I mocked his idols; my caustic remarks about Lenin were blasphemy to him. I was not progressive, I was backward, I was unable correctly to assess phenomena in their complex interdependence because I had only a superficial knowledge of Lenin's works. "If you'd read Lenin," my friend would say in an edifying tone, "you'd understand why Lenin has the answer to every question."

I was not an anti-Leninist, but I did not believe that one person, even if he was a genius three times over, could answer all the questions that had agitated people in the decades since his death.

Years passed. My friend did not stand still; he kept developing. Lenin's portrait disappeared and was replaced by one of Rosa Luxemburg. Bertolt Brecht appeared alongside Mayakovsky. Later on, portraits of Hemingway, Faulkner, Che, Castro, Pasternak, Akhmatova, and Solzhenitsyn either took turns on his wall or were hung side by side. Sakharov too made a brief appearance there. Garibaldi lasted longer than the others, perhaps because it costs more to replace busts.

At one point we quarreled.

Visiting him at home a few years later, I noticed that the decor had changed drastically. Now on the wall there were ikons, portraits of Nicholas II, Father Pavel Florensky, John of Kronstadt, and other faces in cassocks and monastic headgear that I did not recognize. I found Garibaldi, covered with a thick layer of dust, behind the wardrobe.

We talked about one thing and another, and when I expressed my backward views on some subject, my friend condescendingly told me that I was mistaken and that my mistake was the result of my unfamiliarity with the works of Father Pavel Florensky, who had said . . . Then he quoted something which was supposed to crush me. I realized that my friend had not wasted the years in which we hadn't been seeing each other. He had acquired a new, progressive world view, the only correct one, and once again had left me far behind.

My friend's pattern of development is typical of many people in my generation, and in a few of the preceding ones. Former Marxists and atheists are now turning to Russian Orthodoxy, or Buddhism, or Zionism; others to ESP or jogging.

At one time, those people were romantic youths with passionate eyes and brains packed with quotations from the classical works of the only correct world view. Personally, I was more afraid of them than of professional Chekists and informers, who out of laziness or a lack of orders might let something pass. But those devoted to ideals and firm in their principles could rain quotations down on you at best and, at worst, drag you out in front of a meeting, with no mercy for a close friend, a favorite teacher, a father, or a mother.

Now those youths are youths no longer and have grown

disenchanted with those ideals. Some of them have left activism behind to concentrate on their own work; they no longer seek the truth, or if they do, they don't seek it in the works of their former idols. They go quietly about their business.

But there's another category—those who repent quickly and forgive themselves. Now they claim that back then everyone else was like them. They warp the truth. They even slander.

Of course, all of us—the majority of us—were subjected to a certain invisible process. Ideology was drummed into our heads from the day we were born. Some of us were sincere in our beliefs. Others approached ideology with a mixture of belief and doubt, the way people approach religion: if so many learned people (no match for the likes of us) maintain that Marxism is infallible, then maybe it is; they know better than we do. Young people, if they didn't grow up in families of religious sectarians, became Pioneers and Young Communists because they knew nothing else. And it must be said here that not to join the Komsomol was to challenge the all-powerful authorities (he who is not with us is against us). Even so, joining, attending meetings, and paying dues do not preclude an ability to doubt. Not everyone's conscience sat well with dragging a friend out in front of a meeting, a friend who had whispered a joke about Stalin or admitted that his father had not been killed during the war but executed as an enemy of the people. The majority raised no objections, of course (those who did were simply wiped out), they kept quiet and evaded the questions. Many even combined serious Marxism with personal behavior that was entirely honest.

Today, some of those formerly passionate youths believe that everyone was like them—that is, they heard no one but themselves. Some of those who now mouth anti-Communist slogans are once again outshouting everyone else, even though it is they who should be silent now, if only for reasons of taste.

I know a middle-aged woman who as a girl fought so fiercely against ideological heresy in her institute of higher learning that the Party organizers had to restrain her. At a Komsomol meeting in 1953 she accused a friend of not crying the day Stalin died. Now, when she writes in the émigré press "We Christians," I have to admit that this grates on me. For me, the idea of a "Christian" has always been connected with the idea of a "person of conscience." Not all of the newly converted belong to this category.

I'm not at all against people changing their convictions. On the contrary, I fully agree with Leo Tolstoy when he said more or less the following: "People say it's shameful to change one's convictions. But I say: it's shameful not to."

To cling to convictions that have begun to run counter to one's experience of life or history is foolish, sometimes even criminal. Personally, I never trust any convictions that are not accompanied by doubts. And I do not believe that any single teaching can be acceptable to everyone.

My former friend thought otherwise. Passing from one belief to another, he thought he had changed. In fact, he was what he always had been; all he'd done was supplant one set of quotations with another. But he remained as militant as ever. Now he is operating with a new set of quotations, which he intends to use not only for his own satisfaction, not only to move toward a new goal, but also to drag others along with him. He and those who share his views keep parroting the old idea that Russia is a special country; the experience of other nations cannot be applied to Russia. It must go its own way (as if it hadn't). The creators of the new teachings do not find democracy suitable for Russia. They say that democratic societies are breaking down because of their unnecessary freedoms. They're weak, they give too much attention to human rights and too little to human obligations, and these societies are in fact ruled, not by outstanding men, but by mediocre bureaucracies. In place of democracy, they would offer authoritarianism.

I've asked many advocates of authoritarianism exactly what they mean by the term. What they tell me makes no sense at all. They say that authoritarian rule means rule by a wise individual whom everyone will recognize as the authority. But if in rejecting democracy we reject the practice, proven over the centuries, of democratically choosing trustworthy individuals for a limited period of time and with limited power by means of universal and free elections, then what method is there for determining what authority shall be in office and for what length of time? Won't that authority appoint himself to office? And, under his rule, won't society again be turned into a herd of frenzied followers brandishing quotations and machine guns? And weren't Lenin, Stalin, Hitler, and Mao genuine authorities for hundreds of millions of people? And isn't Khomeini an authoritative personality?

All this sophistry about enlightened authoritarian rule could well end in a new form of ideological madness. It is based neither on historical experience nor on reality. Where, in what country, is there even one wise authoritarian leader? In what way is he any better than leaders elected democratically and held in check by the "mediocre" majority? In what way are the authoritarian countries better than the democratic ones?

The advocates of authoritarianism who have emigrated from the Soviet Union provide an eloquent answer to that question by the places they choose to live in. Isn't it curious they always end up in democratic, never authoritarian, countries?

Even now some of the advocates of authoritarianism say that they are the only true patriots (which, at the very least, is immodest) and declare all those who disagree with them slanderers and haters of Russia (just as the Bolsheviks called their opponents enemies of the people). I find it quite easy to imagine how and against whom these people would use the police force of their authoritarian state were it ever to come into being.

Until that occurs, I'll risk saying that no serious problems can be solved without democracy. I do not in the least maintain that Russia is now ready for democratic change. All I know is that if an organism is afflicted with cancer, it's foolish to think it can recover without treatment, or with a treatment that does not correspond to the disease.

End of an Era

While I was writing this book, the old guard finally gave way to the new in the Soviet Union. The laws of nature are implacable and apply to everyone, including the members of the Politburo.

In Mikhail Gorbachev a new generation has come to power. Even if it proves in no way better than its predecessor, it will be bad in its own way. An era has come to a close, one that lasted from the death of Lenin to our own times.

Without in the least intending to touch up Lenin's tarnished pedestal, I will nevertheless remark that there is a large difference, and one of principle, between Lenin and Stalin. Lenin tried to achieve utopian ends by criminal means. To a significant extent, "Lenin's" Party (which had begun to fall apart even while he was still alive) was composed of cruel, dull-witted people, but people devoted to the ideals they advocated, decent in their personal lives, and even capable of self-sacrifice.

Much more a realist than Lenin, Stalin brought ends and means into conformity, that is, he achieved criminal ends by criminal means. He wiped out everyone who resisted the achievement of those ends: peasants, workers, scientists, writers. But, out of fairness, it should be said that he also wiped out Communists—in numbers of which even the most fervent anti-Communists could not dream. Thus, I say there are sufficient grounds to call him an anti-Communist, and the Party he created an anti-Communist party. Under Stalin, there was no graver crime than anti-Soviet activity, but the first in that category and the first to go were people who sought not to undermine the Soviet system but to improve it. All of Stalin's activity, then, can sensibly be termed anti-Soviet.

It should be added that due to the efforts of Stalin and his ideological cohorts, a great many ideas were completely perverted and given contrary meanings. The betrayal of a close friend or parent, for instance, began to be considered an act of courage; lack of principle became principle, cruelty became humanitarianism. Countries without the slightest trace of democracy are called "people's democracies," and one of the most lying newspapers in the world is called *Pravda* (Truth).

When Stalin died, he was replaced by his disciples, his colleagues, his protégés, who had been active and obedient in carrying out his will. The reign of Stalin, his direct disciples, and the people he'd brought up through the system essentially lasted from 1924 to our time.

Now, for the first time in the Soviet Union, there are people in power who did not personally serve Stalin or take part in his crimes. Gorbachev joined the Party shortly before Stalin's death. We'll see what he and the others are capable of.

In the meantime, I'd like to say a few words about the previous generation of Soviet leaders, who have now almost departed from the stage of history. As an example, I'll take the most typical, purest, unadulterated Stalinist—Leonid Ilich Brezhnev, in the years he was in power.

A PROGRESSIVE DADDY

In October 1964, when the news spread that Khrushchev had been ousted and replaced by Brezhnev, Brezhnev's daughter, Galina, was in Koktebel, where she was sunbathing in the company of some well-known writers and actors. (As we know, the children of high Soviet officials have a strange attraction to the bohemian world of the arts.) The changes at the top came as a surprise to everyone, including Galina. People who saw her that day tell how she stood against the wind in her bathing suit, shivering from either the cold or excitement, repeating over and over: "My dad will be progressive. You'll see!"

Her progressive dad, along with his progressive comrades in arms, immediately began turning back the clock of history, setting as their first domestic political task the rehabilitation of Stalin and the restoration of the Party as the infallibly wise, irreproachable leader and mentor of the Soviet people. Soviet propaganda began carefully restoring luster to the pockmarked and bespattered face of our late leader and teacher.

Negative references to Stalin and his terror disappeared from literature. (Why pick at old wounds? The Party has said everything that needed saying; it has roundly condemned the mistakes, and that's enough.)

Positive references, on the other hand, began appearing more frequently, as if spontaneously. After all, it's a free country, and even the Party can't forbid people to love Stalin if they want to.

Documentary films began showing clips of the former supreme commander in chief, and movie theaters resounded with the aggressive applause of KGB agents pretending to be ordinary moviegoers.

At the same time, feature films from Stalin's era began to be released: *The Tractor Drivers*, *Secretary of the District Committee*, *Cossacks of the Kuban*. Those creaky old films were dragged back onto the screen and presented to audiences as examples of high art. This was done in part out of political considerations and in part as natural evidence of the Soviet leaders' taste. Those worthless films were testimonials of their careers, to their stormy youth, when, as a result of the bloody purges, they went from bottom to top—suddenly becoming generals and governors, who could decide the fate of thousands.

The attempt to rehabilitate Stalin was not carried through to the end, because, to their surprise, the Soviet leaders encountered quite appreciable resistance from a significant portion of Soviet society, Western Communist parties, and even the bureaucracy, which had managed to protect itself from Stalin's arbitrary rule. They say that at the very beginning of his administration, having suffered a defeat in his attempt to rehabilitate Stalin openly, Brezhnev decided to rehabilitate him "through channels," but in the end he did not carry this out either, because by then creating a personality cult of his own seemed more attractive.

However, Stalinism was entirely rehabilitated, as demonstrated by the dissidents' show trials. Under Brezhnev, repression did not, of course, achieve the scale it had under Stalin. This is not due to Brezhnev's goodness, but to his weakness of character (in comparison with Stalin). And also to the fact that, given everything that had been exposed, given the various forms of resistance from different quarters and the atrophying of the ideology, such levels of repression in this day and age were simply impossible. (I've already mentioned that mass terror is only possible where there is mass enthusiasm—when an ideology is young and has not yet lost its luster.)

As a personality, Brezhnev was much more the nonentity than Stalin, even though he did his best to imitate him. (Stalin was born on December 21, and Brezhnev on the 19th. That earned Leonid the nickname "Preemie.")

The positive difference between Brezhnev and Stalin is that Brezhnev was a lesser criminal. Stalin was interested in power for the sake of power, but Brezhnev was tempted by the luxurious life that accompanies power. Stalin thought mainly of whom to destroy and how; Brezhnev had other things on his mind.

Now people say that corruption flowered under Brezhnev and they mention the names of various people around him, including his daughter and son-in-law. But that is not fair. The ruling gang (which did not disdain thievery, bribe-taking, or any method of misappropriation) was not headed by Brezhnev's daughter or his son-in-law, but by Brezhnev himself. He was the one collecting Rolls-Royces and Mercedeses and accepting all sorts of other gifts from Western companies and workers in his own country.

There's a joke about a Jewish tailor who said that if he were tsar, he'd live better than the tsar, because he'd do a little tailoring on the side. Brezhnev too lived better than the tsar, because he did a little stealing on the side. His confederates did the same. And nearly always with impunity. If scandals occurred, as they did, it was only because the people involved had displeased Brezhnev in some way.

Nikolai Podgorny, the former head of state, was pensioned off without any special scandal, even though his hands weren't clean in the least. He'd taken bribes to pardon people sentenced to death.

Podgorny is worth a few words. This member of the elect was notable for his intellect even when compared with his comrades in the Politburo. Based on his mental abilities and his skill at dominoes, they nicknamed him "Dimbulb," and for good reason. His pedantry and taste were legendary.

A cameraman who had frequent occasion to film him told me that whenever Podgorny spied Kent cigarettes on a table, he'd immediately pocket a pack. It's said, and it sounds believable enough, that he had a dozen color television sets, which at that time were still rare in the Soviet Union; he had them in his office, his bedroom, and even in the bathroom.

For some reason, many Western politicians until quite recently thought, and perhaps still think, that the Soviet Union is run by narrow-minded fanatics who are concerned with nothing but world revolution and Communism. West German Chancellor Willy Brandt at one time was touched by the fact that Brezhnev told anti-Soviet jokes that featured himself, jokes that if told by ordinary people could cost them some time in jail.

Brezhnev was no fanatic, because there were no fanatics among the leaders of his generation. The Leninist type of fanatic had been cynically destroyed by Stalin, a process begun at the end of the twenties that ended with their complete annihilation in the thirties. Uneducated, uncultured, greedy people were brought into the Party to replace them. The intellectual capabilities of the new leadership were so limited that the overwhelming majority, including Khrushchev, Brezhnev, and Chernenko, had trouble delivering speeches without every word on paper in front of them. I once read a note written in Brezhnev's hand. It was eleven lines long and contained eleven grammatical errors.

In a word, Brezhnev, like the majority of people who rose under Stalin, was a complete nonentity as a personality and had little culture and little education. All of them, or nearly all, were insolent, greedy, vain, and without principle. It would be ridiculous to speak of their devotion to any sort of ideas whatsoever.

I am no Marxist and have no intention of advocating Marxism, but I don't think that even the Soviet leaders themselves are excessively devoted to that doctrine. Marxism professes freedom, equality, brotherhood, and the withering away of the state as its ideal. Marxism rejects censorship. No, I can't believe that Brezhnev or any of his colleagues strove toward those ideals.

They used Marxist ideology as a screen simply because it had been legitimized before they came to power and there was no need to replace it with anything else. They could have used any other ideology with equal success. They quote Marx and Lenin to suit their own needs and reject what they don't need.

As a typical leader in the Stalin mold, Brezhnev was endlessly vain. When Alexander Shelepin was still on the Politburo, he told people, some of whom he did not even know well (could that have caused his downfall?), that Brezhnev was so taken with himself that he could not pass a polished surface without glancing at his reflection.

I left Moscow two years before Brezhnev died. It was ridiculous, painful, and embarrassing to watch endless ceremonies on the evening news in which Brezhnev was awarded medals and prizes, day after day. He was being either awarded the rank of hero of the Soviet Union or a peace prize or given a gold-plated weapon. He eclipsed all his predecessors in number of awards received. He had as many gold stars of the hero of the Soviet Union and socialist labor as Stalin and Khrushchev put together. And they were not distinguished for their modesty.

Brezhnev's excessive vanity was not satisfied by medals, and so he tried his hand at creative writing. The books written for him by teams of writers pressed into service were declared literary masterpieces, comparable only to the best pages of *War and Peace*. Millions of people were compelled to study those books and write reports on them. When experts now calculate how much damage drunkenness and absenteeism do to the Soviet economy, they should also include the damage done to the economy by Brezhnev's literary indulgences.

Western leaders lauded Brezhnev's peaceful intentions and even called him a man of peace, apparently on the grounds that he had not started a nuclear war. Of course, he could not have started one and had no such intention, first because even he did not have enough power, and second because, though a limited man, he was not crazy and was well aware that he had no chance of winning such a war. But just imagine that he could have won, and thereby could have attained the rank of generalissimo and a downpour of diamond-studded decorations. I would have had trouble sleeping under those conditions. Paltry personalities are ruled by paltry passions. The more paltry the personality, the more determined and irresponsible it will be in using all the power at its disposal.

By the way, peace-loving intentions are displayed not by not attacking strong countries, but by not attacking weaker ones. Brezhnev displayed no such peaceable intentions in regard to Czechoslovakia or Afghanistan.

In and of himself, Brezhnev was such a faceless man that he does not deserve as detailed a description as this. But for the course of eighteen years he ruled a superpower capable of destroying the entire world, and during that long period, like Lenin and like Stalin, he became something of a symbol of his time. During the years of his senile administration, Soviet society began a final breakdown. Everything was taken to its logical conclusion. The hopes that had flared up in Khrushchev's time, and that stayed pretty much alive during Brezhnev's first years in office, were replaced by depression, disenchantment, apathy, and amorality, especially after the human rights movement was smashed and every mouth shut. Deprived of any possibility of political, cultural, and public life, the nation responded with drunkenness, thievery (thanks to the example set by their leaders on every level), reduction in labor productivity, and horrifyingly low quality in production.

It can even be said that the "Brezhnevization" of society was in its own way no less horrific than "Leninization" or "Stalinization."

A new generation coming into power in the Soviet Union is undoubtedly an event of exceptional importance. Many people both within the country and outside it have been waiting for this moment for a long time. For that reason, the euphoria accompanying Gorbachev's first appearance is entirely understandable: He is young, healthy, energetic; his wife is interested in elegant dresses, teaches classes in Marxism-Leninism. All of this is, of course, astonishing in and of itself. But now that the initial euphoria is over, let's look at things a bit more soberly. However young and healthy the new leader may be, he's still sitting in the wheelchair he inherited from the old leader. The fight against alcoholism and corruption and the calls for a Stakhanovite movement are old tricks, used by the people before him.

The great increases in alcoholism and corruption are simply the result, not the cause, of the current situation. No serious changes—including a rise in the economy, the introduction of new technology, and improved relations with the West—are genuinely possible without giving people more freedom, without respect for human beings, without a democratization of the nation's life.

Does Gorbachev realize this? Is it what he wants? And even if he wants it, will the Party power elite that supported him allow it?

When Tsar Nicholas I was dying, 130 years ago, he said to his son: "I'm not leaving you the household in good condition." His son (Alexander II) did much to improve that household. He abolished serfdom, introduced democratic reforms into the judicial system, and carried out land reform. But that was the soil on which a destructive revolutionary movement grew. Alexander was killed by terrorists, and during his grandson's reign a disaster occurred, the Great October Socialist Revolution.

But, looking back at the past, one can say with nearly complete confidence that Alexander II simply could not have avoided making those reforms.

The leaders of the USSR now find themselves in a similar situation.